She's Not the Man I Married

my life with a transgender husband

Helen Boyd

author of *My Husband Betty*

SEAL PRESS

Praise for *She's Not the Man I Married*

"Between the covers of this book, you'll hear how love sounds when it's so honest it bleeds. Trans liberation is more certain to 'win' because Helen's on the team."

—Leslie Feinberg, author of *Drag King Dreams*

"This (im)perfect modern love story tackles the big questions—the meanings of gender, why we love the people we love, how we love the people we love—honestly, articulately, and with tremendous eloquence."

—Josey Vogels, sex columnist and author of
Bedside Manners: Sex Etiquette Made Easy

"Thoughtful, sharp, and provocative, this book delves into one of the most terrifying and universal elements of a relationship: change. Helen's courage and insight are remarkable, and we have much to learn from her about redefining gender roles, marriage, and commitment in this century."

—Tristan Taormino, author and *Village Voice* columnist

"Part journal, part queer studies, part liberation manifesto, *She's Not the Man I Married* is a daring love letter from Helen Boyd to her partner, their relationship, and anyone who has dared to love outside of the traditional gender script."

—Abigail Garner, author of *Families Like Mine*

Praise for *My Husband Betty*

"Boyd never expected to write about transvestites and their partners, yet here is her fascinating account of marriage to a crossdresser. . . . Boyd's skill as a writer enables readers to enter a relatively hidden existence easily, and perhaps even to appreciate its complexities. Her account, though initially disquieting to some, well may become a standard text in gender studies."

—Whitney Scott, *BookList*

"A straight woman who has been married several years to a crossdressing man gives a thoughtful account of their relationship (as well as the relationships of other crossdressers she knows) in this forthright and revelatory book. . . . Honest and well researched, this book is likely to become an indispensable guide."

—*Publishers Weekly*

She's Not the Man I Married
my life with a transgender husband
Copyright © 2007 by Helen Boyd

AVALON
publishing group incorporated

Published by
Seal Press
An Imprint of Avalon Publishing Group, Incorporated
1400 65th Street, Suite 250
Emeryville, CA 94608

Library of Congress Cataloging-in-Publication Data

Boyd, Helen.
She's not the man I married : my life with a transgender husband /
Helen Boyd.
p. cm.
Includes bibliographical references and index.
ISBN-13: 978-1-58005-193-4 (alk. paper)
ISBN-10: 1-58005-193-6 (alk. paper)
1. Boyd, Helen. 2. Transvestism. 3. Transvestites—Family
relationships. 4. Transsexuals—Family relationships. 5. Marriage. I.
Title.

HQ77.B63 2006
306.84'8—dc22

2006030698
Cover design by Matthew Silverman
Interior design by Domini Dragoone
Printed in the United States of America
Distributed by Publishers Group West

this book is dedicated to the memory of

peter dee

who in his whimsical way decided that we two were

two someones who needed to meet

& in memory of

gianna israel, for her kindness

vern bullough, for his generosity

gidget, for her humor

minna, for her bravery

&, of course, to betty

contents.

preface.

When I was still putting together the idea of what this book would be, an astute editor told me that there wasn't enough in *My Husband Betty* about me and Betty and our relationship, at least not compared to the information about crossdressing and stories of other couples' experiences. I certainly didn't plan to write a book others would refer to as the "crossdresser's textbook," though I did consider calling it *A Field Guide to Crossdressing* when I was looking for a subtitle because I thought that accurately reflected what *My Husband Betty* is. I didn't intend to leave out so much of our story, and there was no sleight of hand; given the opportunity to write about crossdressing and life with someone trans, I couldn't help but write a book that focused more on practical information and the stories of others because there was so little out there. Our story is between the lines of *My Husband Betty*, there but not there.

Even a few ordinary years can change a relationship and the people in it, but the last few years, since the publication of *My Husband Betty,* have been anything but ordinary for us. We have met thousands of trans people in person, online, and via email; we've met friends of friends, activists, and readers. We've met queer theorists and partners and bois. Betty got to perform with a lesbian theater group, and I've given workshops on sexuality for hundreds of people. These are not ordinary things, but they have become ordinary for us. We both changed a lot once we started meeting people and realized we had become—like it or not—public people.

Because Betty presented as female for the many events we attended, she found more and more time and space to explore her female self, which is what led to her questioning transition more directly than she had before. Like most people who crossdress, she had wondered about living as a woman and had certainly fantasized about it, but she didn't expect to wake up one day and realize that she had actually achieved having a very real life as a female person without necessarily making a decision to do so. It was a little terrifying to have come so far so fast, and unconsciously—a little like being Wile E. Coyote having just run off the cliff without meaning to. She took a few steps back and decided to think more about it, to be more "present," to weigh her options instead of choosing one without considering them all.

We've realized since that even her exploration of her female side was a bit like a Pandora's box, which once opened cannot be closed. Since our exposure to the trans community caused that box to be opened, we thought we should use the resources it provided. We were in a unique position to survey the many ways people seek to make peace with their transness. Once Betty started paying closer attention, she noticed more things that made her hesitate. We became cautious when we recognized how illusory the feeling of safety and acceptance can be when you're most often in "trans friendly" spaces. That is, we're both well aware that the rest of the world is not "trans friendly" or necessarily even lesbian friendly or queer friendly. I suspect Betty will continue to hold off on making the decision to transition until we are sure we can handle being who we are everywhere, that all of who she is can be brought into an only-female self, and that our relationship will survive.

Betty calls her experience as both cover girl and raison d'être of *My Husband Betty* and this book being "Betty of the Book." It's that very public exposure that has made Betty's "to transition or not to transition" issue so complicated. On the one hand, she has met more passing, happy trans women than most. It encourages her to know that life will go on after transition, that it's possible to be both out as trans but living as female, and that transition does fix, for some, the incessant mental niggling that transness is. On the other hand, those very same trans women often mention ex-wives, or the times when they get to see their kids; often they drop other clues that there was a happy marriage in their past that is no longer. It's come to the point where we don't need to ask if transition caused the end of the marriage. In some cases, it's the only loss the trans women regret; many still love their former wives deeply.

We don't know if anything will convince Betty one way or the other that transition is right or wrong for her, to say definitively "I am not transition path" or to take the first steps toward living full-time as a woman. Right now she is at a crossroads, out as trans with a significant female life but physically able to be male if and when she needs to be. We have tried to stop thinking about whether she is male or female and instead have focused on her being her and me being me, leaving the gender labels out of it. It may seem impossible not to know what someone's gender is, but it is amazing how far you can get by simply deciding that that's one question you won't allow yourselves to ask. So far it's working, as we simultaneously plan for a future where she does transition and one where she doesn't.

This book is a sequel to *My Husband Betty*, at least in that our story and my reasons for thinking about gender take up where it left off. Mostly it is a love story, our love story, which, like any other, is not typical. It is the story of how a tomboy fell in love with a sissy, how a butch found her femme, how a boyish girl met a girlish boy. Who is who is not always clear and doesn't always matter. In some ways, that's the heart of this book: the idea that a relationship is a place where people can and do and maybe even ought to become as ungendered as they can. It comes from my very specific dislike of Martian men and Venusian women and the adversarial ideas about relationships that permeate our culture. While I am not interested in a genderless world, I am curious about the ways that gender can be manipulated in a romance, the ways it can be controlled instead of controlling our roles.

The one thing that I want to be clear about is that this is a book of my experience. Not all partners of trans people are or were tomboys. Therefore, I clearly don't represent the experiences of other trans partners; I mention some paths and not others. But the range of experience the nontrans partner in a trans relationship can have is gigantic—essentially there are as many paths as there are partners. We all come from different sexual orientations, pasts, attitudes; some of us prefer identifying as queer and others are gay or lesbian or hetero. We might have met our trans partners after transition, before transition, or midtransition. Some want the protections of legal marriage and others don't. What Mother Flawless Sabrina once said about trans people—"We are like snowflakes"—is just as true of their partners.

This book is not intended to be any kind of guidebook for how to be a trans partner, or how to be in a trans relationship. I know that most partners of trans people ask themselves very serious, often difficult, questions both about identity and their ideas about relationships, and they ask those questions very much in response to being with someone trans. However, the specific circumstances I had with my masculinity, my past as a tomboy, people's assumptions about my being a lesbian, and my acceptance of a queer identity are only my own. They may be useful to other partners of trans people, if only to elucidate how difficult and how deep these questions can be and in whatever ways I've exposed my own process for coming to an answer and a life I can live with.

In one sense this book is indicative of the kind of experience the partner of a trans person may go through. I've observed it on my own, as have other professionals, such as Virginia Erhardt and Sandra Cole and Arlene Lev (three therapists who work with partners, and who have all championed partners' visibility in the trans community). Partners all seem to go through a period of examining and redefining their own sense of gender and sexual orientation. They may start with a sense of being very normatively gendered or not. Some may discover that they only felt they were. Partners may tweak their sexual orientation, or not. It's almost impossible to be with someone trans without thinking about this stuff, whether the transness is expressed through clothing alone, body modifications, legal changes, or all of the above. Change brings self-questioning, reevaluation, confusion. It just so happens that when you are with someone when she decides to transition, or begins to wonder if he'll need to transition, or even if she discovers cross-gender feelings of any kind, the axes of confusion are your own gender identity and sexual orientation. Those same questions may come up even if you meet your partner after transition. Your public (how *they* think of you) and private (how *you* think of you) identities come into play. Your role in your relationship may seem unstable. Your own gender may feel out of place, and your sexual orientation may feel flexible one day and a source of guilt and frustration another.

What I want partners to know most is that all of these questions and feelings are completely normal when your partner is trans. I don't care if they're crossdressing or getting their eyebrows shaped or starting to grow hair in places they never had it before or getting surgery.

That said, the work I have done with partners in various workshops through the years gives me the idea that partners do not yet feel part of the larger trans community. As I like to repeat in workshops: This is not about my husband's life; this is *my* life. We need to be able to express ourselves, to share what's difficult, and to do so without being castigated for getting a pronoun wrong or for—*gasp!*—doubting the necessity of all of our partner's choices. Trans people—our very own loved ones—often pressure their partners into accepting or supporting anything they do, because to do otherwise would be transphobic. Amazingly enough, being accused of such a thing goes a long way to shutting partners up. Some I've spoken to are so paranoid about accidentally using a wrong pronoun that they've simply stopped using them altogether. It pains me to see, maybe because it seems a little too familiar, reminding me of the uneven power balances of so many heterosexual relationships I've known through the years. The "are you with us or against us?" mentality, when directed at partners, is counterproductive and unfair: We've already said we're with you by sharing your lives, your beds, and your families. We often go unnoticed, though, despite being the ones who find the breast forms or the packer, who brush out the wig or figure out if the spirit gum is still sticky. We're not just here, going along, feeling as if these are perfectly ordinary lives, nor do we exult in being partners of transfolk necessarily. Sometimes we are more confused and feel out of control. One partner referred to her husband's transition as a kind of juggernaut she had no power to stop or change or even direct.

I am not altogether pleased with the way the partners of trans people are treated by some therapists, either. I am hoping that therapists may be able to use this book to gauge the depth of partners' feelings when a couple comes in. The heartache, the worry, and the frustration are no less intense than the trans person's. Partners didn't ask for the tumult transness is causing them any more than the trans person did. They deserve more committed support. Often our inability to deal with a change of gender is said to be a lack of love, or a lack of open-mindedness. I felt a tremendous sense of relief when I learned that one of the reasons Kate Bornstein split up with one of her partners was his change of gender. That's *the* Kate Bornstein, trans heroine and gender outlaw. I couldn't help but compare her experience to the way I accepted Betty's femininity but couldn't jump the hurdle of her living female full-time. The difficulty partners have is not necessarily due to ignorance, or a lack of open-mindedness, and I already knew it wasn't because of a lack of love. Partners have a hard time with transition because they do; relationships are often threefold, built on *friendship + romance + sex,* and while it may be possible to hold on to the friendship, keeping both romance and sexual attraction in the equation when transition enters into it is infinitely trickier.

14

It's also my hope that feminists like me whose initial reaction to transness is, "That's no way to solve a gender problem!" might find their gut response a little tempered by my experience. Gender is experienced differently by different people, and as much as I still don't know what feeling "like a woman" or "like a man" means, I do know that many trans people live much happier and much more fulfilled lives post-transition. The same goes for those whose paths are marked by crossdressing, or living dually gendered lives, or genderqueer ones. Neither transition nor gender expression means life becomes easy, or even manageable, but it can become more honest and fulfilling, which is just enough of a respite for people who experience their gender discomfort in acute and chronic ways otherwise.

Because I have a heterosexual history, and the world is still heterocentric, my "default" when talking about relationships is hetero relationships. Betty and I have, however, found great insight and strength from the people we know who are gay and lesbian. Since I've never been half of a gay or lesbian relationship, I can't speak with authority about what it's like to be negotiating gender roles from inside of one. I do know now what it's like to live in a closet, to fear my family's reaction to the news of who I am and who I love, though, and the commiseration we've had from gay and lesbian friends has been key.

She's Not the Man I Married is not intended to be a survey of trans experience—not by a long shot. As much as Betty and I have put a conscious effort into meeting as many types of trans people and partners as we can, there is no way to get all of that experience into one book. I don't think even the most cursory survey of the trans community would fit in a book. That said, I try to touch on different types of experiences throughout, except for one: children. Having quite a few siblings and friends with children, I'm fully aware of what parents think of the opinions of those without children: not much. However, people are desperate for resources on how to raise trans children or how to raise children when a parent (or both) is trans. There are few on hand. To remedy the situation, I started a special forum called "Kids" on the message board on our website to act as a kind of clearinghouse for people with children who are dealing with transness, and I hope that some of you can find stories or resources there that might help, or offer stories and resources that helped you so that others can benefit from them as well.

In addition to the Kids forum, you'll also find plenty of other discussions about gender and transness on the message boards of the website, which also includes my blog *(en)gender,* book reviews, links to more resources, as well as a bunch of other interesting things. Do come by: www.myhusbandbetty.com.

Helen Boyd
December 2006

author's note:
on language
& pronouns
& taxonomy.

I often use "trans" or "transgender" to represent all types of trans people—self-identifying
transgender (TG) people, crossdressers (CD), and
transsexuals (TS)—unless I otherwise specify. I do
so because I talk about their partners' experiences,
which amply demonstrate that what kind of transness
the trans person experiences is not always an indicator of how difficult it is for the nontrans partner. As
a result, I tend to elide the distinctions between crossdressers and transsexuals and all the other subdivisions
in ways that trans people themselves might not appreciate. I don't
do that out of disrespect. I am well aware that many crossdressers
do not consider themselves transgender, and that some transsexuals do
not consider themselves (or crossdressers, for that matter) transgender,

either. I do it more to point out that a CD's wife can have as hard a time accepting her husband's femme self as the wife of a TS might have with transition. That, plus I still find it problematic the way crossdressers and transsexuals self-segregate, playing games of "better than" or "who suffers the most" that aren't productive for anyone. I don't find the self-segregation difficult simply because of the border wars or hierarchies, but because the two big camps in the male to female (MTF) world leave those who might pursue a middle ground with nowhere to go.

I use both him/her and he/she when I'm talking about Betty, and which pronoun I use is sometimes determined by context but sometimes just by how she looked in my head when I was thinking of him. While some might prefer to see instead the gender-neutral pronouns "zie" or "ze" (pronounced zee, works like he or she) and "hir" (pronounced hear, works like him or her), I found that varying pronouns for Betty's gender-fluid life best expressed our reality. I otherwise use the pronouns that the people I mention prefer, and if I'm not sure which they prefer, I tend to err on the side of their target or temporary gender, not their assigned-at-birth one.

For those who don't know the basics, the term "trans woman" indicates a person who is transgendered from male to female (MTF or M2F), meaning that they were assigned male at birth and are becoming or became or will become female. I use MTF for those who are transsexual (who have had the surgery or who haven't, but mainly those who live in their target gender full-time) and transgender people (who constitute, I think, the largest majority, and about whom nothing other than that can be said definitely) and crossdressers (who often retain male bodies but have a feminine or female personality that is expressed through their gender presentation, or not) and transvestites (another word for crossdresser that some crossdressers find pejorative but that is regularly used outside of the United States without insult). You will find other terms in the MTF spectrum such as t-girl, transitioned woman, woman of transsexual experience.

Female to male (FTM or F2M) is the opposite vector from MTF. FTMs are assigned female at birth and move toward a position on the masculine spectrum, which is one way of saying they have some kind of male or masculine gender. I say only as much about FTMs as I feel confident saying, as there are border wars and hierarchies within the FTM community I am not as well versed on. Again, I intend no neglect but only respect for what I don't feel qualified to speak about. In the FTM world, you find labels such as trans man and sometimes butch, AG, trannyfag, genderqueer, and boi.

If you've gotten the feeling that the language is way too confusing and you'll never get it right, you're close. I still don't get it right. Some trans people get upset when you ask their pronoun preference or gender identity, and others get upset when you don't. But the basic rules for dealing with people are pretty much always the same: If you don't know someone's name, ask what it is. If you don't know how to introduce the person, or don't know if the person is your friend's boyfriend or girlfriend, use "partner." If you are unsure as to pronouns, use people's names for a while, until they either have a chance to tell you which pronouns they prefer or until someone who knows them better uses one. If you insult people by referring to them as something they're not, apologize. Do not assume that if you can "see" two or more genders that the person wants any or all of them acknowledged. Respect that people have the right to identify themselves as they will, and it's not up to you to decide what they "really" are. It's not too difficult in the end.

I opted also to use "trans" as a separate adjective when using terms such as "trans woman" instead of as one word ("transwoman"). I chose the former because it expresses something linguistically significant: that "trans" is an adjective, one of many that could be applied to a person, such as tall or skinny or Hungarian American or rich or Catholic or nearsighted. Trans is one facet of a person's self and often not the most important one to him or her, actually. I also use trans woman as a feminist, as a way of acknowledging that while I may be a feminist woman, and a blond woman, I find "trans" only a descriptor of a type of woman, among many types.

A bibliography (page 305) might point you in useful or interesting directions as concerns gender, and you can come discuss those books, or others you've found, at my website, www.myhusbandbetty.com.

girl
meets
boy.

I've been preparing myself to lose my husband for the past few years. He's not dying. He's not leaving me for another woman. If he were, there would be books I could read, support groups I could join. I could seek out the experiences of others and learn from them, find solace in how they managed, tailor their methods to my own personality. I could repeat pithy truths like "time heals all wounds" or "better to have loved and lost" or the more rebellious "his loss." I might find reservoirs of hope and anger that would move me into a new day, a new life, maybe a new love.

There is another woman, in a sense. My husband is that other woman, or he might become her. We don't know yet what decision he will make, but that doesn't matter when loss looms on the horizon. Loss is bad enough. Knowing in advance that you will lose something is worse. Being prepared for a future loss is very, very difficult. But being willing to lose something you love is something like impossible. That's why I've been preparing. I don't want to lose my husband. I don't want him to become a woman. But I'm not sure that what I want is going to decide what happens. What he wants may not even decide our future.

He wants me to be with him if he stays a him or becomes a her. I'd like to believe that if he does decide he needs to live as a woman, I could still be his wife, or partner, or spouse. There's the first problem: I'm not sure what I would be. Legally married, yes, but a legally married woman who'd look like a lesbian to everyone else. I might end up feeling more like her husband than her wife. There isn't any protocol for this situation—no books, not many support groups, and very few people who have lived through this experience. But he loves me and wants me to keep loving her as much as I love him. And I want to, but I don't know that I'll be able to.

Right now it's a little like living with the sound of the other shoe not dropping. I'm not sure there will ever be a time when I can feel assured that the shoe won't drop, but at the same time—I don't want to hear it. I don't want it to drop. I don't want him to say to me that he can't live the way he's been living anymore. But I'm not sure the solution we've come up with for now will last, either. Even if it does, I'm not sure I'll stop listening for that sound I don't want to hear.

When we met, we both felt more than lucky. The way he describes it, our love was like getting the brass ring on the carousel. It was luck, for both of us. We met in our late twenties after we had both survived spending five years with someones neither of us should have spent more than six months with. So many people do that: break off a long-term relationship and then find themselves married within a year or so and so unbelievably happy and so unbelievably surprised at how easy it is when it was difficult for so long. That was how we felt; conversations felt unnecessary, as if we were twins with our own private language, empaths with no need to talk about how we felt. We talked because it was fun, because we found so much joy in being with each other. What we talked about didn't matter much, like old folks who can't hear each other but still enjoy the conversation.

I would have done anything for him. I want to do anything for him, still.

But there's a catch. The she that he is becoming is not the him I would do anything for. I struggle with this love for the man I met, the man I never expected to meet, the man who brought me more joy, more solace, more love and companionship and conversation and laughter and understanding and admiration than I could have ever imagined. If someone had told me I would meet a man who was proud to say I was smarter than he was (whether or not it was true) and proud to have a cranky, stubborn writer of a wife for a partner, I would have said such things aren't possible. I might have thought I'd meet a man who would tolerate my stubbornness, and who in his heart of hearts might think I was smarter than him but never admit it. I met a few of them, and I didn't like feeling tolerated. Betty likes the parts of me that are the least interesting to others and the most difficult. What he likes most about me is that I am no lady; he likes me for being his Eowyn,[1] and he doesn't need me to be his mystical dream of a woman, his Arwen or Galadriel. He prefers me slaying dragons. He prefers someone who has his back and keeps him safe. He prefers me to be the me I am, and I don't want to repay that love by only tolerating her. Right now, while he has both a male and female side, it's easy to love them both. But I'm not sure I would be able to keep doing that if he went away entirely. I love her, but for his sake.

Flannery O'Connor once said that the story of a life is really the story of how a person meets his dragon in the road[2] and what he does when he meets it. My husband's transgender nature is his dragon. I have no doubt of that. Right now, we're both hoping we can feed it small treats and it will let us pass, but it doesn't seem to want either of us to get by. Neither of us will be surprised if the minute we turn our backs after passing it, it will leap and devour him whole, and maybe some part of me with him. Or maybe it will take me as the high toll to be paid to a dragon that wants his skin. Betty must have sensed, when we met, that he had a dragon to slay that he couldn't face on his own; looking back, I didn't know I was being interviewed for the position and got the job with flying colors. I don't mind slaying other people's dragons with them when they can't manage it themselves, but I'm not sure what to do afterward. Shake hands and say godspeed? Have a meal of dragon and part ways? Wrap each other's wounds and find an inn for the night? I don't know if dragon-slaying makes a good foundation for a marriage. I don't know what does.

I've told him that I will be there, that I will stay, that I love him enough to see him through this ordeal. I've also taken all that back. I couldn't make such important promises without knowing I could keep them. I owe him at least that much respect. He has shown me the same kind of respect in return, trying as hard as he can to make peace with his transness. He has remained male at least part of the time, for my sake. He says for his, too, because our happiness is part of his happiness. But I'm not sure he'll be able to keep his finger in the dam forever, if that's what it turns out to be. He seems to be transitioning despite either of our best efforts. When I first noticed that we were called "ladies" when he thought he was presenting as male, when we realized we had friends who knew only his female side and not the male, when friends of ours who'd ended up on similar paths split up, I started preparing to lose him. If you really love someone, you're supposed to set them free, but I don't have the first idea how to do that. I'm not sure he's interested in being set free, either.

Some days I'm convinced I would have been better off never having met him, but I can't even comprehend what I would be like now if I hadn't. I wouldn't be me. In some ways, I'm not. My name isn't even Helen Boyd. That's a name I picked up along the way, a concern for privacy yielding a little white lie that snowballed into a pseudonym. While he's become Betty, I've become Helen Boyd. A nom de plume gave me permission to remake myself, and that is the first thing I learned from the trans community: Given names are not carved in stone. On the way to becoming something and someone else, you may find that a name begins to fit awkwardly, like a pair of shoes after a pregnancy. It just doesn't suit you anymore, and if you're lucky—like I was—and find a good reason to try on a new name, you may find yourself growing into a whole new identity.

When I first found myself with a crossdressing boyfriend, I went online to figure out what marriage to a man who crossdressed might be like. I sent an enthusiastic email to an online group's moderator, and a second after I hit the send button, I panicked: I didn't want anyone to know my real name. What was I thinking?!

I wasn't. I decided to use an email address I'd made up in order to keep Betty's ex from reading my emails instead. Helen's my middle name, and I'd recently named his crossdressing self "Betty."[3] The moniker "bettysgrrl" became my username for any of my online crossdressing research. For a long time, I remained only Helen B. I eventually borrowed Boyd from Edna St. Vincent Millay: She'd used Nancy Boyd as a pen name, a play on the phrase "nancy boy," or a sissy. For Millay, who always signed her name Vincent, it was also a kind of queer veil. She signed love poems to women with that name, so it seemed appropriate for me, too, as my online research was a kind of love poem to Betty in its own geeky way.

It's been a long time since then, so long that now I can say only that I wish I were married to a crossdresser.

It's not that I love crossdressers so much—I do love them, in much the same way a second-grade teacher is inordinately fond of the kid who can't keep his shoelaces tied but who never spells a word wrong—but more because my husband used to resemble something someone might call a crossdresser, even if he always hated the term for an awful lot of reasons.

I wish my husband were "just a crossdresser," even though we both bristle at the condescension in that phrase. No one wants to be "just a" anything. But no, as it turns out, my husband Betty is more than a crossdresser: He is a transgendered person and prefers people call her trans.[4]

Not only did I never expect to be married to someone trans,
I never really hoped to be married at all; I just wasn't that type of girl. No dreams of white weddings (except maybe in the Billy Idol sense), and I had only a brief excursion into playing with baby dolls, mostly because I found a beautiful black-and-white stroller in the crawl space of our garage. Playing at motherhood didn't appeal to me. When I played with dolls it was always Barbie, specifically Ballerina Barbie, who was my favorite, because she was one of the only dolls without that service-with-a-smile

grin painted on her face, and who was, in my elaborate play stories, some kind of power broker who made my Marie Osmond doll work as her poor, much-put-upon secretary. In my universe, Barbie's goal wasn't to meet Ken and get married; she was more like Dagny Taggart.[5]

So much for sugar and spice.

Not that there were many puppy dog tails in my constitution either. Mostly I played outdoor games with kids in the neighborhood and read when I was alone. I wasn't told not to play boys' games, nor encouraged to play girls' games. As the youngest, I mostly did what I wanted, and my parents let me as long as I wasn't underfoot and was within shouting distance for dinner. I've often thought that my lack of awareness that anyone would see anything odd about my own gender is what caused me to marry someone trans; for me, a man dressing up in women's clothes did not create a sense of moral outrage, but instead a curiosity: "So what do you want to play next?" Apparently this attitude astonished Betty, and although she did later confess that I didn't seem like a "typical girl" right off the bat, she never expected me to force her out of the closet, either. I thought I was—if not typical—at least within the bounds of regular. Betty, of course, was not foolish enough to tell me while we were dating that I came off a little dykey, though she did admit to that much after the fact, maybe even after we were married. My oldest friend was probably right when she told me not to wear pants[6] on our first date. I knew I wasn't stereotypically feminine, but I didn't think there was anything particularly odd about my gender, either. I still don't.

But neither of us was paying much attention to gender when we met. I'd grown out of being a tomboy and had adjusted reasonably well to being a twentysomething woman, even if I was more feminist than is sociable, since blonde jokes tended to make me spit nails and expletives. Betty had made herself reasonably comfortable in a closet with an open door. That is, he'd lived in a somewhat rural part of upstate New York for nearly a decade and passed as "one of the guys" around actors, hunters, and tourists—such was her closet. But she had also left that town for New York City, fully intending to explore both acting and gender transgression.

When we met in our mutual friend Peter's kitchen in Hell's Kitchen, we looked to each other like a twentysomething young man who was an actor and a twentysomething young woman who was a writer, neither of us uberfeminine or extremely masculine, both of us bookish, reasonably good-looking, and a little shy.

We looked as if we would make a good heterosexual couple, which is a conclusion Peter had come to before introducing us. Peter certainly didn't know more about our genders than we did, but with Peter anything was possible. Peter was that kind of magic person who divines things that others can't ever see or would take a long time to figure out and that he himself often didn't understand. I'm not sure he knew he was matchmaking. But even he didn't know that gender would become a major theme of Betty's and my relationship. Perhaps we should have. There were those pants I wore on our first date. And then there was the notable fact that he was putting on eyeliner when I called to ask him out.

We met at a reading group meeting, which that night had convened in Peter's kitchen to discuss *The Sun Also Rises,* the Hemingway novel that tells the lost-generation story of poor Jake and his "war wound," and not-so-poor Brett and her trust fund. That it was Hemingway, and that particular novel, turned out to be an uncanny omen. People are always trotting out that picture of the young Hemingway in his pretty frock and long curls, as if that's evidence that the most macho of writer guys was somehow . . . queer. I don't know whether he was or not, but one of his sons was.[7] And that book sure is.

And, as it would turn out, so are we.

But when we first met, we didn't know that. The first three things I knew about my future husband were that: (1) he was an actor, (2) he wasn't gay, and (3) he was leaving town in three weeks. For me, recently broken up from a nearly five-year-long disaster of a relationship, I saw Betty as a great opportunity to start dating again and without having to worry about things getting too serious. He was leaving and he was an actor. I figured he was well rehearsed in casual sexual relationships that ended when a show did. As it turned out, he is probably the least casual about sex of anyone I've ever known. I never did start dating again, and he only left town long enough to do a role he'd committed to doing before we met, and we both opted not to see other people during the time he'd be away. When he returned to New York City, we dated exclusively for a year, moved in together a year later, got engaged a year after that, and got married fourteen months after our engagement.

We weren't in a hurry, but we weren't overly cautious, either. We took things as they came, and while we were having a lot of fun together, we also got to know each other very well. We lived together long enough for both of us to let our guards down and stop being on our best behavior. We had our first fights, interference from a jealous ex, disagreements about where to spend the holidays; we merged finances before we got engaged, but we waited for the engagement to adopt cats. We learned about each other's gender variance within weeks of our first date, but after I learned that he liked to dress in women's clothes, and after he learned that I didn't wear dresses often or heels at all, we still didn't really know how much of an impact gender would have on our relationship.

I've seen a lot of people get divorced or come close to it in the time I've been married, and I've been married nearly six years (though we've been together for nine). One couple split up after a decade together, another after only two years, still another half that. Another couple, parents of friends, separated not long before their fortieth anniversary. Whether I was close to a particular couple or not, I've often found myself wondering why my husband and I are not divorced or even separated. I can't predict the future and say absolutely that we won't get divorced, but when we look at the high rates of divorce among couples in which one person is trans, we're still pretty sure we're beating the odds.[8] Sometimes we don't argue that much, and other times we argue until there's nothing left to say. But still, we're together—we've made it so far, and others haven't. I have a kind of romantic survivor's guilt. Why should we be together and not them? We are both lucky and unusual in that our parents are still married; my parents are a few years past their fiftieth anniversary, and Betty's parents recently celebrated their thirty-fifth. It's not because my husband and I are in love in a mythical way, though our friends believe we are. All couples have problems, some of them critical. I occasionally want to think that we're together because we've worked so hard at our relationship, or because our issues are so complicated that they've forced us to talk in ways that maybe other couples don't.

But I know, in my heart of hearts, that most people work hard at their relationships. Couples want to stay together; they want wedded bliss, good sex, shared lives. Most people want to walk gray-haired and hand in hand on the beach someday after their retirement, and they want, as do I, to still be in love with that gray-haired person at the end of their own hand.

It would be smug of me to think we're somehow special, or that we communicate better or work harder or love each other more. We did have the odd advantage of having to talk about a lot of serious things very early on in our relationship: Our sex life wasn't golden, and my husband liked to crossdress. Other couples seem to fly through the first few years, and then they have children who keep them busy. We haven't flown through the first five years. Instead, we had his ex blackmail us for the first two. For the first five years, he was working a lot—a full-time day job and acting at night, so we barely saw each other. We also had setbacks: 9/11 happened just when we were getting our wedding pictures back, and as a result I entered a depression so deep and dark I had to quit my job, which meant financial struggles. And on and on it went, all the bad interrupted and overwhelmed by really great things: our wedding, his good reviews, my writing success. We never had a dull moment, but we certainly had a lot of complicated ones that forced us to make decisions about very important things. We learned to trust each other in deep ways; we survived a few trials by fire. We were forced to communicate in ways that some couples avoid for a long time.

After all that, my husband felt he might need to become a woman.

Now there's an uncommon relationship problem.

You don't face an issue like transsexualism in a marriage and expect to come out of it together, which is why I'm surprised we have.

Relationships are hard even when they aren't beset with unusually difficult circumstances. That thought has given me solace more than once when we were barely speaking to each other, or when the D word got brought up. It's hard to look around and not realize that we're all wanting to be loved, terrified of not being loved, able to communicate only some parts of what we feel; we're naturally angry or fearful or insecure and tend to focus on what makes us angry or scared or insecure. Maybe we're naturally self-centered or stubborn in ways that prevent intimacy. We all have traits that limit us as partners and traits that help us become good partners. Almost all relationships face communication breakdowns, huge arguments, and at least a couple of monumental crises that seem impossible to get over or get past. I'm no expert; I don't claim to know by what miracle Betty and I have managed to stay together despite all this adversity. But I do know one thing that gave us more tools, more leeway, more fluidity, and more latitude when dealing with our problems—and that was our ability to forget how we were supposed to be as husband and wife. We could ignore gender roles altogether. I can't underestimate exactly how huge that has been, or how thankful I am that in this one way, we were granted a very unusual boon.

An old standby in the crossdressing community, a line that crossdressers tend to use on their wives, goes: "But I'm the same person underneath." The wife, who is standing there looking at a person who sounds like her husband and who might look like him somewhere under the wig and breast forms and press-on nails, tries to parse what exactly that's supposed to mean. She's suspicious that her husband is trying to blow smoke up her ass, the same as a husband who might come up with an ingenious reason why he had to spend his weekend fishing instead of shopping for new sofa upholstery. She might look at him, adjust his wig, and then sigh and take him shopping.

Others just balk.

Some women are just smarter than I am, and when they first hear that line, they run for the hills. Likewise for the ones who hightail it when they hear their husbands say, "I've always imagined what it would be like to have breasts," or "When I was young, I always wished I were Susie Perkins." They call a lawyer, they try to get custody of the children,[9] and they wish their future ex-husbands well, but they want no part of it. Not me. I didn't believe in gender; gender wasn't important.

But the one thing you learn when you hang out with someone who might be transsexual is that almost nothing is more important than gender: not relationships, not children, not employment, not career goals or financial stability. When something isn't right with someone's gender, nothing could be more wrong or more important. When my husband was "just" crossdressing—and not talking about permanent body modifications or a legal change of ID—it didn't affect me in the same way, because it was temporary. Clothes are just clothes. For me, "I'm the same person underneath" was true; stripped down in the shower, my husband might be the prettiest, most exfoliated, least hairy man alive, but he was certainly still a man. Neither of us believed in all the rules about who's supposed to cook or take out the garbage; we weren't our grandparents, after all, but progressive, gender-neutral types who knew that women could be engineers and that men could be equal partners in parenting. But we were still surprised by how huge the chasm was between "man" and "woman." He had to size up that distance to try to make the leap, and I had to decide if I could go with him.

I genuinely didn't expect my husband's shift to upset me. But gender roles are not just about how you perceive yourself, but also about what you expect from others, how they make you feel about you. His gender affects my gender just as mine might affect the next person's. With such an intimate relationship as a marriage, the gendered parts of you that are affected by the gendered parts of others are the most hidden, personal, deep-seated parts—the bits deep in your psyche that don't like to be brought to light, much less changed. It hurts to change such deep parts of yourself, especially when you know that everything you are and want to be is at stake, that the most valuable relationship of your life teeters on whether or not you can pull off a transformation so complete, a transformation of your relationship but also of both of your individual selves. That's a lot of change for a couple to shoulder. I longed for a lobotomy sometimes—to forget how things used to be, were supposed to be, and how I'd wanted them to be—and had to focus instead on how things actually were. Anywhere so devoid of smoke and mirrors is an uncomfortable place; most of us are a little Blanche DuBois in liking a paper lantern over the glaring light of reality.

So now I wake up in the morning wondering whether I can love my husband if he becomes a woman, whether I can accept that people will view me as a lesbian, and whether or not this extraordinary situation might end up being a clear-cut deal-breaker for my marriage vows. Most people would give me their blessings if I find I can't live with a woman, even if she used to be the man I fell in love with. I don't think there's a judge in the world who wouldn't say, "Well, of course" if I explained that my partner's change of sex prevented me from staying "till death do us part."

Even those who hoped we would find a way would ultimately understand. Even my husband would. He might understand better than anyone else.

Some women in the same situation wouldn't have to think twice about leaving. Others might make peace with sharing their lives with a woman, perhaps because they cherished the companionship or had children to consider. But my husband and I have no children, and we have been married for less than five years. I'm not yet forty. There is time, some might say and some have said, for a clean break and a fresh start.

The comfort Betty sought in changing his gender was going to be the end of my own. My personal crisis—in trying to figure out why my partner's gender change might prevent me from loving him—or her—is the basis of this book. To understand why gender was so invisible to me before, and why it's so unavoidable now, I had to try to figure out what gender is exactly, and why it at once means so much and signifies nothing.

Some might suspect me of trying to smart my way out of an unpleasant reality. But here's the rub: I'm in love. It may sound like a romantic fantasy out of the pages of O. Henry, but I meant what I said when I said I do. So did Betty. I at least wanted to make a good-faith effort to figure out whether it was my expectations of our gender roles that had set me up for a fall, or whether there is something essential about gender that I am trying to deny, much to the disgust of my feminist self. Maybe there is a fundamental, important difference between men and women. Or perhaps there is something written into the whole idea of romance that made the future of our romance impossible: something about knights and ladies, something in my head or in this culture that implies that the very notion of what "romantic" means is about men and women. I wanted to know if my need to be in love with a man was a kind of Freudian baggage, or whether it was the frisson of stubble against my smooth cheek that made men the object of my desire.

So, along with gender, I needed to know what desire was, and romance, and marriage. I started asking questions about the purpose of relationships and why people seek them so diligently. So I looked to gender in practice in my own relationship and in others'. I wanted to know how a lesbian couple decides which partner will birth their child. I wanted to discover why or how bisexuals can love either gender, and whether their erotic and emotional drives are equal toward both. I interviewed other partners of trans people to see how they'd managed to love their partners through transition, and I also interviewed couples who were not as traditional in their gender roles in an attempt to find out if Mr. Moms feel less chivalrous, and if their wives who bring home the bacon think less of their stay-at-home husbands for being nurturing. I wanted to know too why so many feminine gay men complain about not being able to find partners who love them for who they really are and why so many straight-acting gay men put "no fems" in their personal ads. I wanted to try to figure out why gay and lesbian culture seems to be the only place for any gender variance. I had personal questions that had long gone unanswered, too, such as whether every heterosexual female tomboy like me had "femmed up" in order to date. When girls ask boys out, or make the first move sexually, does the romance work? It never did for me, not until I met Betty, but maybe that was because he wasn't a man in the traditional sense.

I've felt convinced that at the root of it all is sexuality, that my unwillingness to love a woman is about facing unfamiliar genitals and wondering who is supposed to be on top. I couldn't figure out why loving a woman should seem so unimaginable when loving that same person in a male body was so fantastic. Since I was already comfortable with flexible gender roles, it didn't make any sense why some part of me was dragging its heels and saying no. But in the 21st century, in which the primary ethic is to do whatever you need to do to be yourself, fulfilled, and happy, it's hard not to notice that I'm stuck between a paradox and a dilemma: Either I'd have to change my sexual orientation to accommodate my husband's transition—and do so in an era when gay men have stopped pretending they can change theirs—or my husband would need to find a way to feel female without changing sex. It seems almost laughable, even to me. One voice in my head tells me we're screwed, while another unapologetically suggests I simply haven't tried hard enough.

I had to keep looking, though. I had to know, for sure, that it was impossible for me to love her as much as I love him, before I could leave. And before I could know that, I would need to know why a change of gender could make a formerly perfect romance impossible. Most of what I read about gender in relationships is adversarial: Mars versus Venus and Venus Just Doesn't Understand Mars. But if Mars and Venus made any sense, gay and lesbian relationships would be perfect. Most of my gay and lesbian friends who are in relationships would reject that idea. But honestly, if Mars and Venus were the truth, guys who lived together would understand who's retreating to the cave and why, and lesbian relationships would be soundless exchanges of empathy—nearly telepathic, a complicated system of nods. But they aren't. Gender is far more intricate than that.

But everywhere I turned I found these simplified, nearly Neanderthal views of gender, all of them antagonistic. It's as if we've taken the war of the sexes home with us. Feminism is blamed for all the problems in heterosexual relationships, somehow—as if the mad idea that women are equal has unsettled men in a way they can't get past.[10] In addition to all the Tarzan/Jane thinking that's coming from so-called experts, endless jokes point out that men are numb nuts and women are superior, or that women are flighty or mean while men are just good-natured, trusting

Br'er Rabbits. From Camille Paglia's *Personae* to John Gray's Roman god and goddess, we've set ourselves up as opposites, as if the most important thing were to prove who is innately nurturing and whose biological destiny it is to be CEO. But I don't see that any of that matters when it comes to relationships, when the whole idea is to be happy, not to "win." We have to figure out how to put gender away when we love someone, and to do that we need to recognize what gender is.

For my husband, gender became a bête noire, the dragon in the road that he could not pass. His indecision clogged up our relationship and made us both hesitant about a future we couldn't be certain of. He was scared I'd stop loving him if he became a woman, and I was scared of the same thing. So I had to examine what gender really is, how it affects us, how it plays out in our actual lives—not what it's like theoretically, in the papers of academics, nor what it's like "scientifically," in news articles about what Harvard presidents[11] think girls can't do and boys can.

I once had an older crossdresser tell me, only half joking, that he and his wife seemed to be switching genders in their old age, as his testosterone levels receded naturally while her estrogen levels did the same postmenopause. But Betty and I have always been like that. We've recently found out it's biochemically true, as well; I have a slightly elevated testosterone level that's due to having something called polycystic ovary syndrome (PCOS for short)[12] and Betty's blood work has shown her testosterone is on the low end of the normal range. We used to joke that on the gender spectrum, with female at one end and male on the other, I was a 49 to her 51, but my guess is that even if I become the 51 to her 49, we'll be the same as we are now. Instead of waiting for a lifetime of shared interests and declining hormones to switch genders, we do so several times a day instead, or maybe weekly, or monthly. We've even managed it sexually on occasion.

But we met under the assumption that we both had regular genders, ones that aligned with our bodies. We were also both, theoretically, normatively heterosexual, although I'm not sure I knew what that meant then and I'm definitely not sure I know what it means now. The idea that we both like the opposite sex gets a little complicated because of how we're gendered and because of the difficulty of defining what the "opposite" of that 49 or 51 would be. Still, our romance has been very much a story of boy meets girl: We met, fell in love, went on an exciting first date, couldn't stop talking, and couldn't believe how much we had in common. I could barely tear myself away from my apartment when I was expecting his call in those first few weeks, and I remember us both laughing a lot—laughing with relief at having found someone so cool, so smart, so cute, and someone who was all those things and who wanted to keep dating us. He might have been a little more flabbergasted than I was, especially after he told me he liked to wear women's clothes and I didn't run screaming.

It's only now, after nearly a decade of time together, that I can recognize how much gender has shaped who we are together and as individuals, how much our relationship was a little more *girl meets boy* than *boy meets girl* in that I was the aggressor, the person who made the nervous call, and Betty was more the type who waited by the phone. Some days I have a wife, other days a husband, but I also have a girlfriend, and a boyfriend, and a best friend. Because sometimes I behave more like a husband than a wife, we have a lot of different relationships built into one, and they all operate at once, indistinguishable from one another. Teasing out when I'm being "wifely" or "husbandly" is impossible, in the same way it's hard to tell when your lover is more your friend than your lover or vice versa. It can seem almost crowded in the one-bedroom apartment we share with our three cats. Some days, to be clear, we ask each other what page we're on just so we know how we might spend the evening most in sync. Yet other times our companionship seems like lockstep: If we're talking about Shakespeare, it's a sure bet that we'll both reach for the same issue of Neil Gaiman's comic book series The Sandman[13] at the same critical moment in our discussion. We'll still simultaneously decide we need to reread the series, and we'll argue about who gets to start it first while we both know that he will because I have a tendency to notice a reference to *Beowulf* and spend three days reading that, too. And yet not a word of it has to be spoken out loud, or if it is, it's only in a kind of grunty shorthand, as in, "Yeah, but you, last time," with me finishing the thought with "Right, *Beowulf,* okay."

I had a lot of dreams about twins when we met. We get asked quite often—and quite ickily—if we're siblings. We have the same birthday, same year; our mothers were in labor within hours of each other. I've had old friends compliment me on how good I look on the cover of *My Husband Betty*—and of course it's Betty who's on the cover, not me. Sometimes we think we should differentiate more, and no doubt the word "codependence" has been whispered in our wake.

But while we have moments when our relationship seems more Borg[14] than human, there are other times when we bump into each other opening the apartment door because we never know exactly who is leading. The assumptions about which of us is the husband, or the top, or the lead, were thrown out the window a long time ago, and not consciously. Betty does not have to be presenting as female, and I don't have to be feeling particularly masculine, for me to open a door or pay the cabdriver. Her being out about her transness has meant his looks aren't very masculine, either, which has led to his looking androgynous even when he thinks he's presenting as male. It's a good match for my lack of gender, and while I don't get clocked as male anymore, I'm often assumed to be a lesbian.

We don't know which of us is the husband and which of us is the wife, or we both are both, all the time, or sequentially. Sometimes we're both the husband or we're both the wife. It feels a lot like the kind of friendship most of us experience only as children, when who was in charge wasn't decided by genitals but by whose toys you were playing with or whose house you were in, or by who liked the game the most. We try to work out chores that way, too—by deciding who hates which chores more than the other, or who needs what done sooner. I don't do laundry because I don't have a full-time job and so don't always manage to change out of my pajamas, and she can let a sinkful of dirty dishes pile up and not notice them.

Every other time I dated someone, there was always a tiny difference between how much I liked him and how much he liked me; sometimes I was more in love, sometimes he was. But with Betty, it became clear pretty quickly that we were mutually enthusiastic; at the end of our second date I wondered when we'd see each other next and at the moment I was about to open my mouth to ask, he asked me what I was doing on Tuesday. Things have worked like that, over and over again, ever since.

A sense of what I can only call delight has kept us together despite the difficulties we've been through, and what we've been through isn't what most people would consider a walk in the park. I had been asking him for years if he thought he was transsexual, and he always said no. Then one day he said *I don't know*. And since then, we've been trying to figure out what his transitioning might mean to our romance.

I'd accepted my husband's crossdressing for years before that, so it came as a surprise to me that it should mean anything. I didn't have a problem calling him "she." I was the one who named her Betty. I've picked out clothes, helped with shoes and jewelry, made appointments for her manicures. I was, as far as we were concerned, completely okay with having a feminine partner who happened to be male. Over time it had become a rarity for me to see and spend time with the guy I had met; Betty has changed a lot during our years together, and she has become increasingly out and femme as a result of my writing *My Husband Betty*. We had come to the compromise that I would be okay with seeing the man who was my husband once a month, and even then it was okay if he was wearing earrings and makeup, as long as it was in an androgynous rock star kind of way.

A lot of people must have looked at me as if I were on drugs when the idea of her going full-time caused me consternation. One of my friends asked, "Are you really going to tell me you didn't see this coming?" And I didn't. I honestly didn't. I worried about it and I feared it, but Betty had told me so many times that our marriage, and acting, along with other parts of her male self—yes, that one essential part included—were important to her, and I believed it. I still do believe that all of those things are important to her, but sometimes important things become less important than transitioning. I know transsexuals who've lost nearly everything: loving relationships, contact with their children or parents or friends, jobs, homes, health insurance. They didn't transition thinking they could keep those things; almost all transsexuals I've known expect to lose a good chunk of what they hold dear, and they may hope that they won't and do whatever they can to ensure that they won't, but often they do. It's very rare to hear anyone regret transitioning, even when they regret losing some of the things they valued most in their lives. As one trans woman told me recently: "It's not like I could ever go back to being Brian."

I had deluded myself, and Betty had deluded herself. The more we talked about it, the more flinty I got when we talked. I started to shut down at the prospect of losing the love of my life, and my mind and heart started setting backfires of anger and snarkiness meant to contain the anger and sadness that losing my husband would bring.

On top of all of that, I was angry at myself for what I couldn't deny: that I wouldn't be able to love my husband the same way if he became a woman.

For other people, that might have been obvious right from the start. But I was used to having a transvestite[15] for a husband. I found my husband attractive dressed as a woman. I enjoyed his transness.

My worry was a crushing realization. I wanted to be able to tell him that I would be there no matter what. And for a while, I nearly did. I tried to be encouraging. I had moments when I hoped I might fall in love with someone else to make it "easier" on us both for her to transition without having to worry about me. I thought it would be easier if I died.

The good thing is that I wasn't going through any of this alone. Betty was wondering if it would be easier if he died, too, so that I could find a man to be with again, and be happy.

It's a cold, cold day when death seems easier than what you're facing. A cold, lonely, miserable, heart-wrenching day. Antidepressants were not going to fix it. Money wouldn't fix it. The next-best alternative to death was a partial lobotomy. I fantasized about a plan that would allow a surgeon to remove the parts of my brain that remembered I'd ever met a boy and married a husband; after the surgery I would wake to my loving wife and enjoy her company and feel no regret and just move forward. They could tell me I'd had a tumor that had been removed, and I wouldn't be any the wiser.

Betty and I were in a no-man's-land. Neither of us wanted to break up. I wasn't ready to have a female partner. He knew he wasn't ready to lose me. When he asked me to tell him the truth, I couldn't allow myself to lie and promise I'd be there when he told me the most important thing to him was to be with me forever. And I couldn't convince myself I would still be in love with him the same way if he were to become a woman.

Something had to give.

The way we're living now can sometimes feel as if we're just forestalling what may be imminent—Betty's transition to living full-time as a woman, no matter how she might do that. She has a significant life as Betty and is seen as female by friends and strangers, sometimes when she's trying to present as male. Just about everyone we know is aware that she's trans, though people who always see her as Betty are often surprised she has any male self at all, and others—who have known her only as male—tend to see her as male all the time.

I've often joked with Betty that she will eventually be the only female who shows up at a theater to play a male lead. That may someday mean binding her breasts and applying facial hair with spirit gum and shavings, but theater is theater and allows for such things. We have often wondered if it might not be more useful for her to use a gender-neutral name so as not to confuse casting directors or audiences, but we've come to be such old hands at Trans 101 that there doesn't seem much of a point to doing that, either. Cross–cross-gender acting isn't unheard of, and if anyone could pull it off, it would be my talented and charming partner.

This scheme is entirely mine, though. I'm the type who is always coming up with the plan to end all plans, the "fix" for whatever's wrong. Living in two genders is not easy, and mostly it's unheard of outside of drag communities. In a recent production of Glyn Maxwell's *Wolfpit* by the theater Betty helped found, her experience was frustrating and disorienting, with half the cast using her male name and the other half the female. I could at least relate, as there were nights people called me Helen or by my given name, depending on how they knew me or for how long. My pseudonym situation oddly mimics Betty's identity issue; we both feel as if we have a foot in two worlds. If only one world could contain multiplicity. In our culture, unfortunately, multiplicity is often interpreted as duplicity, and in an era of identity theft and background checks and metal detectors, not intending to deceive doesn't seem to count for much.

I've often had a sense from media people that they are only interested in interviewing me if I'm willing to use my "real" name, and pointing out that Helen Boyd is as real a name as Cher, or Sting, or Jon Stewart, or Mark Twain, or Microsoft[16] doesn't seem to do much good, no matter how old or long or varied the list of people who have stage names or nom de plumes. I get that blank stare, the silence on the other end of line that means I've surpassed their sense of reality. People believe that there is a "real you" the same way that they believe a person only has one real gender, and presenting anything that makes your multiplicity transparent comes with accusations of deception. I have no interest in deceiving anyone, and don't.

What is clear is that Betty and I are actively becoming, but we don't know what exactly; we have no goal but to change together, taking turns or in tandem. We live with an active sense of being unfinished. No one is ever finished changing; all things change all the time. But embracing such vaporous identities seems sometimes too pomo even for a postmodern world. It doesn't come without a sense of anxiety, as when you're driving on a curvy road with limited visibility or stumbling forward by feel in a dark, unfamiliar room. People don't know what pronouns to use depending on how the person they're addressing is dressed; they want one to be the right answer, even when I explain that when my partner looks female, you use "she," and if he doesn't, you don't.[17] But this is just the answer we've come up with, for now. You could see it as Betty halting her transition, or you could say she's transitioning at glacier speed. We have compromised because the fear and sadness I was going through when it seemed certain Betty would become a woman full-time was putting too much of a strain on our relationship, and she, honest about not wanting to lose me, has kept some kind of male self in the picture.

It's confusing, but for us, it's worth it; we prefer complicated together over simple and separate. So far we have been lucky: We live in a city where gender variance is somewhat accepted, or at the very least, many people have met someone transgendered before. We know a lot of people in the worlds of theater and entertainment: drag queens, burlesque stars, and performance artists. As one friend said while trying to introduce me to a friend of hers who is a drag queen, "You two can introduce yourselves. I don't know which names either of you is using tonight." I've gotten used to stepping up to someone whom I'm about to be introduced to and saying, "Hi, I'm Helen," to spare someone that moment of stuttering. Betty does the same. While it's nice to have a demimonde—who doesn't want to have a demimonde?—it is not the only world we need to travel in. We have work lives and families who don't live in New York; we have young nieces whose parents may or may not be okay with their kids knowing their uncle sometimes looks like an aunt; we want to travel with IDs that won't be questioned by overzealous security guards. So while the path we've chosen is holding for now, in this place and time, we are not sure it's a lasting solution. When we think about who we will become and how or where we will be living ten years in the future, the best we can do for now is guess, and hope. It's a little like that scene in *Raiders of the Lost Ark,* when Indiana Jones finds out the Ark has just been put on a truck to Cairo, and he's got to go after it. His friend Sallah wants to know how exactly he's going to do that, and he responds, "I don't know. I'm making this up as I go."

Likewise, for us. There are days that "making it up as you go" feels adventurous and freeing, and others when it feels restrictive and very, very tiring. But it's what we've got, for now.

two

confessions of a grown-up tomboy.

When your boyfriend tells you he's going to wait outside while you buy a pair of summer sandals, you don't think anything of it. Guys are supposed to be bored outside of shoe stores, waiting slouched on mall benches near the potted palms. They're supposed to wander off, into an electronics shop, or a hardware store, or a sports equipment emporium. They're not supposed to care if you buy clogs or mules, sling-backs or flats. They're not even supposed to know the difference.

So when I popped into a shoe store on Eighth Street to buy a pair of mules, I didn't think twice about my boyfriend waiting outside. The store was a little crowded—almost too crowded for me—and I understood not wanting to be in a gaggle of women buying shoes on sale. For me, it was a necessary errand; I would find the only three pairs that appealed to me—

which were almost guaranteed to be the plainest the store had—and leave with the pair that made the most sense. I don't really shop for shoes; I buy shoes. I go into a store knowing what I'm looking for and I leave with a pair that's close enough.

I bought my shoes and came out to find Betty looking kind of pale, and tired, and a little angry. I asked her if I took too long. I asked if she were hungry, or thirsty, or wanted to go home and take a nap. I asked everything except the right question. Finally she blurted out that I didn't understand how difficult it was for her to see me buying women's shoes in a woman's shoe store with other women.

It never occurred to me that Betty remained outside because he wanted desperately to be a woman shopping for shoes, and that the women around me who oohed and aahed and modeled for each other and pointed out that Kenneth Cole was having a sale the very next week actually caused Betty so much envy that she wouldn't and couldn't come in. My practical response was, "This is Eighth Street. No one's going to care if you want to go in and try on a pair of women's shoes."

I didn't get it. I didn't get it even by a long shot, because guys are not supposed to have identity crises when their girlfriends buy a pair of summer sandals.

We talked that day and into the night; talked as we walked, from Eighth Street to Broadway down to the Brooklyn Bridge and then across it. We stopped and cried together a couple of times. Betty told me how stupid she felt because of this desire to be a woman, how it didn't go away, never went away, no matter what she did. She'd been out and crossdressing with me on her arm for a few years at that point, so I was completely surprised. From what she had told me and from what other crossdressers had told me and from what I had read, going out *en femme* should have relieved her angst. And it did, she admitted, it did. But she needed me to understand that going into a store looking like a man to buy a pair of pumps was not what she wanted. I suggested she dress and we go shopping for shoes instead. She shook her head sadly, no. Dressing as a woman wasn't what she wanted, either, though sometimes that was okay—at least better than being a man buying women's shoes. She just wanted to feel like one of the girls, one of the many picking up Jimmy Choos and clucking over details. Now it was my turn to shake my head sadly, no. I had never felt like one of those girls, never one of the women. Every woman in a shop looked up when I walked in; salesgirls knew I wasn't one of them because I didn't wear the right amount of makeup or carry a purse and because I wore black oxfords.

I certainly couldn't tell Betty what it felt like to be a woman—at least not one of those women. I am a woman, but I can't guarantee I feel like one; I suspect I don't, or that I feel similar only to a subset of women who are a little bit more like me—bookish, practical, direct, and not into shoes. I'm *supposed* to be into shoes. I've not laughed at more jokes on TV sitcoms about women and their love of shoes more times than I can count, and I've dropped out of conversations because shoes became the subject. I've asked women if the shoes they were wearing were comfortable only to be told that comfort had nothing to do with it. I've also taken off shoes other women call comfortable after twenty minutes of foot pain. I just don't get it. I feel like the guy on a recent commercial who looks up at the three different shoes his girlfriend is showing him and who sees only three of the same shoe. To me, a pair of pumps is a pair of pumps. I find most fashionable shoes designed for women kind of silly, and Betty sometimes loses her patience with my sarcasm when she's looking at shoes. I often lose my patience when she tries to describe her transness, the feelings and desires it creates in her, because so much of what she talks about—such as fitting in with the other women in a shoe shop—is so far away from my own experience of being a woman. She talks about wanting to fit into that group of women as if it were an indicator of her innate woman-ness, which makes me wonder, sometimes, if I'm a woman at all.

The whole issue of what a woman is comes up a lot in my life because of Betty wanting to fit in with women and because trans women I know ask me if they "feel" like women because they've always felt like women on the inside and want to know if their outer and inner have become the same. I've tried to find something in me that "feels like a woman," and Shania Twain hasn't done me any favors. I don't feel like a woman, ever, really, except maybe when I actually have my period or when I feel an odd twinge in one of my breasts. To me, other than feminist stuff, being a woman has primarily been about what body parts to check for which cancers and knowing that I could become pregnant if I have unprotected sex. I am thankful for multiple orgasms and find it amusing that women's clitorises are the only body part—male or female—that has no purpose other than pleasure. But to me, being capable of multiple orgasms and having a clitoris fall more into the pros/cons kind of categories; having a clitoris doesn't make me feel like a woman internally. I've never been the Gaia-worshipping, menstrual-blood-tasting type. I don't identify with the yoni; I have no natural sense of yin. I don't feel comfortable in formfitting clothes; I hate heels; I'm usually uncomfortable when I realize someone is looking at my ass. I don't write in lavender ink, or dot my *i*'s with hearts. I don't like perfume because I'm allergic to most of it, and I've never been much of a giggler. I don't have any interest in having a baby; I like children okay but wouldn't want any living with me. I am quite fond of chocolate, though.

Such stereotypes. But when I consider how someone might "feel like a woman," what else is there? I know I'm a woman; I have the requisite parts.[1] But feeling like a woman strikes me as being something else altogether; I assume it must mean feeling feminine, or sexy, or playful, or compassionate, even. Maybe goddesslike or nurturing or gentle. I don't really understand what it is I'm supposed to feel; if someone asked me if I felt like a man I'd be just as confused.

Sometimes I'm thoroughly convinced I'm innately androgynous and don't have a strong internal sense of gender; maybe some people do, the way some people are strongly left-handed and others are insistently right-handed and other people really are ambidextrous. If I woke up tomorrow with a male body instead of this one, my day wouldn't change very much, at least as concerns what I might be thinking about or what I might do with my time. (Well, okay, the day *after* wouldn't be much different, because the first day I'd be too fascinated with my new penis to do much of anything else but play with it.) How I would be treated would obviously change in ways I can't predict and maybe don't want to know.

I've asked a lot of other women if they feel like women, and some of them say they do. Women often mention they feel like women because they like the company of other women and don't so much like the company of men. But as far as I can tell, that's not about feeling like a woman; that's about figuring out who communicates about what in ways you like and are comfortable with.

Betty's attempt to figure out what exactly she's after in wanting to be a woman is completely confounding for both of us. I feel like someone who lives in a rainforest who's trying to understand why Eskimos (and Vermonters) have a dozen words for ice and snow. I once found myself trying to explain to a Burmese monk how cold it would be in Tibet, where he was going on a short visit. It's very difficult to explain how cold snow is to someone who feels chilled in seventy-degree weather; he didn't understand how a human being could physically survive being that cold, though by the end of the conversation I had convinced him he couldn't wear sandals and should bring every article of clothing he owned. My sense of gender is similar to that monk's sense of cold: They tell me I should wear these kinds of shoes, and these kinds of clothes, and I might not ever like it, and in the end the idea of it will probably be more fascinating than the reality.

In my universe, gender is an external thing; because of the parts I have, they tell me I'm a woman. Because of the sexism in the world, the parts I have cause some people to think I'm not that bright, or logical, or powerful, or strong. But I've never experienced being a woman internally. I've had trans people tell me that the reason I don't have a strong sense of gender is because I've never had a problem with mine, and that—well, that just makes me laugh. I've always had a problem with my gender; I just can't imagine changing my sex because of it. That would be like jumping out of the frying pan into the fire. Kate Bornstein gives women an extra 100 points in her gender quiz[2] just because it's normal to think about gender if you're a woman, because gender is a pain in the ass if you're a woman. The sexism of the world makes gender a problem for every woman, but that doesn't make me feel like a man. That's a leap that trans people make that baffles the rest of us. I certainly have gotten to know enough trans people to know that their internal sense of gender is really very intense, and very painful, and very much directs them to change their sex if they want to be happy. Talking to people who have changed sex makes me certain I'm not trans, but it doesn't mean I don't have a problem with my gender.

I was a tomboy.

I was called "butch" by the neighborhood bully when I was seven. I don't remember doing or saying anything that encouraged him to say it. I didn't beat him up no matter how much I might have wanted to. His insult seemed directed at who I was, not inspired by something I did. I had convinced my mother to let me have a Dorothy Hamill bob haircut like every other tomboy who grew up in the seventies, and I had a license plate with my name on it hanging from the handlebars of my yellow Schwinn that I tore all over the neighborhood on. I had stopped my bike and was standing in front of my banana seat, legs astride the bike's works, a dirty pedal pressing against the back of my calf; the bully stood in front of my bike, holding the handlebars, his legs on either side of my front wheel. I see that scene in my head now as if it were filmed by Spielberg. Two children—one purportedly female, the other male—who looked a lot alike. Me and the neighborhood bully shared more than a haircut: We were both blond, both chosen first by the older kids for neighborhood games since we were both fast and played to win. We both had older brothers we couldn't embarrass by being lame players. Neither of us could afford to throw like girls, and we both had long eyelashes and yellow-brown eyes.

He flipped the plastic license plate dismissively, made like he was going to break it, and said instead, "This should say butch."

I wanted to protest that butch wasn't my name, but I didn't know if it was a name at all. The first rule of childhood was never to admit you didn't know what a word meant; years of ridicule might follow. So I didn't say anything.

I never asked anyone, and I didn't tell anyone that story. I shoved it to the back of my mind the way you do with things in childhood that confuse or upset you. Betty's transness has encouraged me to think about things I hadn't thought about for a long time, like having grown up a tomboy, and about things like what women are, and what they do, and what it means to be one. It didn't happen on purpose. What happened was that I found myself playing a part—a part I enjoyed and that terrified me—when she presented as a femme. Something in me responded unconsciously to her femme; I became, in my own postheterosexual kind of way, her butch. Soft butch, to be sure; I'd learned to pass as a regular girl and couldn't undo that. I had to squelch my feelings about being the more masculine one of the two of us. For a while I'd get all dolled up with her, and—as had happened earlier in my life—I got tired of it really quickly. I longed for pants, and shorter hair, and flat shoes. I longed to be what I now see as a kind of essential or organic me. But when Betty and I met, I thought I'd grown out of being a tomboy; I thought it was in my past, a "phase" I'd gone through.

But the more and more Betty presented as femme, the more and more it was obvious I was well suited to be her partner; I wasn't a lesbian, but Betty wasn't exactly a woman, either. I was just butch to her femme—not butch in the grand scheme of things, because "butch" is a specific identity, specific to lesbians, but rather masculine relative to her feminine gender.

Sometimes things that feel natural and good can be terrifying. Sometimes who you are is exactly who you don't want to be. Sometimes, admitting that you're different is more than you can manage.

But being with Betty made me even more aware of how much I wasn't one of those women in the shoe store, and how I never had been. I tried. I've given more pairs of heels to the Salvation Army than I'd care to admit. I picked up a love of corsets and makeup when I was passing as a so-called regular girl that I might not have developed otherwise. One high school friend actually classified me as "boy crazy," but I ended up with Betty, and I loved her in makeup, and I started to wonder about how much I liked boys, and what kind of boys I liked.

What I came to when I looked back to my puberty and prepubescent years was the man I've always jokingly credited as having turned on my hormones: Adam Ant,[3] with his lip gloss and dandy clothes and high cheekbones. My first high school crush had delicate features and long jet-black hair. The guy I dated before I met Betty had long curly hair and big lips and high cheekbones. They all had a certain ferocity, too, a kind of delicate anger, much like Johnny Rotten's. Other women didn't have a similar long line of pretty men in their pasts, which kept me thinking until I found that scene from my childhood. I can still feel that bike pedal up against my dirty calf.

I don't know when I learned what butch meant, and I didn't have a lightbulb moment when I did. I did know to be cautious around that neighborhood bully after that encounter, and as the years went by I came to understand that he was the kind of boy to avoid at all costs.

Half a decade later, the girl who became his girlfriend called me a dyke. We were just beginning junior high at that time. They were made for each other.

I didn't understand that his problem with me was that I was a threat to his standing as the neighborhood's fastest runner or maybe that his future girlfriend preferred me to him. I hadn't been told yet, as I would be in fifth grade, that beating a boy in a foot race wasn't something nice girls did—forget crowing about it. He hated me because I didn't let him win, and because a boy who is beaten by a girl doesn't just lose, he is humiliated.[4] Had someone explained to my child self that I was expected to submit, I might have made a different decision. But I was dense that way. It never occurred to me to let someone win a game because you wanted the person to like you. I was used to people liking me because there was a better chance of their team winning when I was on it. But those two future terrors were princess and crown prince of the neighborhood. I was supposed to pay allegiance to their royalty. As a child, I'd always felt I was both prince and princess; I never saw any reason I couldn't be and have it all. Puberty was one hell of a wake-up call, because I suddenly felt I was a failure for being good at the things I'd been good at as a kid, and I also began to learn that I wouldn't be allowed to do certain things at all because I was female, like become a priest.[5] After my genderless childhood, it was kind of hard to take all the rules about what I was and wasn't supposed to be good at, what I could do and couldn't, how I was and wasn't supposed to sit, talk, stand, or look.

A lot of tomboys have a hard time with puberty—I still can't finish reading *The Member of the Wedding* because it's so personal and so painful and so familiar. It was as if my body were committing treason by developing breasts and hips and gaining that layer of subcutaneous fat.

Breasts made running uncomfortable; my thighs made wearing shorts uncomfortable. The women in my family seem to hit puberty by getting fat—almost overnight, it seems—and I was entirely unaware that I'd reached that coming of age until other people commented on how round I'd become. Round was not what a kid who had the longest long jump wanted to be; round meant not athletic. The more jokes I heard people make about other girls with "thunder thighs" or fat asses, the more self-conscious I became, even if those comments weren't directed at me. It was simultaneously upsetting to not have breasts yet when the other girls did and to have them at all by the time I did. By junior high I dreaded gym, not for the sports—I still liked running around like a nut, and I ran full-on into a mud puddle playing flag football when I was twelve—but because I hated changing in a locker room full of girls.

A locker room full of women, in high school, was even worse.

Like most teenagers, I worried that I wasn't "normal"—that I wasn't developing at the right time, that I'd get my period at the wrong time, in the wrong place. I secretly hoped I would never get it at all. It sounded gross to me, and mostly it still is. I'm used to it, but I'll never like it; I do not celebrate my oneness with the moon and her tides—not by a stretch. When I first heard about Seasonale, an extended-cycle birth control pill, I lined up for it: a period four times a year instead of twelve was like manna from heaven. I actually asked my gynecologist when I was fifteen and having really terrible cramps when he would be willing to give me a hysterectomy. (One of my older female relatives had recently had one.) He chuckled and told me I'd want babies someday. Twenty years later I asked my gynecologist for a referral to a urologist so that Betty could get snipped; she chuckled and told me I might still want babies. I don't. I never have.

But the worst fear of every teenager—of not being "normal"—was actually true for me. Painfully, frustratingly true. I didn't have proof of it then, but my instinctual need to keep my body covered, even in all-female spaces, was entirely right. I wore tights under my jeans on gym days, and I skipped gym if I'd forgotten to wear them; being an honor student had its perks, as it was easy to come up with extracurricular activities that demanded my attention, and kindhearted gym teachers let me go. It turned out that I had something called PCOS (polycystic ovary syndrome), but I wouldn't find that out until I was twenty-two, when a gynecologist had the sense to ask me smart questions when I went in for a possible bladder infection. She poked my bladder from the inside, and when I didn't scream she knew it wasn't infected, which makes me laugh to this day. She asked me about my acne, and how easily or not I lost weight, the regularity of my periods, and about the general hairiness of my body. She kindly explained that I might have a syndrome and it would take only a simple blood test to find out. I left thinking nothing of it, especially since I didn't have the bladder infection.

When I went back to talk to her about my blood test, she told me I had PCOS. PCOS's symptoms are like a recipe for a teenage tomboy: higher testosterone, irregular or absent periods, hirsutism, increased acne, high sex drive. She said I was a textbook case, and that treatment was simple: All I had to do was go on birth control pills. So I did. But the one thing the pill wouldn't fix was how testosterone had already affected my body: I was hairy. I remember leaving her office that day, still kind of underwhelmed by the whole diagnosis and treatment, when I glanced down at the piece of paper I had brought with me to the front desk before paying. There it was, one word that remains stamped into my memory: *hirsutism*.

She may as well have told me I was a werewolf, or a she-wolf, or a hag.

I had worn those tights to gym class all those years ago because I was afraid I was hairier than other girls, even if I wasn't sure. I'd spent all those years feeling that there was something very wrong with me, and it turned out there was. Once I went on the pill, I stayed on it, and even now I worry about what's going to happen to my body when I hit menopause. I got waxed by Russian women instead of Asian women, who often—politely and demurely—made me feel like a freak. I made a lot of jokes about being half-Italian while trying to ignore the looks of surprise on cosmetologists' faces.

One in eight women have PCOS, and a lot of them don't know it until they end up having trouble conceiving a child because they don't become hirsute or don't have any of the other visible cues of a body that's polycystic. Some women are plagued with male pattern balding, one aspect of the syndrome I'm thankful I don't have. Now hirsutism and balding in women with PCOS are often treated with spironolactane, which is also taken as an antiandrogen by transsexual women, which underlines exactly how masculinizing PCOS can be. Others become diabetic, have gigantic libidos, struggle with weight loss. Admitting I have it is probably the hardest thing I've ever done, because it was the one thing—when I looked back on the years before I was diagnosed—that made me think that there was something wrong with me, that I would never fit in. It's only with age and experience that I've come to believe that almost every woman (and man) I know has a story about why she believed she didn't fit in, either; it's just that most of them didn't eventually get the blood tests to prove it.

Betty's desire to be like those women in the shoe store was a desire I couldn't understand. It wasn't a desire I had ever had because I knew as a kid, and as a teenager, and as an adult, that I wasn't one of those women. They didn't have high levels of testosterone in their blood. They didn't have facial hair and irregular periods. Looking back, I wonder if I have no internal sense of being a woman because I took a break from stereotypical femininity at a young age. It wasn't a happy partnership. Then again, I was a tomboy long before I hit puberty and developed PCOS, and I don't know what caused my being a tomboy exactly. I'm not really sure I think it matters, either, and I prefer to think of it as a natural variation, not an error.

One of the mistakes I made was thinking that my tomboy self ever had to change. Trying to change who I was at the core is an experience I share with a lot of trans people: years of pretending to be something other than what I felt I really was. My feelings were not nearly as insistent or as acute, but I still got trapped in thinking that being gender normative had something to do with being grown-up. After all, Peter Pan can be played by a woman because he's only a boy, not a man. In that way, I grok crossdressers; something about them just feels better in their skirts and heels than in the clothes they're supposed to wear and do wear on most days. When I see Betty in stilettos and jeans and cute mohair sweaters with dangly earrings and blown-out hair, she looks as if she feels good in her own skin. That's one of many reasons it's hard to deny her transness; all it took for her femininity to bloom was taking the flowerpot out of the closet. But has it hurt to see my husband take to femininity like a fish takes to water? Of course. I had sought out whatever native femininity I had, and what was there wasn't much: I took to femininity more like a fish takes to a bicycle. I could assuage myself with feminist diatribes about the beauty myth, but my honesty compels me to admit that the reason I'd become a punk rocker during my teen years was precisely to avoid giving up my tomboy ways. I found what I like to call my "Left Turn at Albuquerque."

Lucky for me, there was a left available; I turned thirteen in 1982, just in time for new wave and punk rock to go subverting gender all over the place. Annie Lennox was the sexiest woman anywhere, and she wore men's suits and had a buzz cut, and she wasn't a lesbian either.[6] And there were Boy George, and Pete Burns of Dead or Alive, Adam Ant, and Nick Rhodes of Duran Duran, who wore only slightly less makeup than his bride at their wedding.

That left turn ultimately only delayed the pain—it didn't permanently get rid of it. Because when I did start to try to fashion myself in more feminine ways, I found that one of the disadvantages of having had an "alternate" youth as a punk rocker is that I'd never otherwise fashioned myself in any way. Having had mohawks and a shaved head and various incarnations of buzz cuts and ratted-out goth hair à la Siouxsie Sioux, I didn't know what kinds of haircuts looked good on me, or even where to get a haircut. I had no idea what kinds of clothes communicated which messages. My band T-shirts and trousers or cargo shorts and combat boots mostly radiated a clear "leave me alone," which was useful at the time. But once I was in college and looking to date, I was going to have to communicate something else. I upped the femininity of clothes I already liked: It was easy enough to buy button-down women's shirts instead of men's (although it took a while to get used to having the buttons on the wrong side), and I bought them in brighter colors, and in silk. I'd always liked jewelry, so I started buying pieces that were more ornate and less industrial; I even bought chandelier earrings (which have, unfortunately, become fashionable again, but which has also meant that

Betty and my various nieces were willing to take them off my hands). I discovered Mary Janes, which are flats, a little fetishy and a little punk rock. I learned how to wear dresses, at least once in a while. But it did take conscious effort and deep breathing. For a while I couldn't walk into a class late for fear everyone would look up to look at me and what I was wearing. I may as well have walked in wearing oversize blue rabbit ears for how self-conscious I felt. I slid around the edges of rooms for a while as I built up my confidence in those newfound duds. Mostly, it worked, despite that I often felt uncomfortable, or in drag—at least it worked well enough that I started dating a lot more. I didn't feel very much in control, and as a result I often ended up in a kind of default: T-shirts or blouses and jeans, or gender neutral. After years of signifying loudly as "alt," it was kind of nice to be Jane Doe, instead. My appearance ceased to be a source of conversation or speculation. Men held doors open for me all of a sudden—and I'm still working out how to respond. But the problem was, my new appearance was also false advertising.

If there had been a place for me in the heterosexual world as I was, I don't think I would have tried to be more stereotypically feminine. It was the social pressure that did me in; I wanted to have sex with guys. In my twenties, I saw my ability to conform—to pass—as "progress." I was finally becoming normal, a "regular woman"—except that it just complicated my life. On dates, guys wanted to talk about how pretty my eyes were when I wanted to talk about Woolf's use of parentheses. On one date, I simultaneously thought: (1) I should cut my pretty hair off so he could take it home and make love to it, and (2) if I still shaved my head and wore combat boots I wouldn't end up on such horrible dates. What was even more ironic was that I'd stopped shaving my head and wearing combat boots because men thought I was a lesbian, but during that date I realized that if I didn't shave my head and wear combat boots, they made all these other assumptions about who and what I was that actually offended me. The choice was between loneliness alone or loneliness on dates. Despite the long blond hair and dangly earrings, I still had the personality of the Angry Young Man, as it were.

I was assumed to be a lesbian because people still conflate gender identity and sexuality. They also tend to think—quite incorrectly—that all lesbians are masculine and that all masculine women are lesbians. People assumed I was a lesbian because I was more masculine than the average girl. I was masculine, *therefore*. . . . I spent a long time trying to figure out if I were a lesbian because everyone else thought I was. It took me years to settle the question in my own head, which I did by having the stunning realization that you needed to want to have sex with women to be a lesbian. I didn't. *Therefore*. . . .

Despite my efforts to feminize my wardrobe, I discovered that gender is also communicated by way more than clothes. Years of combat boots encouraged a very steady gait; I tended toward sitting positions that had one ankle crossed over the other knee. My voice is naturally deeper than the average woman's, too. That is, people still picked up something about my innate gender, even if I didn't show it in my choice of clothes. I've noticed that women who are more feminine in terms of their body language can wear more masculine clothes and not be assumed to be gender variant. One friend has admitted that my adolescence was more like a boy's than a girl's—especially when you throw in slam-dancing—and my clothes reflected the extreme of the kind of gender-bending that was going on then. On top of all that, I had

my PCOS to deal with. It's not a big surprise to me that the percentage of
FTM transsexuals with PCOS is much higher than the national average
of women with PCOS.[7] I had higher-than-average levels of testosterone
in my blood all through puberty, when secondary sex characteristics are
helping create your body—and sometimes I wonder how much it shaped
my personality, too.

I was asked out more often by women than by men; if someone told
me I had a secret admirer, she was almost always a girl, usually a pretty
baby dyke whom any proper lesbian would have dated on the spot. I had
my chances, more than my chances, and all of them were cute. Definitely
there were times when it was obvious to me that my social life would have
made a lot more sense if I were a lesbian, because in that universe there
was a place for a woman like me. I recognized myself instantly the first
time I heard the term "soft butch." Butch conjured an image of women
much tougher than me, much more masculine and assertive, who were
lesbian. I was an effete city-dwelling metrosexual to their longshoremen.
But at least in lesbian communities that were populated with femmes,
butches, soft butches, and all the other lovely varieties of gender women
come in, there was a place for me that made sense; lesbians seemed to
have met people like me before, which wasn't as true when I was in the
straight world. Maybe it was just the higher percentage of feminists to be
found in lesbian communities, but in my early twenties those spaces felt
like home, and yet, somehow, they also weren't. I knew it because young
lesbians asked to borrow my trousers but were baffled that I didn't like
girls. Going back to those spaces now, with Betty on my arm, has been a
little like a queer homecoming.

Maybe not surprisingly, my own experience with learning

femininity and sorting out which kind of woman I wanted and needed to be is one of the bases of my sympathy for crossdressers and trans women; having to learn "femininity" as an adult is awkward at best. As I've watched newly out crossdressers or trans women who are beginning to transition or starting to crossdress in public, I'm amazed at how quickly some of them surpass me in their apparent ease with feminine clothes. The difference between them and me, I've decided, is that they have a native inclination, or maybe just a love of the stuff, that needed only time and space to flourish until it became second nature;[8] for me, all the time and space in the world wouldn't have helped.

I ended up with a kind of gender-neutral look. I've come to the conclusion that that's just who I am. Sometimes it feels as if I've got an unconscious system of internal checks and balances in my head: If I put on a mannish suit, something in me chooses a darker lipstick, longer lashes. If I put on a skirt, I want to wear combat boots with it. It's my own internal yin/yang, always self-adjusting for gender balance but with an eye toward remaining just this side of female. I think everyone has a range within which she feels comfortable. I prefer an androgynous place; that's when I feel "like myself." When I put on formfitting dresses or heels I feel as if I'm in drag, or in a costume. The same way that guys refer to tuxes as penguin suits—expressing exactly how costumed they feel in men's formal wear— is the way I feel in the ubiquitous LBD (little black dress).

I certainly don't regret pushing my own limits. It was useful to feel I could pass as a "regular woman" if I needed to or wanted to. When I did put my trousers back on, it felt a lot more like a choice than a default decision made out of fear. Ultimately, it gave me a lot more flexibility in terms of clothes; I wear dresses when and if I need to or want to and actually feel okay. When it comes to wanting to feel confident, though, I still rely on trousers.

One of the most important days I chose to wear trousers was my first date with Betty. I called Lara, my best friend from high school—we had learned how to wear "regular" clothes together, as she'd been my partner in punk rock—and she knew me like no one else did. She also knew my wardrobe. She recommended that I push the feminine side a little, and she laughed when I told her the next day that I'd worn my favorite pair of trousers despite her advice. Betty and I had already made plans for a second date, I explained, so I'd wear a skirt then, and I did. Betty, alas, did not get to wear her favorite skirt until the fifth date or so. The funny thing is, I don't think she even noticed I was wearing a skirt on our second date; we were too busy getting to know each other to care about what the other person was wearing. Not surprisingly, we spent a lot of time on that first date talking about our mutual love for the gender-bent eighties and its music.

Feminism has expanded our cultural notions of what a woman is and can be. Now there are a lot more aspects and experiences that describe who women are and what they do, and what they like, and how they think, than when I was a young girl. Some describe me. Others describe the kind of woman's experience I don't understand and have never felt part of. But my predicament with Betty was that she aspired to those parts of woman-ness I had never felt part of, those parts where I couldn't be any kind of guide, because I was a tomboy growing up, one who'd only reluctantly given up my tomboy ways—because I was one of those unlucky tomboys who happened to be heterosexual. Ironically, I succeeded: I met and married a great guy, although now he's telling me that he wants to be a woman. It didn't seem the cleverest move on my part to have given up being a tomboy for this, and yet it makes perfect sense. Unconsciously or not, Betty had found in me a kind of fellow traveler. We've come to understand that there will probably always be times and places where we both would be much more comfortable if we could switch bodies, but as it was, we are with each other: both of us gender misfits of a sort.

That girl—that tomboy—grew up and married a man who longs to be a woman who fits in with other women in a shoe store. And yet for me those women may as well be the ones who called me dyke, and who dated guys who'd call me butch. That's a broad brushstroke, but part of the experience of growing up a tomboy is being able to identify who will ridicule you for who you are. For many girls, giving up tomboyish behavior is part of growing up; they start to feel superior to the girls who haven't given it up, and their gender markers—the high heels, the makeup, the trendy fashions—are how they broadcast that they're ready to be women. I suffered at the hands of girls who would prove themselves more "mature" than me by pointing out exactly how graceful and girlish I wasn't and how graceful and girlish my proto-gay male friends were. But the existence and behavior of mean girls has been pretty well documented by now: Thank god for Margaret Atwood and Tina Fey.[9]

A lot of women who wear silly shoes are kind and smart and funny and respectful of people's differences; some are tougher than I ever was. Because I passed for so long as a "regular girl," being with Betty has called up very old reservoirs; it's my tomboy self who has been navigating the world for both of us. I innately avoid the kinds of people who might call my husband awful things, and unfortunately or not, the feminine girls (and macho-in-training boys) of my childhood were those who were most likely to do so. Picking on gender-variant people is not restricted to femmy women who wear high heels, but since they were one of the first groups in my childhood to inspire caution in me, they do still show up on my shit list.

The irony is that my own husband looks just like those women, sometimes, and acts like them, too. But the difference between them and him is that he appreciates having a tomboy around, even when she makes fun of his taste in shoes. In that, Betty is a lot like the femme lesbians we know who regularly date butches, and a lot like Kate Bornstein, who, in the middle of a performance, squealed gleefully, "Don't you just love butches?" in a way that only she could. Betty wouldn't ever have predicted my own exploration of gender would reveal my more masculine self, but she knew something, something unconscious, and slowly, over the years, what had drawn us together started to become clear. It was more than a fellow-traveler feeling, more than having a mutual freak flag and letting it fly; it was a sense that we were something else, a kind of couple that no one even knows exists.[10] We are, or were, a heterosexual couple who are simultaneously a butch/femme couple. The butch/femme dynamic has been accused of aping heterosexual gender roles, but the first time I met a butch/femme couple, I didn't see it that way. What I saw instead was a way of articulating gender roles that wasn't dependent on genitals. When I see a butch woman, I see a woman who owns her masculinity, who has declared it her own, and who has not only taken off the sign that says "for men only" but who has burned it to ash.

Coming from the straight world, where the culture assumed that Betty had to be the butch because she was the man, and I was the femme because I am the woman, "butch/femme" was about the most liberating idea we could imagine: a relationship based on gender roles that suited the people in the relationship, not the system around them that told them what to be, or how to be. But owning that, for both of us, has been tremendous. It's meant that Betty has had to try to make peace with being a male who is a femme; for us, as a couple, it's meant learning about a lesbian history where we feel like interlopers; and for me, it's meant trying to make peace with the gender in my life—not just Betty's femininity, but my own masculinity. Being around people who are trans and otherwise exploring their gender has made me realize how apologetic I've been about who I am. I hid it for the sake of dating; I hid it for the sake of getting a job; I hid it the same way I hid my leg hair from those high school girls, because that was what was expected of me as a heterosexual woman.[11] But the more time I've spent with transgendered folks, and genderqueers, and queer women and drag queens, and lesbian femmes and trannyfags,[12] and of course the more time I've been with Betty, the more permission I've given myself to figure out what my gender is all about. It's also made me think a lot about what it takes to create a space where people can be who they are when they're gender variant.

Betty has never pressured me to be anything other than what I am, which is one of the many reasons I love her. But I can't say that's true for everyone. It took me a lot of work to femme up to make society happy, but now I end up in the awkward place of feeling chastised for expressing my masculinity. Sometimes, people imply or tell me outright that my own masculinity encourages Betty's transness, that maybe she'd feel better about being a man if I were a little more feminine. And by that

I assume they mean more submissive, docile, sweet, cheery, pretty. I have no idea why they think Betty married me in the first place if what she was looking for was a submissive, docile, sweet, cheery, pretty woman. I have times and moments when I am all of those things, but they're not really what you'd call my "selling points." Betty knew that fully when we decided to get married and when she proposed. Shoot, she knew it when I called her to ask her out.

I used to feel a little gun-shy about telling people that I asked him out on our first date because it's so unseemly, not the way it's supposed to be done. More than once after I've mentioned it I've gotten that "Oh, it's pretty obvious who wears the pants with you two." Sometimes the innuendo is playful and complimentary, and sometimes it's judgmental and harsh. Because, like with so much else, my asking Betty out was completely natural to me and something I had previously tried to stop doing. By the time we met, I'd spent nearly a decade encouraging myself to be the most feminine I could. I had broken up for the last time with the guy I had spent the previous five years dating, and not dating, and dating again. We had broken up for the umpteenth and final time because I thought that when we agreed to an open relationship, that meant *both* of us could and would see other people. I forgot to read the small print, where it says an open relationship is supposed to be open only for the guy, or his fragile ego will be broken.

It was a few months later I met Betty, his cocksure lean against Peter's kitchen counter like catnip to a lion. He introduced himself and I bit my tongue; I gathered courage and tried not to stare at the handsome stranger while the group of us discussed *The Sun Also Rises* and the ill-fated Jake and Brett. War wound, indeed.[13] As we all left the meeting, I gathered the nerve to suggest we all go for a drink in order to get to know him a little better, and before I did, Betty abruptly went west while the rest of us turned east. My plan was thwarted. His unintentional coyness goaded me into being the pursuer.

I didn't require much goading. I'd asked my first boyfriend out, too. I'd vowed since then to stop being a Sadie Hawkins,[14] especially after that first relationship turned out to be a disaster. It wasn't until after we broke up that it became apparent that he wasn't able to fall in love with me precisely because he hadn't pursued me. When a man says, "It's such a compliment to be asked out," he actually means, "You're emasculating me." Maybe I just wasn't lucky enough to meet the kind of guy who wouldn't ultimately feel emasculated by being asked out by a woman, but I certainly tried enough times, so for me asking a guy out just became another instance of gender transgression, another time when I failed to read the fine print, another example of the way I got in trouble because of my stubborn belief that gender wasn't a good enough reason not to be what you are.

One of the frustrating things about growing up gender neutral is that you transgress gender without intending to. In first grade I got in trouble for chasing after a boy to kiss him, but I thought I got in trouble for kissing someone without his permission. I didn't understand then, or for many years after that, that the problem was my aggression, and that I had subjected this boy to it. As it turned out, the problem wasn't the aggression but the gender transgression. If I had been a boy and he a girl, everyone would have thought it was cute.

I really never did learn my lesson, even if I pretended to, and like some kind of recidivist, I kept doing it. I did learn to ask nicely. It's not as if I didn't have good examples. My steadfast father asked my mother to marry him seven times, though like me, my mother didn't want to get married—which was a far more controversial notion in 1950 when she was twenty than it was for me in 1989. But we both did get married in the end, though I got married as the result of asking a guy out, while she did it the "right" way, by resisting my father's overtures and forcing him to "win" her. It is supposed to work the way my parents did it, the way it does in movies and pop songs. The expression is boy meets girl, after all, and not the other way around. Some might say that I got what was coming to me by being so masculine about my desires, instead of being coy and flirtatious the way I was supposed to be. I had upset the natural order of things, and some would say, *No wonder you ended up married to a trans person.* But at the same time, I wonder how many women passed by the chance to be with a handsome, sweet, talented guy because they were busy standing around batting their eyelashes and waiting for him to make the first move. For once, my masculinity meant I won a round.

But when we met, I thought I had finally found a man liberated enough to be okay with being asked out. Had I been able to see him when I called to ask him out, seen the eyeliner in his other hand, I would have known—that it wasn't *finally* but *of course:* Masculine Woman Meets Feminine Man. We were meant for each other. But of course no one tells you that's even a possibility, a mold, a template. What they tell you is that we don't exist. No one noticed in the beginning except us; Betty passed for a man and I passed for a woman. And oddly enough, we really were those things—just gender-variant versions. But everyone said we couldn't be, even Papa Hemingway: Girls like Brett and boys like Jake were doomed, stopped in a traffic circle by a cop with a baton that signifies "phallus."

So of course I'm vulnerable to the idea that if I weren't so masculine in key ways, Betty might feel more "like a man" and thus have less gender confusion.

But when I'm told *It's your fault,* or *You should be more feminine so his dick might feel bigger,* or *Let him take charge,* I have the same response that I had as a kid to that bully who called me "butch," and it is still a response that comes from my gut, not my head. I don't let boys win because I'm a girl. I don't consider it my job, as Virginia Woolf once so fabulously put it, to reflect my husband back at him but at twice his natural size. Too many men actually believe you. It goes straight to their heads. Women have been throwing the game for centuries so that men will feel important and love them the most, and it's gotten us a bunch of pumped-up egomaniacs who actually believe women aren't as competent or interesting or intelligent as they are. Not all men are so gullible; plenty are fully aware of how equal women are. Betty is among them and has no problem with being emasculated, for obvious reasons. But believe me, I've met plenty of girly boys who are threatened if their wives even suggest that those shoes don't go with that skirt. Some guys need to know everything—even when the subject is something they know little about, and even if they're wearing a dress.

Maybe my mother should have pruned my masculinity out of me at a much younger age when I wouldn't have felt the pain of the pruning, removed it like an invisible foreskin from a still-squawking infant. But she didn't. My mother hated any weakness of her own, and she didn't encourage weakness in her daughters. She, like so many women, treats men something like children—entertaining to have around but not necessarily competent. It's the women who put the meals on the table and wipe the children's faces and make the dish of Swedish meatballs for the woman down the block who just lost her husband. Women, my mother might say, are what keep the world that matters going, the world of children and family and community. She grew up the eldest daughter of a single mom in the 1930s, and for her, being a woman had nothing to do with sitting around watching soap operas. She admired her mother's strength. My grandmother, and my mother, and probably my grandmother's mother, never had any room in their lives for princesses, and they didn't raise their girls that way: Velvet dresses don't hold up to too-numerous washings, and neither do their velvet needs. You could say that my mother was made of corduroy and she expected children made of the same stern stuff. For anyone raised working-class, a woman's gender is not about pale skin and Mallomars and gossip; it's about working extra jobs and getting what needs doing, done. For that you need any skill you have and can't be picky about your tools or reject any as too masculine or too feminine. My masculinity is who I am, by nurture and nature.

Having found a partner who appreciates both my femininity and my masculinity, the suggestion that I should cop only to the feminine, for his sake, strikes me as absurd. Tempting, sometimes, because I could hope that path might lead to saving our marriage and his existence as a man. But it's not a rational idea, because his transgender nature was apparent (to him, at least) long before he met me; if it did work, it would be only temporary, if that. Plenty of transsexual women have very feminine wives, and that didn't stop them from transitioning. And even if my acting more feminine were the magic trick that would keep him from transitioning, I still couldn't do it. Betty wouldn't want me to, and the smell of the sham of it would stink up our lives.

We love each other as we are, as the couple who both love *Raiders of the Lost Ark,* for the archaeology, the history, the dialogue, and the clothes. What I could never say to anyone until I met Betty is that when I said I loved the clothes Indiana Jones and Marion are wearing at the end, I really meant I loved Indy's clothes. Yes, Marion's were great—as smart 1940s women's suits are—but nothing compared to that fedora and double-breasted suit Indiana Jones is wearing on the steps of the Federal Building. Betty understood. She spent her whole life knowing she was supposed to become something like him, and wear those clothes, no matter how much she wanted to be Marion. If I'd had the vocabulary when I first saw the movie at age twelve, I would have known to say that I didn't just like Indy's clothes, I wanted to feel like I imagined he felt in them. His consternation over what the government types would do with the Ark was a good match for my worried, angry, earnest self. I was the type who would grow up to have a friend in Marrakech who knew where Incan icons were sold. I wanted to know my way around a Nepalese bar and know how to translate obscure texts written in obscure languages.

But every message I got was that traveling alone as a woman was dangerous, and that I was supposed to be batting my eyelashes and distracting someone into buying me a drink. I tried. It's not that I can't bat my eyelashes; I'm told I do. What I can't do is put that on when it's needed, and for me, that requirement became the too-tall wall of what femininity is: the conscious use of such feminine wiles. I just didn't have it, and Betty is a natural. We know when we watch *Raiders of the Lost Ark* together that she is more often the one cleaning the mirror and I'm the one who falls asleep, world-weary. We have both spent most of our lives wearing the wrong clothes, acting the wrong way, and trying to keep ourselves hemmed in by our correct gender, and we're both tired.

What I don't understand about Betty—and what I don't understand about transsexualism in general and probably never will—is that gender actually means something concrete to Betty, and it's connected to which sex he is or presents as in her daily life. I don't really understand how anyone comes to the conclusion that changing sex will fix a person's gender issues. It seems to work. People who feel "more female than male" seem to get on in the world better in a female role. Having seen enough transsexual people find relief in doing so has convinced me that transsexuals have a medical condition—not a mental disorder—because many of the most pragmatic and rational people I have met spent years trying to resolve their gender issues in other ways. Jamison Green's[15] experience living as a butch, or androgynous, for many years before transitioning mirrors a friend who did the same thing as an MTF. In other words, I've seen transition work for people who would have loved to find any other solution, and who actively pursued more nonmedical ways to fix things. Transgender people experience gender discomfort differently from other people who are gender variant. It may be a difference in intensity, or brain sex.[16]

My response to gender issues—as someone who isn't trans—was to stop taking gender so seriously. I lived by that adage of RuPaul's: *Either you're naked or it's drag.* I didn't believe in gender as aligning with my sex for most of my life, for two main reasons: the tomboy thing, of course, and because I am a feminist. I had to believe: I was as good as a boy, I was accepted by the boys, I may as well have been a boy, *and* that it didn't make any difference that I wasn't a boy. Then, when my husband started wondering if he might need to become a woman, and started presenting as more and more feminine, something in me balked. The tomboy in me said, *Ewwww, a girl.* The heterosexual woman in me said, *I don't want to have sex with a woman,* and the feminist in me said, *Why are you being so stereotypically feminine?*

All of a sudden, because of my husband's crisis with his own gender, I had to admit that gender meant something. I wanted to believe it wouldn't be a big deal to have the man I love become a woman. After all, the scripts on wedding days are all about souls entwining—not genitals and socialization—but I still expected those souls to be somehow androgynous, genderless—not hung up on being called "she." But the more my husband actually shook off his socialization as a man, the more something in me retreated. The more I encouraged him to find an identity that felt comfortable and natural to him, the more unnatural he seemed to me: His manners changed, as did the way he used his hands; he flipped his hair and started using a new voice. "She" felt constructed, not natural, but he insisted he felt more "himself" when he presented as a woman.

I kept hoping that the constructed femininity I was witnessing was a phase, because I felt as if I were living with Britney Spears. It was like sleeping with the enemy.

And while I've seen many transsexual women become less stereotypical and more "natural" about expressing their femininity as time went on, I didn't see how I would make it through the rest of my life living with Britney Spears. Actually, I wasn't sure I could make it a month. So even if Betty were the type of trans woman who ended up being more tomboy than Barbie, that process would take time—and at the end of that process I might discover that Betty really was that uberfemme, or we might discover that being with any kind of woman wasn't quite what I needed in a romantic partner, either. Likewise, she might discover she liked men; she wouldn't be the first trans woman to go on hormones who suddenly noticed the frisson of stubble.[17] I understand the attraction of stubble, since it was the main reason I didn't want Betty to remove her facial hair permanently. I caved in and bought her laser sessions when I realized that if I'm jonesing for stubble that much, I can always rub my face against her legs a day or two after she's shaved them: This life requires creativity.

But I'm also criticized—by MTFs of all people—for not loving the glories that are the feminine. I've seen crossdressers and trans women put pressure on their wives to enjoy it as much as they do, but what MTFs don't always realize is that we gender-neutral or tomboy types accept gender variance because we're a little gender variant ourselves. More than one wife of a crossdresser has noticed the irony of being a woman who accepts her husband in a dress but who is simultaneously being told that she should wear dresses more often. I've seen those women out in outfits their husbands have bought them, and the phrase "living doll" has popped into my head, and not in a good way: What I see way too often is an MTF who wants to experience certain ways of being a female but encourages the wife to express or "wear" it instead, even if the wife is obviously uncomfortable. It's a little too obviously sexist for me when a wife encourages her husband in his gender expression but is simultaneously discouraged in her own by that very same husband. Having men in size 12 sling-backs mock my "librarian shoes" is probably the worst kind of experience I've had in the MTF community; it's one of the reasons I often prefer FTMs and their (usually) lesbian girlfriends, because they don't care so much about my shoes.

What MTFs don't usually get is that my sarcasm around high heels and other feminine accoutrements is just the tired frustration of being a woman who never liked those things and who never cared much about being pretty. It's okay for men to not care about their looks. But if I actually say, "I never really liked the beauty contest part of being female," people look at me as if I'm a radical "womyn." Sometimes other women—women who are more like me, or women who are very tall, or very short, or who have large noses, or who are overweight—understand what I mean. Other women really do love the glamour game; they check to see how many heads they turn when they walk into a room. Some people find that sexy or powerful; I find it leads to plastic surgery and botox, but who knows? Maybe they're right, and I'm really missing out. I don't think I am, though, not if Tyra Banks can explain that she used to get made fun of for having a big forehead or if Marilyn Monroe could worry about her fat hands.

The pressure to be "correctly gendered" wears on you, and those who inhabit something close to the ideal encourage a kind of scornfulness in me that I don't like but that's hard to choke back. I just get tired of the fact that not liking heels and not caring about being pretty seems to mean to so many people that I don't like being a woman, or that I hate men, or that I hate women, or that I need a makeover. (When was the last time you saw a television talk show featuring mothers who brought in their feminine daughters to have them be a little less femme? Never. But the shows where mothers drag their tomboy daughters onstage to be made over into the little princesses their moms know they truly are and want to be are endless.) I'll admit to a native scorn for people who follow rules without question, or who are so naturally what they're supposed to be that they don't notice there are rules—which may explain why it's easy for me to like men who are feminine, but not as easy for me to like women who are; feminine men have to push back against the constant messages that what they are is wrong the same way that I have. There's a natural simpatico there.

Betty becoming a woman bothers me sometimes because, if she did live as female full-time, she'd be just another femmy woman who fits tidily into expectations of female gender. Now she has to deal with some of the same crap I do.

Being pretty always struck me as a mug's game. Compliments based on what I do mean more to me than compliments on what is essentially genetic good luck—my parents' accomplishment, if anyone's. Being blond and white, maybe I could afford to not care about being pretty. But maybe, just maybe, there are really good reasons that some women don't care about being pretty, the same way some nice guys don't care about being macho, reasons that aren't sour grapes.

The first time I remember actually feeling the compliment of being called pretty was when I was goth—dressed in black and well-read on the subject of vampires, around the age of sixteen—and two other goth girls approached me in a record store and told me they wanted to be like me, because I was cool *and* pretty. That meant something to me; I remember feeling that "they like me, they really like me" kind of tingle when they told me. Because they were strangers, because they were fellow goths, because they saw my beauty the way I wanted it to be seen.

Because I was once a pretty blond girl, Dorothy Hamill haircut notwithstanding, I also got the feeling that pretty was just shorthand for saying well behaved, or polite, or meek, even: *Pretty Is as Pretty Does.*

There's also the issue of age and beauty. Now that I'm approaching being a "woman of a certain age," I'm glad I exited the pretty contest a long time ago, because it's depressing watching friends desperately try to hold on to their looks as they age. Even more depressing is hearing a movie reviewer go on and on and on with complete and genuine surprise at how attractive Sharon Stone is at forty-eight. If it's surprising that Sharon Stone can still turn someone on at forty-eight, the rest of us are *f-u-c-k-e-d*.

Deciding I wasn't going to care about being pretty—or trendy, for that matter—was a little like that *Seinfeld* episode in which they compete to see who can go the longest without masturbating, and after about five minutes, Kramer barges in and announces, "I'm out!" For me, it was liberating to say, "I'm out!" of those competitions. I had other things to do. There is a time limit on how much you can get done in a given day, and being pretty in stereotypically feminine ways requires time. I know how long it takes because I've done it. I don't want to spend an hour or two getting ready every day, and I don't want to have to increase that time to "keep up my looks" as I age. It's much easier to have set a precedent that I am who I am, and if I have crap skin that day, I do; if my hair looks like crap I wear a hat; if I end up wrinkled then so be it. I make a point of looking attractive in ways that suit my personality.

I've had a lot of encouragement not to be so "done up," too: I grew up with a father full of charm who would say, "Why gild the lily?" every time he saw my mother or any other woman applying makeup. In a lot of the subcultures I've hung around in (environmentalists, punk rockers, students, lesbians), women who didn't "need" makeup were considered prettier anyway, and they were valued for giving priority to other aspects of themselves, such as toughness or commitment or creativity or smarts. Ultimately, my rejection of pretty was more a simple cost-versus-benefits equation: The return on pretty isn't significant enough for me to devote much time to it. Pretty doesn't get me anything I need, and sometimes it gets me things I don't need, such as doors opened and chairs pulled. It got me dates with guys who wanted to have sex with "a blonde."

I wouldn't ask a man who doesn't prefer hockey jerseys and Coors hats why he rejects his masculinity, and I don't ask crossdressers that, either. I wouldn't tell him it's easier to get on in the world being a "real man." I'd tell him to paint watercolors and wear silk and carry a man-purse if he wants. And while I know those guys are out there, and they have to deal with being told those kinds of things too, for me as a woman the messages are insistent. And while there seems to be a cultural drumbeat that's starting to embrace women being tomboys, the message is clear: It's okay to be a tomboy as long as you *also* wear heels and knock 'em dead in that slinky number you got on sale. For me, that takes all the pleasure out of being a tomboy, and all the comfort. I've tried to care about pretty for everyone else's sake. I don't perceive myself as a failure as a woman, and I don't think I'm copping out because secretly I believe I don't measure up. I don't appreciate having the kind of coy, understated, indirect kind of power flirting gets you, or sex appeal, because I've found so often it's based on the assumption that either you're stupid or he is, and that's just too cynical a worldview for me. What I want is to find a way to be an adult tomboy, to feel free to reject the girly things I don't like, to embrace the ones I do, and to allow myself whatever masculinity feels right to me. I don't want to hear about "what a waste" my looks are, or my blond hair is; I don't think I'd necessarily look nicer if I wore blush or skirts or heels, and I'm absolutely certain I wouldn't be sexier if I did, because feeling like a Barbie doll diminishes and doesn't augment my confidence.

I don't want my gender to restrict who I am or what I wear or what

I look like. I don't have any interest in being correctly gendered. I don't really want to believe in gender at all. At the very least, I think we need to expand what we mean when we say "man" or "woman," "masculine" and "feminine." We need to decouple feminine from woman or female, and we need to realize that the assumptions and unwritten codes of what these words mean is what makes so many of us unhappy and limits our own sense of who we can be. My masculinity has never caused me to doubt that I'm a woman, even if my woman-ness, and specifically my heterosexuality, caused me to deny my masculinity for a time. I don't really want gender to be dependent on genitals at all, and I'd like for there to be more room, for more people, to express who they are without it being such a big deal.

My venture to express my own masculinity has taught me how powerful a force gender is, how loudly and unconsciously we hear the messages we're sent about who and how we're supposed to be. Gender is like a strong tidal undertow. I'm a pretty strong swimmer: I was quite emphatic about not being strongly gendered, grew up in an era when gender variance was celebrated and fabulous, and had to deal with the masculinizing effects of PCOS. I also live in a place (both socially and culturally) that accepts gender variance—that is, in New York City, but also in LGBT and more liberal social circles.

People can't even be who they are naturally because of gender; our choices are so delimited so early on that we don't even know what we're missing—unless of course we're butches, or genderqueer, or crossdressers, or have another deep internal reason for bending gender to our own ends. Even then, the binary makes itself felt: Crossdressers often feel uncomfortable with their less-than-masculine appearance in male mode and object to being seen as homosexual or effeminate; transsexuals limit the ways they express themselves in order to fit in, at least for a while during and shortly after transition. And while gay and lesbian spaces "allow" for more gender variance, gay men obsess over masculinity and treat femme gay men as if they are embarrassed for them, while femme lesbians are often disrespected just for being femme. Still, the gender variance permitted in gay and lesbian circles is a good indicator of what is possible in terms of gender expression, and my guess is that the same spectrum of gender expression is natural to straight folks, too, but the deep homophobic tic of our culture is such that they dare not show it.

Being by Betty's side, and exploring who I once was, am, and might be has made me much more aware of the pressure to be one or the other in acceptable, socially approved ways. It bears down on everyone. I see it every time the beautiful love of my life comes home and looks exhausted from hearing a run of "mister, miss, ma'am—what are you?" questions all day. It is almost impossible for Betty to present as a feminine male because her femininity means she is often just read as a woman, instead, because "feminine men" aren't allowed to exist. Gender can be excruciating for transsexuals who don't pass as their target gender. There is no way we see the full range of gender expression in human beings because our socialization, and the world, precludes that.

People are much more susceptible to the undertow when they aren't aware of it. They may even try to escape it but just tire out with the effort. The effort it has taken me to buck any of this makes me worry for all those weaker swimmers who are swept up in that tide, too far out to swim their way back to shore.

I can't shake the feeling that even though I understood this intellectually, it took something this personal for me to see again what feminists have shown us, over and over again. How much would we have lost, or never had, if Marie Curie had allowed herself to be hemmed in by the gender constraints of her era? How can we know what kind of beauty or statesmanship or art or scientific discoveries we might be squelching, even now, in letting kids grow up so repressed by their gender? No Calamity Jane, no Marlene Dietrich, no Quentin Crisp, no Walt Whitman. The world would be an awfully dull place if the gender variant didn't occasionally insist on being who they are, because they need to develop such strong personalities just to be themselves.

three

the
opposite
of 49.

People ask: What would you do if Betty got "the surgery"? I never ask what people mean because I know what they mean: They want to know how I would feel if my partner didn't have a penis anymore, but a vagina instead.[1] I never know how to answer their question because in it two separate issues collide: (1) What if my lover's genitals were no longer the kind of genitals I prefer to play with?, and (2) what if my male partner became female? Most people don't seem to understand those really are two different questions, and that my answer to one has nothing to do with my answer to the other, but most people don't live in a world where women sometimes have penises, and I do. Instead I answer:

That would be the least of it, if she'd come that far.

That would be more than I could handle.

That would be it for our sex life, but I'm not such an old dog that I can't learn new tricks, so maybe we could make our sex life work. I hope I would be smart enough and self-protective enough to leave before then. I assume that I would care enough, and love her enough, to encourage her to find someone who could be with her through an ordeal such as that, someone she could love and trust and feel safe with. But I'm the only one who could be that for her, and I'd have to be there, no matter how much it might shatter me, and then I wonder if thinking that way means I'm some kind of masochist. I am a mess of contradictions: I really have no idea how I would feel, and I just hope it won't come to that.

But for many women whose partners are trans, it does come to that. I've talked to women who stayed; I've read about them,[2] seen interviews; I've met them at conferences and gotten to know them via email. Some should have left long before surgery ever happened. Some of them have deep scars from doing something so self-sacrificing, and they seem kind of shell-shocked, there but not there. Others are so angry they terrify me in that "there but for the grace of God go I" kind of way. The ones who baffle me most are the ones who seem okay. They're not happy about it, but they're not angry or scarred or bitter or gone. They stay with their partners and help them recuperate after the procedure. Because there is, on top of everything else, the very fact of surgery: blood loss, expense, risk of losing your life, recovery. Some of them try to make love with their postsurgical partner despite the change in genitalia.[3] Others don't imagine trying but live with their spouses as something more "like sisters," in a deep but platonic bond.

Maybe it's my age or my sensibility, but I don't know how anyone who was ever in love and deeply sexually attracted to another person doesn't feel bitterly disappointed if her partner becomes "like a sister" to her. Betty and I have been asked if we're siblings no matter how she's presenting, and the question seems just as obscene now that we're viewed as sisters as when people thought we were brother and sister. While I understand what kind of bond couples are talking about when they say they live "like sisters," it's not one I'd want with my husband. I would have partnered up with one of my gay friends if I wanted someone to cook with and watch movies with on Friday night.

Some of these couples do whatever it takes to manage. I've heard of couples who threw out wedding photographs they once treasured. I can't comprehend what kind of mood you can be in when you throw out wedding photographs and don't hate the person standing there next to you in those photos. Even if you do throw out all the reminders, how do you erase all the goals and hopes of the life you planned together? I can't imagine them not sneaking up on you from time to time and knocking your legs out from under you. I'm lucky: Most wives of transsexual women don't have the luxury of the time I've already had. Most transsexual women take no longer than two to five years to complete transition,[4] and Betty hasn't made up her mind if she will or won't.

Maybe you don't forget but instead just let the feeling dim, like after any kind of breakup. But even if that's the case, I don't know how you do that when you haven't left, when the person you loved is still there but so different from the person you fell in love with that he or she is not the same person at all. Maybe you never fall in love with this "new" person in the way you were in love with the old one. You might still love the person but not be in love with him, and the feeling you had might still be there under the surface, a kind of longing to be in love, a pining for what was, what might've been . . . every day you see the person who reminds you of what you had and what you don't have anymore. The woman who was once your husband is in your house, in your bed, and in your life.

And on top of all that, you haven't given up on loving your spouse, still, and you haven't stopped liking who he is and trying to forgive her and maybe coparent with her, too, if you have children.

When I think about Betty becoming a woman, I question whether I will be able to get over the sense that I met this really cool guy but lost him. He would be replaced by this new person with a vagina and breasts but with mostly the same personality and facial structure as the husband I fell in love with. And she'd continue to be by my side, to remind me every day of that really cool guy I met, and fell in love with, and lost. Having met the guy of my dreams was like winning the lottery, and sometimes Betty's transness feels like the awfully steep tax you have to pay on that kind of money. If she transitioned, I'd feel a little bit too much like Frances Hodgson Burnett's *Little Princess*—in the middle of the book, when she finds out she's lost everything.

Yet—many women would already feel this sense of loss if they found themselves in my situation, in the way that I'm living with my husband as he is now. As she is now. They would feel as if they had already lost that cool guy they'd met; they would feel that an effeminate, androgynous someone had been left in his wake. And they would struggle with the reminder of that loss every single day. They would feel as if their husband were already gone.

Perhaps ironically, this gives me hope, because I've made it this far. I do accept my husband's innate femininity and celebrate it by supporting her expression of herself.[5]

For me, all Betty has done so far is strip away some layers of artifice to reveal who she truly is. Yet, I don't want him to keep stripping until all that's left for me to see is that my husband was never a man at all, and that who I fell in love with was something he had constructed during the course of his life to get along in the world. I don't want to find out that the man behind the curtain working the levers of the great Wizard of Oz is a woman. Despite our love for each other, and the intense connection we feel, I sometimes miss the guy whom I used to kid for having such an "upstate wardrobe"—his collection of flannel shirts—and sometimes I feel that I fell in love with Betty's clothes instead of the person in them, even though that's not true. Still, clothes are a very important way people express gender, so those flannel shirts really do connect me to the guy I met and fell in love with, and the tight jeans and tops really symbolize how much he's changed. I regret ever having encouraged a more urban, metrosexual kind of look for him and long for the flannel. Gender is something like clothing. Clothes can be changed depending on context, or the people you're around, or the environment you're in, much like gender, and gender can reflect your class and your upbringing much the way clothing can. Both can also be entirely inaccurate about the way they communicate the person you feel yourself to be inside.

Sometimes the density of memories seems the biggest problem, which is why the lobotomy sounds like a good idea. I can imagine accepting other scenarios more easily than transition per se: Betty's having a physical accident in which he lost his penis, or maybe they'd have to remove it for medical reasons[6] and the only replacement option is a sensate vagina. If

I woke up one morning and Betty had magically turned into a woman overnight, I would manage. I'm not sure how it would work, but I'm pretty sure it could. It's the notion of losing what I've had for something unknown, and that I don't know that I want, that's immeasurable to me. I don't want what's behind Curtain Number 3. I'm just not that sort of person. I wouldn't take the risk on what was behind Curtain Number 3 if all I had to lose was a blender, and I already had what I wanted. I don't gamble. I don't understand the idea of it. I'm one of the few people who played the slots in Vegas only for the free drinks. Put another way, my grandmother didn't raise a fool; and maybe, again, my working-class roots are showing: A bird in the hand is worth two in the bush.

If the man you love becomes a woman, it's impossible to know whether you will have the same joy, the same love and laughter, the same romance, or whether you'll just be angry, and bitter, and single. A moment might come when Betty leans to kiss me and I'll involuntarily recoil. That's when I will know: *I should have gone before now.* But I might have different, or even better, kinds of joy and love and romance, because I'd be living with someone who has become who she truly needs to be.

Yet the question people ask—What would you do if he got "the surgery"?—isn't about having a female partner, or a feminine one. It's not about gender. What people want to know is how I'd feel as a heterosexual woman if my partner turned his penis into a vagina. But genitals are the least of it. Genitals are just parts you learn how to touch when you love someone. Genitals are only a doorway to something else far more inexplicable than surgery or marriage. They matter, of course they matter, but when you're wondering whether your husband might become a woman, they seem a little bit like an afterthought. Ask any lesbian or heterosexual man: There's a lot more to loving a woman than a vagina. There's smell and taste and the softness of skin. But still, a vagina is a vagina, and there's a reason men fear them. As a hetero friend of mine once said, "I just haven't made that kind of peace with my own hairy clam to go getting to know someone else's." When I present my sexuality workshop at conferences, there's a point at which Betty chimes in and admits for me: "And Helen likes penises, mine in particular." And it's true. In working marriages that's usually on the "pro" list, but when you're with someone trans you start feeling apologetic for liking your partner's genitals as they are.

Luckily for us, Betty isn't interested in getting genital surgery, but that causes a whole other raft of problems if she does want to transition; it means she'd be a woman with a penis: Emergency room attendants might freak out about her body, depending on where we are and what kind of training and experience they've had; most states require genital surgery to make gender changes to identification documents;[7] and she'd need to take antiandrogens for the rest of her life, and in high doses, to "combat" what testicles produce, which can cause health risks such as heart disease. One wife I met at a conference was in a hurry for her husband to have the genital surgery because she worried about his gender and genitals not matching if he were in a car accident, and because the idea of a body with breasts and a penis upset her more than a body with breasts and a vagina would.

When I think about Betty living as a woman full-time, I wonder how much being a tomboy interferes with my ability to love a woman. The irony of having been assumed to be a lesbian seems particularly acute to me, since my being a tomboy was about liking boys, hanging around with boys, doing boy things. I must have been a gay tomboy. I always had trouble with that wanting to be/do dynamic of desire. When Sting came on the scene, people didn't know if they wanted to be him or fuck him. And that is the essential conundrum of crossdressers, and people like me, who not only like the way they themselves express their own gender, but who admire people who express theirs in similar ways. Maybe other women are clearer about separating the desire to be and the desire to have someone. I'm sure there's a psychologist out there who's now coming to the wild conclusion that I've got some kind of identity disorder. Let me tell you: No kidding.

But genitals really are the least important part of gender, especially when it comes to romance and relationships. With sex itself, genitals matter. There is no easy word for the rest of what constitutes gender: behavior and presentation and role and identity and tone and sensibility and personality. Even physically there is so much more: I'm not sure I'd make it to the surgery because breasts or curved hips might turn me off as much as a vagina could. Then again, I thought I would be long gone before Betty permanently removed her facial hair, and before she quit acting[8] to explore her gender identity, and before she had more of a life as a woman than as a man. But I'm still here, and I'm still in love. Maybe I'm just very slow, or very stubborn, or have too much attachment to memory. I've been told more than once in my life that I'm remarkably loyal. Maybe a Buddhist could teach me to live in the moment, or maybe someone should tell me I'm nuts for staying this long. On one day I'm convinced staying is entirely and overwhelmingly what I should do, and on the next, I'm entirely convinced going is the right choice, which may go a long way toward explaining why I'm where I am.

I often think about why people stay or don't stay in relationships, and I've come to a relatively simple equation: People stay when they get what they need out of the relationship, and they leave when there's too much they're not getting from it. That may be about the most unromantic thing you can say about love, but since the world tried to sell me on the whole Knight in Shining Armor thing, I'm not convinced by any of the rest of its tales, either. Love to me is a little more mundane than single people and teenagers and newlyweds think it is. What it is is hard work. It's fantastic in the same kind of mundane way, too, in the way someone who loves you will listen to a story you've told more than once before, and attentively, keeping an ear to what bits you change. It's in the little details such as Betty's caring which version of a story I tell that I find hope. We care about each other in deep ways, and we find the peaceful, silent times when we're together in the living room—but each reading our own books—romantic in their own bookish way. When we first got engaged, a column about romantic astrology predicted that two Tauruses together are very stable, but that the end result of being so rock steady might be horrendous boredom—a thought that makes me laugh now. Getting to know someone in the way Betty has allowed me to know her has been challenging and profound in a way I never expected. For some, it might be a little too challenging, but boredom is definitely not an issue.

At the same time, who can say that their relationships are so permanent that they will be the same a year from now, five years from now, two decades from now? No one can. Fifty percent of people who get married, intending to be married forever, don't stay married. There are no guarantees. Living in New York through 9/11 made the issue of whether or not my husband might become a woman less of an issue than it might have been because the unexpected horrors of that Tuesday helped me realize that there are days here when walking out the door seems just as full of chance as where we'll be five years from now. Hell, transsexualism looks great in comparison to what *can* happen. In its own odd way, Betty's transness has made me feel very pragmatic—on the days I'm not a sad, raving lunatic who is convinced that if I were just normal, this wouldn't be happening to me. Irrational, but there it is. It's a useful distraction, pretending the transness is your own fault, when there is no chance it could be: Betty was trans long before I showed up, but blaming myself was a nice way to stall for a while, to distract myself from feeling any of the negative emotions that were sure to follow. Other women who have trans partners blame how normal they themselves are for this unwanted and unexpected predicament; even those husbands who spend fifty-plus years as men and who wake up one day to realize the difficult truth have been trans since long before they got married.

Although science has not come up with consistent evidence that transness actually is biological or innate, that's the way many trans people describe the experience. When they retrace their sense of their own gender, they often had only a vague sense that something was wrong. They mention later that they always knew, for all those years, but they weren't quite sure what they knew, or what caused the sense of wrongness.

It's not hard to imagine why these people haven't been quick to leap to any conclusions or say what they're feeling out loud when they do. As recently as thirty years ago, mentioning that you were possibly transsexual was a good way to gain entrée into electroshock therapy, and expressing a need to crossdress didn't mean you fared much better. Someday, perhaps, people will start to realize their own transgendered natures much earlier in life and do what they need to do long before they get married. Transsexuals who transition later in life often end up ruining their own lives and everyone else's with the change required, but if they had some inkling, they could at least let their partners know that their gender doesn't fit quite right, that transition might be a possibility in the future, so that the partners can go into the romance with their eyes open.

The lousy chances a couple has of staying together now are based on the partner's not knowing transition is in the cards, or might be. If partners knew up front, those statistics might be very, very different. An interviewee on an *In the Life* show about gay marriage said, "If you let us marry each other, we'll stop marrying you," which is, in the end, the lesson behind *Brokeback Mountain*. The same idea is applicable to transsexuals: *If they're allowed to transition at younger ages, and to come out as transsexual before beginning an adult life and making adult commitments, they won't marry people before they know they're transsexual.* They wouldn't go into marriages thinking romantic things like "Love will cure me," the way Jennifer Finney Boylan did.[9] They won't break so many hearts, including their own.

Betty crossdressed, and still we didn't know. It certainly

would help if being trans weren't considered perverted or immoral or unnatural, because if she's any of those things, then the same people who think she's crazy will think that I've completely lost my mind for staying with her. Sometimes when a wife of a transsexual woman says they're "like sisters," she's also saying, "This doesn't make me a lesbian"—as if the people who judge transsexuals or gays or lesbians as being immoral are really making such fine distinctions, as if they've designed different circles of hell for the people they consider perverts. Some of the wives I've met online and in person say exactly that. One couple I met pass themselves off as the surviving wife and sister of the same man to explain how they came to have the same last name but look nothing alike. And of course, staying with one's trans partner doesn't make a woman a lesbian—if only it were that easy![10]—but the rest of the world sure will view her that way, and she should sure be ready to be viewed that way if she wants her romantic relationship with her partner recognized publicly and socially.[11] Some don't need that and don't mind having a relationship that is primarily private, so living "like sisters" is perfectly satisfying to them. It wouldn't be for me.

Lesbian couples are more comprehensible to people than trans couples who don't fit into the gay mold. Thanks to increases in gay and lesbian rights and visibility, people know what same-sex couples *are*— not so of your average trans couple. Both halves of a lesbian couple are considered so-called perverts by the people who go around judging such things. They often have an equal share in dealing with discrimination, whether it's about marriage rights or employment opportunities. But being the nontrans half of a trans couple sometimes makes you seem more nuts than your trans partner because—after all, I could have a "normal" life if I wanted. Betty's the one who's stuck with this. But either way, it bothers me to hear partners who say, "I'm not a lesbian" a little too often or too loudly, because being a lesbian seems quite sane in comparison to being the partner of a trans person. I tend to get a little extra prickly about homophobia within the trans community, because there's a history of it,[12] and while the T has been added to LGB, albeit reluctantly or largely symbolically in the names of many gay and lesbian organizations, there's often little effort on the part of the T to learn anything about gay and lesbian lives.

That said, when you're read as half of a lesbian couple, then you're expected to act like a lesbian and dress like one (whatever that means), and of course you're expected to have dated women and to have had a coming-out experience and not to enjoy sex with men. Even if the expectations are incorrect, and based on popular prejudices, there are expectations. In a sense, after the trans person is passing in the target gender, the couple need to learn how to pass as whatever it is they've become if they don't want to explain who they are all the time. For lesbians who date FTMs, that can mean getting along in straight crowds, which is a huge challenge for some couples I've met. But for me and Betty, it would mean passing as lesbian, or bisexual, or queer of some stripe, and that requires knowing something about what those kinds of couples are like.

Despite my years of being a faghag[13] and lesbian hangabout, it was an entirely different experience the first time I walked into the Lesbian, Gay, Bisexual, and Transgender Community Center in New York City's West Village.[14] My intention was not to walk into LGBT spaces pronouncing my heterosexuality. I wanted to meet other women like me and learn from them. But I didn't find any; they weren't there. What I found instead were assumptions about who I was that were all wrong: When Betty wasn't with me, people assumed I was the lesbian partner of an FTM or they thought I was newly masculine spectrum myself. I'm often read as queer anyway and have come to accept myself as queer, but other female partners of trans women are not and do not. Because I wanted to help create a space for other partners of trans women who came from heterosexual backgrounds (and for the male heterosexual partners of posttransition trans women, too, eventually), I found myself being more vocal about who I was so that others might find it a little easier to walk into LGBT spaces that weren't quite ready for this weird influx of heterosexual people.[15]

I'd felt all sorts of safe in my heterosexuality as an ally, but when my own straight privilege started disappearing, things took on a whole new light. All of a sudden I didn't feel safe kissing Betty in some neighborhoods. The bit that's most alarming is how differently we're treated now. We used to be a feted couple, smiled at by store owners and retail clerks. Now we're followed around and asked if we need anything a dozen times. And when I call Betty "doll"—loud enough for her to hear me—everyone else looks up. We get odd glances, looks of surprise, looks of derision, or sometimes just amazement that I would be so bold about acknowledging our relationship in public. It sucks. It sucks gigantically. We were used to people asking how long we've been married, whether we're planning to have children, and how we met, but now it's as if people think we have some nerve being public about our love. What it feels like to me is that people are okay knowing we're a couple, as long as we don't do anything to show it.

We're the same people we've always been. Betty treats me much the same way she did, though with a slightly higher-pitched voice, and I started using "doll" in public so that I wouldn't out her by using her guy name when she was presenting *en femme*. Now it outs me; my fear isn't in her getting read or outed as male anymore. My fear now is that they can't tell she's trans, and we'll be treated like any lesbian couple who talk to each other with affection in public. It makes me want to pass our relationship off as a friendship sometimes, because the treatment afforded us as a hetero couple was so much kinder and more welcoming than the treatment we get when we're perceived as a lesbian couple. Maybe people who grow up lesbian-identified get more used to this injustice, but it's a fresh wound for me and makes me very angry because I know, firsthand, how the other half lives. Some days I want to take every last ounce of straight privilege I ever had and make out with Betty in every sports bar I can find. Because Betty's gender has changed I've suddenly gone from admirable to socially unacceptable? Because of gender?! How does that make any sense?

The irony of the whole situation is that my loyalty and commitment to Betty could be interpreted as being quite conservative. Our commitment and loyalty to each other really *is* that. Betty and I are both very monogamous and pretty traditional about love and relationships. But when we appear together in public, we're clocked as queer, lesbian, or radical. People who see us on the street, or in stores, don't encourage us to buy each other things. They ask us if we need help in ways that ring more like "Please don't touch things in here," and "Please leave quickly; you're making our other customers uncomfortable." I'm not talking about South Dakota, either; I'm talking about New York City.

For Betty and me, it's been a revelation to gain some understanding of what it means to be treated the way a lesbian couple might be. The worst of it is that I thought I understood. I didn't. I suspect there are a lot of straight allies who are under a similar delusion that they understand what it's like. They don't know the half of it. I've been an ally of lesbian and gay people since I was a teenager, when a guy in my high school came out and caused a ruckus and I told him I'd go to a meeting with him to support him. (Sometimes I wonder if I just naturally attract trouble.)

My best friend and I both went, and only later did we figure out that he'd invited us to go with him in hopes that we would come out, too. I was always surprised when people thought my best friend and I were a couple, or that one or the other of us was a lesbian; at last check, neither of us is. I'm not sure why I had such a native like of gay folks, except that I was reading Henry James and Joe Orton back then and listening to people like Marc Almond and Jimi Somerville, who were singing about gay life and gay literature—Bronski Beat's "Smalltown Boy" is still one of the saddest ballads I know—and because that was 1986 and HIV and AIDS were finally being addressed publicly, even in sex-ed classes. Our next-door neighbor was an early victim, so I was already well aware of the disease and the stigma.

Some women are born faghags, and I was one of them. I can't really explain what's required in being one, because I was not typical. I never fell in love with a gay man; I tend to like men generally and gay men in particular because of a kind of simpatico I found with them. The faghag/gay man friendship is one of the reasons we should change how we describe sexual orientations, because "hetero" and "homo" end up putting odd bedfellows together. As Tom Stoppard muses in The Invention of Love, the word homosexual is half-Greek and half-Latin, which makes it a confusing term in the first place, even if we seem to be stuck with it. It would be much more accurate to define sexual orientation as either "androphilic" (loving men) and "gynephilic" (loving women) instead, as then you'd have gay men and straight women on the andro team, and lesbians and straight guys on the other. It might bridge the gap between gays and straights, too, and help further eliminate homophobia—on the assumption that more than one straight guy has been convinced that lesbians are okay by sitting next to one watching sports in a bar.

What's interesting to me is that I've met many wives of crossdressers who are natural faghags but who honestly wonder how it is they ended up marrying crossdressers. Not all wives of crossdressers, but enough that I've been a little surprised that they don't know that they're faghags. For me, it wasn't a surprise that I'd married a feminine man, because I'd always liked feminine men—men who wore makeup, drag queens, and performance artists like Klaus Nomi. But there are women who have no exposure to feminine gay men, or drag, at least not to the degree where they're aware that they're faghags, and so they end up marrying men with a slightly feminine side without realizing what they're doing. They don't think about gender-bending or anything like it, and they don't recognize that they're drawn to guys with "a sensitive side," or who are otherwise less than macho.

One of the loveliest women I met after *My Husband Betty* came out was a young wife from Texas. She was Christian, and she was a faghag through and through. Her church elders must have known it, since she had been sent out by her church to "find" the gay folks. Her mission was to bring them back to God or to encourage them to be celibate or ex-gay or something like that. She had a big laugh, big hair, a kitschy sense of glamour, and a snarky sense of humor. She was worried about what being with a CD might mean about her own sexuality. She was also a happily married woman who believed in "till death do us part" and was willing to indulge her husband's sexual fantasies for the sake of their marriage. She asked me how she could make his desire to be treated as a woman in the bedroom sexy for her. I suggested that she maybe use the idea of a "lesbian taboo"—that is, her own internalized fear and excitement of doing something deemed "perverse," such as having sex with a woman—to see if that would turn her on, since she was uncomfortable with lesbianism but found her husband attractive *en femme*. Well, it worked. It worked so well that she found herself getting turned on by lesbian scenes in porn films, and she was so upset by the idea that she could enjoy watching that kind of "immoral behavior" that the two of them decided to give it up: He quit crossdressing, and she stopped fantasizing about lesbian sex.[16]

Their choice made me think a lot about desire but a lot more about perspective. As a young teenager I was comfortable with homosexuals and certainly (at least) with other people's homosexuality, and it never occurred to me to see it as sinful or wrong—and that despite growing up Catholic in the suburbs of New York City. Our next-door neighbor of many years—the same one whose son died from AIDS (though infected by needle use)—also had a gay brother, and my parents were fond of him and his boyfriend of many years. My parents—as Betty and I found when we told them about Betty's transness—were not the types to be put off by something as arbitrary as sexual orientation or gender identity, and they found a reasonable and discreet form of homosexuality they could live with in that friend's brother and his long-term boyfriend. I didn't grow up with people who imagined homosexuals could be anything but homosexual; the matter was more what you did about it.[17] That is, it'd be a little easy as a smug, sophisticated, worldly-wise New Yorker to dismiss that young woman's response to any queer desires she discovered in herself and her husband, but I also wondered if I would have reacted exactly the same way if I believed homosexuality was wrong, had been raised by people who taught me it was wrong, and was living in a culture that was convinced it was wrong. She was, quite simply, trying to be a good Christian, and that's not something I could fault her for—

especially since I often wish a lot more Christians would work a little harder on that plank in their own eye before dealing with the speck in someone else's, which is what she did. She saw her own desires, deemed them immoral, and shut them down.

But it also made me wonder about desire and how we react to it. These things get very murky for the wife of a trans person. If you're a woman who is turned on by lesbian scenes in porn films, are you a lesbian? Are you a lesbian if you desire your husband when he's crossdressed and looks like a woman, even if you know he has a penis and otherwise-male body underneath "her" clothes? If you are in love with and make love with a woman who has retained a penis, are you a lesbian? Are you a lesbian if you were one before your FTM partner transitioned, and are you still one after he does?[18] Are you a lesbian if you mostly date men but find yourself in love with a woman? Whether or not someone is heterosexual, or a lesbian, or something else altogether, tends to revolve around the idea of what a woman is, or when an MTF becomes a woman exactly, or whether or not a vagina is required for a person to be considered a woman legally or socially, and that's not a question I can answer exactly.

Those questions point out how impossible that whole same/opposite paradigm is for anyone involved with a trans person. In a documentary called The Aggressives[19]—so named for the usage among masculine women of color—one of the AGs mentioned that, dressed and presenting as a guy, she had had penetrative sex with a pre-op MTF. She was the man (but a man with a vagina) and had sex with a woman (who had a penis). In other words, a biological female who was playing the role of the aggressor and presenting as masculine had sex with a biological male who was presenting as female who still had a penis: *Her penis went into his vagina,* or rather the person dressed as male was penetrated by the person presenting as female, which meant, at least as far as their genitals were concerned, they were having heterosexual sex. If you judge their sex by their genders, they were having heterosexual sex, too, but what they were doing isn't even close to what is usually meant by the term heterosexual. If both people are trans, they should end up back at heterosexual, but they don't. Betty and I make a distinction between "straight" and "heterosexual," but in the case of trans people, even heterosexual can be further broken down; if I decided to become a man and transitioned, as did Betty, we'd be heterosexuals on the surface of it, but in reverse and only if no one knew. But we wouldn't be straight by any means.

Straight is a political thing, a mindset, a way of thinking about life and sex and desire. Sometimes it's more like a way of not thinking about sex and desire but assuming that everyone else is like you and that your desires will not become complicated in any way. That's why straight men get so confused if they fantasize about playing with a penis other than their own, or when an ostensibly heterosexual woman has a dream about breasts that is more sexual than she's comfortable with. Even now, I am utterly baffled at how I find women sexy although I have no interest in actually having sex with a woman.[20] For me, it's just the idea of it that's intriguing, or erotic—which is exactly what it was for the young Texan wife. But for some, even the idea of having a homosexual thought is terrifying. Accepting that you may occasionally have a homosexual desire is very different from being okay with homosexuality in general, which is in turn very different from making peace with being seen as a homosexual in the world.

About a year after we met, Betty's theater company was doing a production of a play called *Winterset*, which is about the trial and execution of anarchists Nicola Sacco and Bartolemeo Vanzetti.[21] I had done my senior thesis on them and continued to read about their case whenever it came up. Betty told her director, who promptly asked me to come speak to a group of students at a local college where they were going to perform the play. I could explain the history of the case while the theater company talked about the play's dramaturgy. I hadn't met many of the actors Betty worked with then, and I hadn't met the director at all. On the morning of the presentation—Betty and I weren't living together yet, so she wasn't with me when I was getting dressed—I showed up in a pair of trousers and a button-down shirt with my hair in a barrette at the nape of my neck. Betty—then very closeted, and very much in guy mode—looked at me and blanched. I remember him saying, "Everyone's going to think I'm dating a lesbian" out loud. He said it like someone who was in the closet, as if my looking like a dykey feminist professor were going to out him, magically and instantly, to his entire acting company, as if my trousers were really code for my own gender variance and would out him as queer by association. What I assumed he was thinking was, *They're going to know I'm a transvestite.*

I don't know if anyone actually did think I was a lesbian that day (or if anyone thought Betty was a transvestite, or a closeted gay man with a "beard"),[22] but it was kind of amusing to me that years later I was actually described by Tristan Taormino as looking like a dykey feminist professor in her column about *My Husband Betty.*[23] When I sent the column to friends, many people—in addition to congratulating me on a good review—wrote to tell me that she was dead wrong, that I didn't look dykey at all, though I did have a kind of professorial bent. Objection after objection, from old friends, recent friends, other wives and girlfriends of crossdressers. For me it became a case not so much of "the lady doth protest too much" but more of "too many ladies doth protest too much." Explaining that I was flattered to be described as a dykey professor by someone who likes dykes didn't get very far. I still consider it a compliment. But the way I looked to Betty that day in that classroom made him nervous, in the same way the description of me in that article tweaked others, in the way that a road sign that reads No Shoulder makes drivers pay closer attention. I was dancing a little too close to the edge of the straight cliff, and people sought to pull me back.

They didn't succeed, and I found myself a few short years later walking into the LGBT Center in Manhattan as me, for myself; not as an ally or a faghag or the friend of a lesbian, but for me. And it was terrifying but necessary. I not only wanted to help make a space for people from hetero backgrounds who found themselves under the T, but I had a lot I wanted to learn. When I was seen as the wife of a crossdresser, most of the expectations people had about me were also all wrong: that my husband's crossdressing made me unhappy, or that I didn't find it erotic, or, after I'd cleared up that actually both of those things were untrue, that I was *really* a lesbian. And often that assumption was confirmed in some people's minds by the way that I acted or dressed. It was a revolving door of expectations I couldn't fulfill and got tired of explaining. After a while, when someone said, "So you're a woman who loves women," with a sly wink, I just said yes, and occasionally added, "but only recently." If someone said, "As the wife of a crossdresser . . . " I just said yes, and added, "but Betty prefers to identify as trans." "But you're straight, right?" *Yes. Kinda. I'm legally married and historically heterosexual.* "But you like women?" someone might ask. *Sure, I like women, but probably not in the way you mean.* Or otherwise they'd want to clarify their assumptions about how I looked: "You dress like that because you're a dyke/lesbian/butch, right?" *Sure thing, whatever you say.* When it comes down to it, there is no word for what I am as concerns my love for Betty. Besides that *crazy* option, that is. Since it would take an hour to go through what the people asking me these questions mean when they say lesbian, heterosexual, and masculine, I just say yes. Like queer Uncle Walt in his *Leaves of Grass*, I contain multitudes.

Others are judgmental in more considerate, complimentary ways. I've had more than one person tell me how courageous and strong I am, how brave and cutting-edge. I'm not any of those things. I'm just another person living my life and trying to make my way in the world, a person who has found out that love is complicated and life is difficult, but that companionship is worth all the king's ransom. The rest is just me mining Betty's transness to find out what it means to me, and for me, and even what it means about me.

I've also had people assume that I'm a doormat, that I'm merely tolerating all of this because I need a husband so bad. Amusing, considering I never planned on getting married. What I planned was a series of monogamous relationships with brilliant men around my age: actors, maybe, but musicians and photographers and philosophers and urban-studies types. I just have never had that "stand by your man" personality, and honestly, I can't stand by my man if my man isn't a man, can I?

Every once in a while, someone in a support group for partners of trans people will get up the courage to ask, "But *really*, why do you stay?" It's usually asked by someone new to the group, new to transness, who is looking at the prospect of having her husband become either a part-time or full-time woman, and who honestly can't imagine herself staying, and who can't come up with one good reason why any woman would. I've told several women friends they could date crossdressers when they complain to me about how hard it is to find a boyfriend or a husband, and that's about all they hear before they change the subject. It's rare to find a woman who would even be open to dating a crossdresser, let alone one who would want to.

But it's good for partners to cut through the sentimental stuff about love and being soul mates—not because that stuff isn't true but because so many of our romantic roles are so gendered they don't always hold up when your partner is trans. We need to get to the more pragmatic issues at stake. I appreciated having one of the older women whom I met in an online support group admit that she stayed because her partner transitioned so close to their mutual retirement age, and that neither of them had the funds to live separately, among other reasons. She added that after a few decades' worth of marriage, their extended families had become irretrievably mixed into one big family. That's a practical answer, one I believe more than the ones full of love, though I have no doubt her honesty and pragmatism are also both informed by her love for her partner, too. In the 1970s, Deborah Feinbloom[24] said that partners of crossdressers must all either have low self-esteem or be latent lesbians. That was a little too clinical, a little too cold an analysis, but over and over again I hear things from partners that make me wonder, not about the lesbianism, but about the self-esteem. But it's not as simple as that, either.

Not too long ago, I read an essay[25] about why trans people with female partners seem to have more stable relationships than trans people with male partners. It felt as if the author went out of his way to come up with explanations, but he avoided the obvious one—that women are more likely to try to work it out. I often wonder what that means about women. My feminist alarm bells went off: The obvious answer is that it's in our socialization, that women are raised to value relationships and family more than men are. Women seem to put relationships and family before career and status, or at least on par with those things. We derive status and pleasure and place in a community via our family connections; the first time it occurred to me that my mother wasn't just my mom or Mrs. My Dad, but actually had a first name, astonished me. I remember feeling shocked by the realization that my mother was a person, like me, and not just someone who'd been invented or come into being as a result of my father's need for a wife or my and my siblings' need for a mother. A lot of us have grown up thinking of individual women as someone's mom, someone's sister, someone's girlfriend or wife, and not necessarily as independent agents in their own right. Even women think that way about women, sometimes.

I also worry about the economics. As one thoughtful trans woman put it, "Women are much less likely to have the life skills, confidence, earning power, and education to support themselves (and their kids). So they hang on to the ship." They might feel too old or overweight or unattractive to find another partner, or they might realize that already being a mother might put off prospective suitors. They might have—as many women do—given up years in their career to raise those kids, and they would have to go back to school or an entry-level job to get back to where they

111

were when they left to have the kids. On top of all that, transitioning can cost tens of thousands of dollars, so the family bank accounts may be empty by the time a wife needs to leave. Since transitioning people face significant job discrimination, the former man's earning power may never return to its previous levels. Staying with him and scrimping to get by can look like a great option compared to being single and destitute, especially if the woman was rejected by friends and family for staying with the trans person in the first place—friends and family who might have otherwise been a good network of baby sitters. That is, often a woman who is married to someone trans tries very much to stay and suffers a lot of the same consequences her partner does, socially and financially and in terms of estranged family, so that by the time she makes up her mind to go, she may have already burned bridges that another divorced woman or newly single mother would have.

Maybe there is a maternal instinct involved with those of us who stay to work it out, since trans people often need to be protected, taken care of, and encouraged. One of the important, albeit Freudian, aspects of a relationship is the way two people tend to parent each other. One of my trans woman friends refers to the heterosexual relationships trans women often have with women like me when they're still living as male, before transition, as being something like a midwife relationship: The trans person finds comfort, and support, and love, and encouragement, all in all a safe place for him to even realize his transness. Because women are the way we are, we help out; in effect, we help the trans woman give birth to herself fully grown. This has merit, but it's not the whole of it either.

A lot of us simply don't want to be single (again). We don't want to live on what we can earn ourselves because we're still getting that sixty-nine cents on a man's dollar. Some don't want to be single parents, and others are just plain used to their partners. Crossdressers' wives stay, too: Grayson Perry's[26] wife was quoted as saying something along the lines of "perverts are very loyal," which gives a little bit of insight into why she stayed—loyalty weighed in as a stronger "pro" than the "con" of being married to a man whom others view as a pervert. (Her comment makes it obvious that she also came armed with a sense of humor.)

Once I get past the "because Betty loves me and I love her, and we're soul mates" stuff, I end up back at "because I can." Nothing Betty has done so far has caused me to fall out of love with her or to think that I would be better off without her in my life than in it. "Because I can" feels more like "because I want to," especially as I've been trying to eliminate bad or dependent reasons for staying; I'm here because I want to be, not just because I don't want to be alone. The irony is that I first accepted that I had made a choice when I started to remind myself that I could go and leave all of this behind any time I wanted to. I can, but I don't, and that's a choice.

Some women stay because they do discover an innate bisexuality, or realize that they are, and probably have been, lesbians without realizing it. It's only when they discover that they find their trans person attractive as a woman that they look back into their pasts and remember a crush they had on a woman. Some stay simply because it turns out that having their husband become female simply isn't as bad as they thought it was going to be, and the relationship still meets their needs. Others find such huge relief in going from being the partner of someone who is angry, frustrated, and depressed all the time to being the partner of someone who is okay with herself, happy, and far more productive than she was before she transitioned. Maybe what they want and need out of a relationship is more

about companionship and building a life together. Others are the type
who have personalities that roll well with the punches, and others have
been through enough bad stuff in their lives that, in comparison, having
a partner transition really doesn't rate. It really depends so much on the
woman, her worldview, her priorities, and her basic personality.

All relationships are moderated by how close the relationship comes
to what the person expects from it, and how much she gets out of it vis-à-
vis how much she puts into it. I spent my whole life dating men for whom
I had to put in 85 percent to their 15 percent. Betty puts in a lot more.
She can talk. She likes politics. She values having a smart wife who's a
writer. She plays me songs she thinks I'd like, sends me links to websites
that might be useful, and kisses me every morning before she goes to
work. In a nutshell, I feel treasured. I try to return the feeling, of course.
Betty is also monogamous to the bone, which was as important to me as
my commitment to monogamy was to her. She understands, as a basic
premise, that relationships are full of compromise, unexpected joys, and
friendship. For her, no matter how difficult I am, at the end of the day
she knows she's lucky to have a friend who is her lover—as am I. But she
wouldn't want me to be only her friend, and she wouldn't want me as a
lover without our friendship and romance, either. The good thing is that
when it comes to these kinds of questions, we tend to see things the same
way. We both like the bells and whistles of romance, the thrilling flutter of
it, not just the companionship.

Sometimes the obvious answer is the closest to the truth, even when
it isn't the whole truth: The only real secret of any successful relationship
is that both people want to be together more than they want to be apart,
and they do whatever it takes.

I thought I was liberated about gender roles and what I
expected of a husband until Betty's transition went from possible to
probable. I suddenly felt uncomfortable about having a female partner—
for various reasons. I expected her to be different than she is now, that
she would become more traditionally gendered as a woman than he is as
a man. Aside from joking with her that she couldn't transition until she
learns to put her socks in the laundry basket, I felt a kind of panic that
having a female partner would mean that we'd be lacking a man to do the
things men are supposed to do—take out the garbage or kill bugs—even
though Betty doesn't often do those things, and sometimes I do. When we
would talk about it, I couldn't figure out what it was, exactly, that I was
worried about. I'd lived on my own or with roommates my entire adult
life: I could fix things (or hire someone who could); I'd paid my own
rent; I'd cooked my own food—not well, but well enough; I'd always
had a job. I wasn't concerned that I wouldn't have a man to take care of
me anymore—because a man hadn't ever taken care of me. Betty and
I didn't have a very gendered relationship to start with, so I was a little
surprised by how much I worried that having a female partner meant I
was going to have to take out the garbage or balance the books—when I
already did both. Her uberfemme thing didn't help, but at the same time
Betty still carried the heavier bag when we were traveling, was still taller
than me (a lot taller in heels), and still treated me like the girl she always
wanted to meet.

It was my fear of being seen as wearing the pants that was causing so
much anxiety, ultimately, about her transition. I liked having some power

in our relationship—to make financial decisions or choose where we went to dinner. I'm like other women in that regard. As the knight puts it in "The Wife of Bath's Tale":

> *Women desire to have the sovereignty*
> *As well upon their husband as their love,*
> *And to have mastery their man above . . .*
> *In all the court there was no wife or maid*
> *Or widow that denied the thing he said . . .* [27]

But of course, even in Chaucer's time, this statement was a secret told to the knight by an older wife in answer to his question about what women most desire. But so many women can't admit it like that old wife did, because then their poor husbands get accused of being whipped—as Betty did many times before anyone knew about his gender stuff. My discomfort was with everyone thinking I was the one in charge, and some days, it still is. I'm not alone in that. So often women are used to pretending the man is in charge, even when the woman is. Many of the good relationships I know of are ones in which the woman has a little more power than considered "normal" for heterosexual couples. Some are more obvious about it than others, though my friend's husband, David, likes to repeat, "A happy wife means a happy life"—and that implies that the woman gets her way. A lot of people are not that up-front about it, so even when the woman does call the shots, no one admits to it. When they do, it's only under the pretense of a joke or after a lot of bourbon, as our friend Phoebe pointed out.

Betty and I don't have a Dominant/submissive [28] relationship, either (though that works for plenty of couples, too; the lovely Minna once explained to me that D/s relationships are more transparent and up-front about power dynamics than most couples are willing to admit to). One crossdresser asked me if I were a domme because I told her that I liked deciding when Betty and I were going to have sex, which made me wonder afterward if that was all it took in some people's minds for a woman to be seen as dominant. What might look to others like an imbalance of power is actually a balance of power, but we are so used to seeing women in a slightly more submissive role that an actual balance seems odd. I was certainly used to being more submissive with boyfriends; one of the liberating things about my relationship with Betty is that I don't have to pretend. Unfortunately, before Betty, I had feminized my behavior—meaning that I tried to cop a more stereotypical girlish quality. I stopped asking guys out, to start, but I also tried not to pick the restaurant where we were going to dinner, or the movie. Simply put—I dumbed down. Once, when I was complaining about the new feminine clothes I was trying to wear, an old friend of mine said, "You're already smarter than 99 percent of men—do you really want to estrange the 1 percent who won't be intimidated by your intelligence?" Luckily, though, it doesn't take 1 percent of men to fall in love; it only takes one man. In my case, that perfect man may turn out to be a woman, and way too many of my friends find that far too easy to believe.

It took me a long while to figure out how gender and power were intersecting for Betty and me. I had trained myself to be more submissive, and I certainly worried that my natural ability to wear the pants in our relationship was going to screw things up. I had never let myself be who I am with a guy, because everything told me I wasn't supposed to be the way I was naturally. It was difficult to come to terms with outbutching Betty by a long shot. Granted, I do try to bring out her native tomboy, if there's one in there, because I won't have an "I broke a nail" partner. Interestingly, when I first started saying out loud that I was more the husband than the wife, people giggled nervously and corrected me a lot. They said, "But you're not masculine," or "Betty's still stronger than you," or another kind of affirmation of my femininity. Some of my characteristics are very feminine, but that didn't mean I couldn't also wear the pants. Still, I've been a little astonished at the ways in which people have effectively said, "Don't say that out loud" when I talk about being the one in charge. It's as if I were embarrassing *them* somehow. This has been one of many experiences over the past couple of years that has made me realize: (1) tomboys are okay as long as they are children, (2) masculinity in women makes people nervous, (3) heterosexuality was no place to figure out how to be who I am, and (4) most people don't want to talk about how their relationships are gendered.

People don't want to recognize gendered issues in their relationships because a discussion about gender roles can bring up feminist problems.[29] But we can't afford the luxury of not discussing them. We need to talk about the many problems that come up in a relationship that are gendered, even ones that don't seem to be. When a woman complains about her boyfriend being "a mama's boy"—which seems as if it's about maturity—she's actually complaining about how her man isn't living up to her expectations of how an adult man should behave, especially in terms of how much he needs or doesn't need validation from other women. It's almost as if, as a culture, we've chosen to ignore how many ways gender shapes our lives. One night I caught one of those now-myriad home-makeover shows on television. The family in question had suffered because the husband and father, a firefighter, had been injured in the line of duty. He needed a wheelchair and was on disability. While he was casting around for an alternate career, his wife had gone back to work full-time and was feeling the pressure of being the sole breadwinner. When she talked about the loss she felt—of how her husband, once a big, strong, and brave man, had become dependent on her—she expressed a kind of embarrassment. Not just of him, or for him; she also seemed embarrassed by her own feelings. The sorrow she felt seemed outweighed by her struggle to respect her husband now that he couldn't "do" anything.[30]

As I watched the show I thought, *This is about gender but they're not going to say that.* And they didn't.

Before anyone gets up in arms that I'm conflating disability with woman-ness,[31] hear me out: I knew the wife was talking about gender because she talked about her husband the same way I talk about mine, in a voice tinged with deep love and sadness, anger, and embarrassment. She sounded a lot like other partners of trans people I've talked to through the years, and she sounded a lot like a woman I know whose boyfriend was traumatized by a car accident he was in. In other words, she sounded like a woman who was exhausted with wishing that things could go back to the way they were. I know the sound of that wish too well, because it's the sound of my own.

I'm sure that firefighter's wife was as surprised as I was to find herself reaching to respect her husband—and just as surprised, too, to discover how out of reach it sometimes felt. Granted, Betty wasn't ever the strapping, heroic firefighter type, but he certainly could play one on stage, and he did play something like one in his day-to-day life when he was passing as a "regular guy," before anyone knew he was trans. The firefighter's wife wasn't under the illusion that women can't be the breadwinners, and neither am I. She was proving she could be because she had to, and I had a lifetime of paying my own bills before I met Betty. But our partners' changes revealed something we'd formerly been unaware of: our expectations of what a husband is and does. For more traditional people, this might be a no-brainer because they think *a woman needs a big strong man by her side, a man's job is to bring home the bacon,* and other Cleaver-era family values. But many of us—I'd even guess most of us—believe that feminism helped change those old-fashioned ideas. Those changes in our gender roles have been incremental, however, and the modifications made somewhat slowly, and over time. Sometimes those changes seem to be more public than personal, too.

I don't know what happened to that firefighter's family in the long run. They got a cool new refurbished house, and the husband got a home recording studio so he could learn how to do voiceovers, which he seemed to have a knack for. Maybe by now their world has been set to rights and he's working steadily again, bringing in something like the income he used to. Maybe she's gone back to working part-time and making sandwiches for their kids' lunches. Home makeovers don't resolve the kind of crisis that woman was going through; she probably needed to do a whole reassessment of who she was and what she was and what she expected out of marriage and life, just like I did. Let's hope her husband regained a sense of potency in his life, forgave himself for his injuries and bad luck, and took the bull by the horns. That's what guys are supposed to do, anyway, though they can't always: Men are breakable, too. If that wife and I ever met, we could talk about the time when we hoped things would return to normal—and the moment we realized they never would.

Betty and I have ended up in a kind of no-man's-land, where we aren't straight anymore, but we're not lesbian either. He isn't quite the "husband," and I'm certainly not the "wife." I have to remind myself of what other people mean by "husband" and "wife" because we've mixed them up so thoroughly that they're nearly unrecognizable. Meanwhile, my husband grows more feminine every day. Some days he feels more like my wife than my husband. It's become a kind of a joke for us; any day now, I'll expect dinner and my slippers waiting when I get home from a hard day at the office. Neither of us is sure yet if that's the picture we both see of our future together, though we speculate that we might take turns at being the housewife if and when the mood strikes us. By then, her expecting her slippers might feel as if we were switching roles. We were quite surprised the first time we experienced a preview of that possibility.

A few years ago we saw an exhibit about Kafka on the Upper East Side. On our way home, we found ourselves on Lexington Avenue, which has more boutique stores than anywhere else on this planet, all of them featuring high-priced leather goods, or silk scarves, and shoes upon shoes upon shoes. I had to remind Betty that we were already spending more money than we had on the museum entry and dinner. Eventually, we found a lovely old steak house, the kind that looks more like an old Irish bar from the outside than a restaurant. Once we were seated and warmed up a little by the nearby fire, I started talking about the Kafka exhibit. Betty, on the other hand, was still talking about the shoes she'd seen, and about how she longed to have enough money to buy what she wanted when she wanted it. He was dressed as a man, and I was dressed in my usual gender neutral. I started talking about art and politics and how it never says he turned into a cockroach in *The Metamorphosis*, and Betty was talking about Kenneth Cole shoes and occasionally throwing in a comment about having played the painter in the play *The Trial,* or about the R. Crumb version of it, which I'd given to him for opening night.

Me: "I'm really amazed at how he insisted on being alone to write and turned all those women down, even the ones he loved."

Betty: "What I need is a pair of stiletto boots."

We were both listening to what the other was saying; we were just feeling enthusiastic about very different things. We had a moment when the waiter brought our drinks—mine, scotch; hers, beer—when I might have been wearing a smoking jacket and she a silk chenille dress. It was— eerie. I felt as if I might retire to my study after dinner while she retreated to her quarters to phone a friend. When we were getting ready to go, the waiter gave me the check. He wasn't the first one to see who we really were, even then: The person who married us in Brooklyn Civil Court ended our ceremony by saying, "You may now kiss the groom." We hadn't said a word about Betty's transness to our savvy female judge, and we were both as "correctly gendered" as we've ever been around the time of our wedding. Betty even had short hair, and mine was long enough to put up, and yet that judge still managed to see through our gender conformity to the truth of who we are together.

While we're both quite comfortable with these moments of gender switch, most other people aren't, and we can't stay holed up in our apartment forever, or hang around only in queer circles or with family and friends who understand us. It would be easier if we could, because the most difficult things about this life are the looks of disapproval we get, and knowing that people will most likely think Betty is crazy or perverted or just out of control, and that they'll think I'm just stubborn or stupid or codependent instead of realistic and supportive, like the firefighter's wife.

But I understood every inflection in that woman's voice, every connotation and denotation and wish and sorrow and impulse. Her story is also my story, even if mine isn't hers at all, which is exactly why I don't think I'm courageous or brave or crazy; I'm just married, and I'm finding a way to complement my spouse, though maybe in ways that other people find quite bizarre. But my journey here has brought me to uncharted territory, and sometimes I'm stunned by how terrifically and terribly alone I feel. Our companionship relieves that and often makes us feel stronger as a couple, in a kind of "us against the world" kind of way, which is often what it feels like when we're at a party or on the street.

We have changed together as a result of Betty's transness. As more than one trans person has pointed out, transition is not about one person when the trans person is in love: Both people need to transition when someone is changing gender, and each person does it in his or her own way.

four

snips & snails
& sugar & spice.

At a recent party Betty and I attended, and after the party guests had had a bit to drink, a friend of a friend of our host plopped herself next to me and Betty on the couch. I knew what was coming. We'd met her before, at a previous party, and she'd asked a lot of questions then, too.

"So, when you two make love . . . " she started. She did add the requisite "if you don't want to answer, that's okay" caveat, but still: not fun. What's not fun about it to me is the assumption behind the question. She assumed that (1) because we look different from others we have an outlandish sex life, (2) because we look different she actually has the right to ask us about our sex life (and it bothered me that she seemed to not be aware of that), and (3) we had the kinkiest sex life of any of the couples at the party.

I wanted to ask her, "Well, how do you and your husband have sex?" But I didn't. Normally I don't mind questions when someone seems genuinely curious and open-minded. What bothered me was the tint of "I'm so normal and you're so not" to her questions. Her husband and she did not strike me as totally "normally gendered": She came off as kind of aggressive, bulldoggish, and he seemed kind of sweet and passive.

I find it kind of funny when people are so willing to present themselves to me—of all people—as "normally gendered." If anyone's going to see anything gender variant about anyone, I'm a safe bet. I am always on the lookout for gender variance in other couples, and not just while I'm researching, but because I'm fascinated by the way gender plays out between people. I should come with a warning label: ABANDON GENDER CERTAINTY, ALL YE WHO CONVERSE HERE. I'll find even an inkling of gender variance, if it's there.

Being around trans people makes you wonder about everyone you see. Betty and I have been to a lot of transgender conferences, which draw trans people of many flavors. There are trans women out there whom no one would ever know were trans. I've occasionally mistaken them for partners instead of recognizing them as trans themselves, which always makes them blush.[1] I've had conversations with men I hadn't met before only to be told later that they were trans.[2] When we get back from one of these conferences, we're not really sure about anyone we see, or at least not so sure we'd put money down on our guess. I get on the subway and wonder about the gender of a lot of people on the train with me. A tall woman might catch my eye, or a woman with a square jaw. A short guy who's got a little bit more butt than other guys keeps me guessing. Someone may hold himself differently, perhaps because he's recently from another culture and not yet gendered in an American way. If the people I was looking at knew what I was thinking, they would be terribly upset—insulted, even. Yet I'm really not very sure what anyone is anymore. When I see really obvious markers of gender—tattoos on muscled arms, beards, or conspicuous cleavage and high heels—I start to presume that the person is transsexual, because trans people often use such conspicuous gender markers to pass; if you're looking at a woman's cleavage, you may not be as quick to notice her large hands. Your average woman would nearly knock my block off if I asked, "Excuse me, ma'am, but your gender markers seem so intent on convincing everyone you're a woman. You don't happen to be transsexual, do you?"

Although we live in New York City—and in what seems to be an especially queer neighborhood in Brooklyn—it's probably the case that most of the people we see were born in the gender they're presenting as. But, you never know.

Some days I'm astonished at how thoroughly someone can change gender, and in some cases, sex. When we see someone who is visibly trans, we assume that we will always know when someone is trans. We don't, and we won't. Thousands of trans people are out there whom you can't tell are trans at all. The term used in the trans community is "woodworking:" Once people transition and pass as their target gender, they fade into the woodwork. I wouldn't have thought it was possible except that I've seen too many people who do it. Betty has a hard time being read as male these days; he goes out thinking he's dressed like a man and before we know it, someone's calling us "ladies." It's not something you take lightly when you see it over and over again, and frankly it's undermined my sense that gender is such a certainty—especially culturally.

Yet there's still this chasm between what I've seen and what people believe about gender. I'd grown up wanting the chasm to be entirely illusory. People take gender very, very seriously. Every year around Halloween, letters are sent to agony aunts in newspaper columns: "My son wants to go as a ballerina; what should I do?" or "My husband wants to go as a hooker; what should I do?" or even "My daughter won't go as a ballerina; what should I do?" The answers are less satisfying than they used to be, as so often the answer is something along the lines of "He'll probably grow out of it" or "Lighten up, it's Halloween." The tone of the letters shows me that these parents are scared: scared that their children or partners will cross that line and become ungendered, or wrongly gendered, or freakishly gendered.

I've come to know a lot of ungendered, wrongly gendered, and what some would call freakishly gendered people. I get email from self-identified hermaphrodites, and I'm friends with a few women with penises and men with breasts. I've been to conferences full of people who are cross-gendered, queerly gendered, and dually gendered. They're really not very scary. Sometimes they are scared, because the world often isn't very kind to them. It is often outright violent, or discriminatory, or intolerant, which is why it can be so important for someone to pass as his or her target gender. Being identifiable as trans, or gender variant, can target you for harassment and worse. Often trans people embrace gender in a similar way to the people who write those concerned letters to advice columnists, because they've longed their whole lives to be normal, to fit in, and to feel as if they fit in. They want to know the rules, and they want to follow them. Ironically, gender can be much more stereotypical in trans circles than it is in the rest of the population, because for trans people, figuring out how to fade into the woodwork is a means of survival, literally life or death.[3]

If all the stealth or closeted trans people—and I mean all of them, the trans men and women who transitioned five, ten, thirty years ago, plus the genderqueers, the crossdressers, and the drag queens—went to work one day with a shirt or a button on that said, "I'm trans," a lot of people would be very, very surprised. Tens of thousands of people would be wearing those buttons one day, and there would likely be hundreds of thousands of people who knew them who would suddenly realize that they knew someone trans, and who had thought they didn't.

My sense of gender has eroded, changed, and been re-created much like the way the Grand Canyon was created by the continuous pressure of water cutting rock. On the one hand I see gender as variable, changeable, not a constant, and certainly not necessarily connected to what genitals a person has. But on the other, I see the insistence and sacrifice with which transsexuals aim to live in their target gender, and I wonder if there is an innate sense of gender, an innate sense that I don't notice because I don't believe there are important differences between men and women. I see important differences in the way we're treated, behave, dress, and in terms of what role we play in reproducing—all of that and more—but no significant *innate* differences. I have no scientific evidence; I've just known women and men my whole life, like everyone else, and what I see is a lot of range in talent, intelligence, strength (both emotional and physical), and creativity, but I've never noticed that those things "pattern" on gender lines.

Maybe I've known unusual people, but the research I've read that has concluded that women are innately different from men always strikes me as deeply flawed,[4] or the writer has left out some other significant factor, such as race or class or culture. Like religious faith, maybe it's just something I know in my gut and can't explain or find evidence for. If you go back through the historical record and read the hysterical things[5] people have said about the "innate" differences between men and women, it becomes obvious that the people who came to these conclusions were biased, and that observation gives you pause to ponder what kind of blinders we still may have.

What I most want to know is what women they're talking about, because I know a lot of women, and a lot of types of women, and from what I've read, the one thing people who study gender seem to agree on is that there is more variance *among women* than *between women and men*.[6] That means that some women are stronger than some men and other women; some men are weaker than many women and other men. What it really means is that comparing "men" to "women" is like comparing apples to apples. Some women are taller than other women and some men, or they're louder, shorter, faster. Others are smarter, more logical, more aggressive, and more violent. While I can't really see the use or understand the value of always pitting women against men (as if it's a contest), I still want to know why we all read this stuff about "how women are" without asking, at least, *Which women exactly are you talking about?*

Surely the same things cannot be said of me and a woman in Mumbai, India, peeling garlic for her family's dinner, or a teenager in Chinatown who reads all the papers for her immigrant parents, or a woman who was laid off by the recent GM closings, or the woman in Mexico who might end up with that same job. There isn't anything to be said about all of us that *is* true, except maybe when you get to the bare bones of it and talk about breasts and uteruses and reproductive capacity.

Except, of course, not all women have breasts or uteruses or reproductive capacity.

Sometimes identifying a woman is a little like that old idea of how you identify porn: You know it when you see it. But people often see crossdressers and think they're seeing women, and people see men who were assigned female at birth and who are able to pass as men, such as Billy Tipton, who everyone thought was a man his whole life, including his five wives, and who was revealed only upon his death to have female genitals.[7] Justice Stewart's definition[8] doesn't hold up for porn, either, but people expect obscenity or erotica to be difficult to define. Everyone defines those things in different ways, and what we might label obscene now wouldn't be labeled obscene in another era or in another country. But the category of woman isn't supposed to be one of those things. It's supposed to be a static, immutable category. "Woman" is meant to mean something inclusive that implies some similarity in experience, or biology, and even worldview. But imagine the kinds of women that exist: corporate women, housewives, porn stars. There are still Ladies Who Lunch, lesbian separatists, race car drivers, granola types. If you throw in ethnicity or class, forget it.

The category is intersected by so many other facets of identity—race, class, religion, culture, nationality, education, occupation, marital status, sexual orientation—that you'd have gotten very lucky if you pulled two women out of a hat and found they had anything much in common. That's why people try to define what a woman is biologically or physically. There are those things that women are supposed to have in common that define them as women. But the funny thing is that even that isn't a sure thing. We think we know what "a woman" is, and people like to talk about what women do, but I still haven't found a definition for "woman" that includes all women, and all types of women, not even a biological definition. Yet we all think we know what a woman is. I did—until I was asked to write a definition and found I couldn't.

Depending on who you talk to, a woman is an adult human being who

• can give birth to a child,
• has XX chromosomes,
• has a uterus, ovaries, and a vagina, and
• who has subcutaneous fat and other secondary sex characteristics of women, such as breasts.

As it turns out, there are actually eight categories for determining the sex of a child:

1. chromosomal sex (XX or XY)
2. antigenic sex (whether or not there is an HY antigen on the XY chromosome)
3. gonadal sex (ovaries or testicles)
4. prenatal hormonal sex (what hormones were dominant when the child was in the mother's womb)
5. internal morphologic sex (presence of ovaries, uterus, or not)
6. external morphologic sex (penis or vagina)
7. pubertal hormonal sex (whether testosterone or estrogen is dominant during puberty and so affecting secondary sex characteristics), and
8. assigned sex (whether the "IT'S A BOY!" or "IT'S A GIRL!" sign gets put on the parents' front door)[9]

Sex is simply your classification as a biological human being. How you are sexed, which is usually at birth, depends on the size and shape of your genitals (i.e., if you have a penis or a vagina) and is based on an assumption that the size and shape of your genitals imply alignment with your chromosomal sex and the expectation that your internal reproductive organs match your genitals.

But the issue is that sex itself is problematic, and that's the part that even pretty well-educated people don't seem to understand. There's a reason there are eight variables, and most people believe that they always line up. For most of us, the eight variables do line up, so we take it for granted that they always do. But there are significant—in the statistical sense—numbers of people for whom those eight variables don't line up. I lose a couple of points because of the seventh variable, because I had PCOS starting at puberty, which meant my body was somewhat dominated by testosterone and not estrogen, resulting in both male and female secondary sex characteristics.

The more we find out about chromosomes, the less the first variable is always true, as we already know there are women who have XY chromosomes, XXY chromosomes, and all sorts of other variations. I don't know for sure that I have XX chromosomes because I've never been tested, but I assume I do because I have a vagina. But that's no guarantee: Women trained as athletes have gotten to the Olympics only to find out they were disqualified for women's events because they were chromosomally male; this situation became such a problem that the Olympics does not test chromosomes anymore as a way of clearing an athlete to compete in the men's or women's events.

Women who have had complete hysterectomies don't have ovaries or a uterus, but they're still women. Some women are born without them, or with ovaries that are more like testicles that never dropped, but which "pass" for ovaries in an otherwise-female body. Sometimes the gonads are a combination of ovary and testis called ovo-testis. (People declared male can have the same tissue in place of testicles.)

Sometimes a girl is born with a sealed labia and a large clitoris and is declared a boy in the delivery room. Sometimes boys are born with what are referred to as "micropenises" (and yes, doctors have a special ruler for measuring), who, if they are otherwise of indeterminate sex, are "turned into" girls. (One surgeon actually crassly stated, "It's easier to dig a hole than build a pole." Charming.)

All sorts of natural variations occur on these qualifications, ones that are only now coming to light thanks to researchers such as Anne Fausto-Sterling and Alice Domurat Dreger.[10] This chasm between the sexes is supposed to be "natural," but any biologist can tell you that our bodies are not as mutually exclusive as we like to think. Men have nipples. Women have hair on their legs and underarms (and sometimes on their upper lip, cheeks, chin, and chest, and they also have treasure trails[11]). Even our reproductive systems have the same building blocks: Ovaries and testicles come from the same set of cells, as do the clitoris and penis, and the labia and scrotum. Our most gendered parts—our genitals—differentiate only late in fetal development.[12] Menstruation and breasts don't even show up on the list and are not required for a body to be declared female, so all the menopausal women, the postmastectomy breast cancer survivors, the amenorrheal, and anorexics are safe. It surprised me that these two markers of woman-ness are not required. Next thing we know heels and skirts won't be, either, and then we'll never be able to figure out who's a woman and who isn't.

Even if we tried to add a few caveats, we might end up with a definition such as this:

> *Women are adult human beings who* often *have a chromosomal configuration of XX, who* usually *start menarche between the ages of ten and sixteen, whose secondary sex characteristics* sometimes *include breasts and subcutaneous fat, who* may *or* may not *be capable of conceiving, carrying, and birthing an infant starting around the time of menarche and until menopause, which* generally *occurs sometime between ages forty and sixty.*

If a biological definition has to be that circumspect, how can we possibly talk about what women do, how they communicate, or what they wear in "generalized" ways? If we can't even define a woman physically without caveats aplenty, it seems unlikely that we can define "woman" culturally or politically. That's why it bugs me when an article or study tries to talk about "women." They have to leave out types of women to present any information at all.

But if we could qualify those statements by adding "socialized as female," we'd exit the realm of sex and enter the realm of gender. "Socialized as female" means someone is considered a woman or a girl and is feminine. Of course, all of those things mean entirely different things in different cultures, and even at different times within cultures.

What exactly gender is, and how you define it, is a big question. Conservative people might define your gender as the social role you play depending on which genitals you have—a male or masculine gender role if you have a penis, female or feminine gender role if you have a vagina. But there are plenty of people with penises who live out very feminine roles in their lives, such as "Miss J" Alexander of *America's Next Top Model* or the late Quentin Crisp. Whether these men live more like women because they're raised to be like women or because they have some innate femininity, I don't know. So you could say that gender isn't dependent on genitals, or that gender, because it's a cultural experience, is variable based on time and place. Many women alive now would not have been classified as "feminine" one hundred years ago—so much so that their status as women might have been repealed in the same way gay men were once considered not "real men" because of their romantic and sexual partners. Still other people think that our sense of gender is too restricted when we base it on sex; that actually, there are five genders, or twelve, or three hundred, or as many as there are people on the planet. Still others talk about gender being performative: that your gender is inferred by your social interactions, and not a "thing" at all, but something more capricious, like the weather.

I grew up with a feminist understanding of gender, which was more about gender roles than about gender per se. The general gist of the way feminists define gender is that people should be granted equal opportunity no matter their sex, which is based on the idea that women have the same or similar competencies, talents, and native intelligence as men. When it comes to brains or business-running or star-finding or athletic achievement, women have always had the potential to do what men can do but were never given the education or opportunity (and actually, often achieved or surpassed men's accomplishments without either).

That is, one of the feminist understandings of gender is that gender is an old-fashioned idea that got women's ability to birth babies mixed up with their general mental and physical competence.

Which it is.

But gender is a lot of other things, too.

Gender is mostly described by the words "feminine" and "masculine," and although many rue the day that gender was built upon the sexual binary, and some rue the day that the sexual binary ever came to be accepted as fact, those two words tidily summarize what we mean by gender, most of the time.

People like to think sex is definite, while gender is variable and cultural. However, the words are often used interchangeably[13] and they're not really the same. Sex refers to the physical characteristics that cause a child to be declared a boy or a girl at birth; gender is role and identity, which is usually determined by how the person was sexed at birth. Usually, too, each person comes to accept the way she or he was sexed at birth—or not.

An awful lot is riding on what sex people think you are, because they expect your gender to match. There are plenty of people who fit the stereotypes of what men or women are supposed to be. But most of the time we talk about gender as if "man" and "woman" are perfectly natural categories and "masculine" and "man" always go together. They don't. As a result, you'll occasionally see a ninth category for determining the sex of a child listed:

9. Developmental establishment of gender identity and gender role, which is a formal way of saying that the child agrees with the sex

it has been assigned and so agrees that it is female, or male, and so will learn how to be a girl/woman or a boy/man.

Interestingly, Number 9 is the first time the child has any say in the matter, and also interesting is that whether the acceptance of one's gender identity happens or not, gender has come into play. Transsexuals don't accept a gender role and identity that's based on their genitals and insist their brain sex—how they experience their own gender—is more relevant. Tomboys don't accept being told they are femininely gendered; neither do butches. Conservatives would say gay men do not accept their gender role and identity because part of a man's gender role is having sex with women, or procreating, or a combination of those things. Someone's sexing is like a bill presented to the president, and gender identity is the stamp of approval, or its veto. Most people approve their sexing; they decide internally and easily that the sex they have been assigned seems appropriate, and so they accept the gender role and identity assigned to them. Even then, people may only be agreeing to being what they think of as a "woman" or a "man" and not what someone else thinks. I'm quite clear on being a woman, as long as I don't have to abide by John Gray's ideas of how a woman acts.

When you read an article about "how men are" or "how women are," there are usually statements: Men don't talk about emotions; women are nurturing, or curse less, or tend to work part-time if they have children. It's not just in the books; this shows up in the kind of jokey emails people send to their friends and family, and on T-shirts: One I saw recently said "No Cash, No Car, No Chance" in sparkly cursive—definitely a T-shirt designed for women. Yet, a block away from the store where that T-shirt hung in the window, I talked to Delia, our local diner waitress, who works two jobs in addition to parenting her child and who gave the father of her son a car so he could pick up their child at daycare. I asked her about men being breadwinners, and she told me men are the lazy ones; it's the women who work, because no one else is going to take care of their children. Without her mother's help and two jobs, Delia wouldn't be able to get through a week. She knew the reason her son's father had gotten angry about her taking the car back (after he failed to show up at daycare on time) was that it became clear to everyone else that she'd bought him the car in the first place. Talk about a double standard: A woman whose male partner buys her a car can stand tall and be proud of what an excellent breadwinner he is, but a man whose female partner does the same is told she's humiliating him with her ability to take care of not only herself, but him too.

A lot of women are like Delia,[14] and yet we all walk around thinking that it's "normal" for men to be the breadwinners and for women to cover childcare. Delia is both father and mother to her son; she said she hates hanging around a whole barbershop full of guys when she has her son's hair cut, but she does it, because she wants him to be around guys sometimes. I started to wonder how much what we think about gender roles is actually true, and how much of it revolves around what we want to be true, or what we think is "right."

But it also made me realize that there's an implicit assumption about who a woman is in books such as *Men Are from Mars, Women Are from Venus*. Let me put it this way: To write any book about gender, there are going to be sweeping generalizations about the "woman" the author is writing about. It's rare to see even in those ubiquitous email jokes any reference to any kind of specific woman (except maybe blondes). The joke never starts, "So this working-class Puerto Rican woman was talking to her half-Italian blue-collar husband. . . . " No, it's always just "A woman says to her husband. . . . " So who is "a woman" in that joke? A blue-collar former factory worker in Flint? A society woman on the Upper East Side of Manhattan? A Filipina doctoral candidate? Or maybe an African American bus driver? For that matter, who is the husband?

There's an assumption that race and class don't matter when it comes to gender, but they do. Delia is a good example. So am I. When you read about Norah Vincent's impersonation of a guy[15] in a bowling alley full of working-class guys, and the conclusions she came to about what men talk to each other about, and how, you wonder if maybe they would have talked more to a guy who seemed more like them, or to a woman who could bowl, even.

I was very comfortable as a student at a public college where a lot of my fellow students were African American, or from the larger African American diaspora. I could never put my finger on why I felt more comfortable there than at Fordham or the New School or when I visited friends at predominantly white Barnard or Cornell. In the City College English department, Latinas read Virginia Woolf elbow to elbow with me, and then we read Michelle Wallace together. And when Wallace wrote that white feminists' demand for jobs didn't make sense to her in the 1970s[16] because the women in her family had always had jobs, a lightbulb came on over my head. The women in my family had always worked, too. It was a watershed moment for me when I realized that class had always been what got in the way of my friendships with white women whom I was supposed to feel comfortable around but didn't. I'd always understood and gotten along well with the women at City College, whether they were from Ecuador or India or Bed-Stuy (so much so that one Stanford-educated white female professor asked me how I had bridged the race difference). I worked, and they worked—in high school, during summers, while in college. Students at City College often took semesters off to work full-time and save up for the next year's tuition. I often felt I had more in common with the smart, working-class men of color at City College than I did with the white middle-class women I was "supposed" to have more in common with; and for some of the men who came from countries with more traditional gender roles, my tomboy status should have mattered more, but it didn't. There was an overarching solidarity at City College that wasn't based on race or even culture; it was based on how to afford school and how to make your way through the bureaucracy that financial aid created. Conversations about financial aid applications were remarkably bonding.

Even things that seem universal, such as standards of beauty, can be remarkably different for different women from different classes, races, social groups. Whether a woman lives in a city, a suburb, or in a rural area makes a huge difference. I'd have given my left leg for J. Lo to have come around and made bigger butts hot a decade before she did, but I was lucky instead to go to an international school where many different types of beauty were appreciated. In Brazil, more women get their breasts reduced than augmented, and they get their butts lifted and augmented instead. In Indian erotic poetry, the mark of a sensual woman is the line of hair from navel to pubis, but don't try telling your waxing lady that.[17]

Again, there are always variations not just on "what a woman is," but on what makes a woman pretty, what she does, how much she works, whether she's been to college, if she curses a blue streak, or if she expects to be supported by a husband. On those grounds alone I read those jokes about gender and roll my eyes. Don't get me started on jokes about dumb blondes; every time people tell me "it's just a joke" when they notice that I'm gritting my teeth, I want them to trade lives with me for a minute and realize what it's like to grow up a smart blonde. (I'm half-Polish, too, and the Polish are of course the only other group still regularly portrayed as stupid in common humor. What a combination.)

But when I read articles and books talking about "what women do," I can't just roll my eyes; I wonder how many other women read things and just assume the authors are talking about some other kind of woman. For years I read articles and wondered what was wrong with me because so much seemed off; now, I talk to other women, and it's more as if we are who we are, and the articles are talking about a mysterious "typical woman" who doesn't exist. "A woman" in those jokes, and in books and articles, is something like a middle-class white woman. The assumption of who she is and what she does might rely on the medium, the author, the researcher, the target audience. But the whole idea that "women" are all "the woman" in question is more than a stretch—it's absolutely impossible.

I felt a little bit better when an African American friend of mine explained, "When I read 'women,' I read 'white women.' Because when it's black women, they always say black women or use some other code that means black women—like urban, inner-city, underprivileged." As a minority woman, she's learned to read the "code" to know when they're talking about her in terms of her race. My friend went on to mention a study that showed that African American teenage girls read mainstream teen magazines such as *Tiger Beat* and aren't as negatively affected by them because they discount half of the advice as being not for them. In that case, not being the typical teenage girl is a positive and keeps them from feeling pressured into having boyfriends or dieting themselves to death.[18]

I've got a couple of theories as to why people read gender jokes and books such as *Men Are from Mars, Women Are from Venus,* and actually relate to them. First, there's the horoscope analogy: People agree with what reflects their own situation and ignore what doesn't. The assumption about how women tend to be more in touch with their emotions is a good example. I talk to women all the time who tell me that they don't know how they feel, or are afraid to examine how they feel, or simply don't want to admit how they feel because they don't want to upset their husbands or feel forced to make a difficult decision. When women seem to be expressing how they feel, perhaps they're either trying to talk themselves out of an emotion (especially negative emotions such as anger) or because they are trying to figure out what's really bothering them, not what seems to be. When I harp about a sock that isn't in the laundry basket, my problem is usually not the sock. Dealing with whatever is actually bothering me can be much more scary, so I blame the sock. Women are better at fooling themselves into believing they are more "in touch" with their emotions; otherwise why would women blow up after weeks of seething about something without even realizing they were seething about it? Is that being "in touch" with your emotions? Not in my book. The higher incidence of depression among women might also indicate that women's emotions are not getting expressed; any therapist can tell you that depression is often the result of bottled-up feelings. The flip side of the same coin is that men more often commit murder and are more prone to road rage, and last I checked anger (or jealousy, or frustration) are emotions.

That's not to say that men *are* in touch with their emotions. But the way these books are set up to be adversarial about gender make it seem that if men aren't in touch with their emotions, women are, or vice versa, and that it's the diametrically opposed ways of being that explain why men and women have a hard time communicating. I'd argue instead that communicating is hard. Emotions that make you feel sad or angry or uncertain are difficult to bring to the surface. When what you're feeling might upset your partner, your happiness, or your relationship, you're even less likely to say it out loud. Instead of a sock it's that asshole driver, but in either case, people often find themselves raging about something that turns out to be completely beside the point a day later.

Second, people prefer excuses. They want to know their relationships have failed for reasons that had nothing to do with them. A writer who sets out to tell women that they can't find boyfriends because they're more interesting in "getting" a man than relating to one isn't going to sell a lot of books. It's a rare woman who will admit that she's after a guy with money because she doesn't have the confidence to make it herself; she wants to hear that it's her "biological imperative" to find a good provider so she can cut herself some slack. Do we really need to tell men that it's their biological imperative to have sex with as many women as they can? Considering overpopulation and STDs and deadbeat dads and testosterone's tendency to encourage a high sex drive in the first place, supplying men with an easy "out" by telling them it's their biological imperative to have sex with as many women as they can seems to just encourage crappy behavior. I find it amusing that people find excuses for their bad behavior by pointing to residual cavemen genes, since I thought the whole point of civilization was to maybe get past our most basic urges, or least indulge them responsibly. We didn't learn how to read and build buildings and invent elevators so that we could just live according to the dictates of our caveman brains.

People read those books and jokey emails simply because we all want to know how to be normally gendered. We want to fit in. Books such as *The Rules* make it plain what women are often looking for: not just how to be a woman, but how to be a woman who has a boyfriend or husband, and for men, how to be the boyfriend or husband women desire. You can look at cultural trends to see this at work: If being happy means being desirable, and being desirable means being thin, women try to lose weight. Men take drugs that cause erectile dysfunction in order to keep their hair, and then take more drugs to fix the ED.

The problem is, we don't recognize or identify these worries or decisions as gendered. We think they're about beauty, attractiveness, aging. But what we don't notice is that we're constantly surrounded by gendered jokes about sissies and masculine women. I was always aware of women-with-facial-hair jokes, and ones about European women "growing their own socks." Closeted crossdressers blush when they hear jokes that mock guys who wear panties. On top of that, we've got magazines telling us how to look and act, all of them geared toward men or women, but rarely both. Articles about parenting often use "she" pronouns and otherwise seem geared toward women only. Watching sports can make it seem that there are no attractive men in the audience, while the attractive women—especially if they happen to be the players' wives—are featured prominently.

Often people read these types of books as a kind of checklist, making sure they're "normal" and just like the other guys. I'm not dismissing the need to fit in—we all need to, in various ways, for various reasons—but in terms of relationships, is it really more important to be like all the guys you know or to relate better to your wife? The assumptions about who we're supposed to be, what we're supposed to like, look like, act like, and even where we're supposed to work are determined all the time by the culture all around us. For women, for whom fitting into social networks might make it easier to find a babysitter or a job, it may be even more important. A friend's mother, while going through a divorce, admitted that she knew she should have gone back to work, but in her world, she fit in better with the other mothers by being a stay-at-home mom. Her husband, as it turned out, wanted a woman he could talk to about business, and who—in his opinion—could talk about subjects other than PTA meetings and bake sales. She fit in so well with the other women that she found herself not fitting in her own marriage.

Because I talk to transitioning women so often, I've become aware of how absurd it is to try to define "what women do," or even what they look like, much less try to nail down what it means to be a "typical" woman. Trans women often want to fall into the realm of "typical woman," but I don't know what that is. Is the typical woman white or black? Tall or short? Thin or curvy? When someone born and socialized male is trying to parse what she needs to change in order to be a woman, she wants answers, and I have none. Sure, women generally have higher voices than men, but not all of them. When Betty and I were traveling with two trans women not too long ago, I was amused that I had the deepest voice of the four of us. Women usually have bigger hips than men, but not always. Sometimes they have longer hair, less body hair, and breasts. Unless a woman born female is gender variant in obviously masculine or androgynous ways, it's not likely she'll be told she's "not really" a woman, but sometimes when people learn a trans woman is trans, they can be very willing to toss her back into the "male" category. We might not hold every woman up as an exemplar of woman-ness, but we wouldn't call them men because they aren't, either.

And that's the problem with the binary. Close counts only with hand grenades and horseshoes—and gender. Because we have two choices, and only two choices, everyone has to fit in one or the other. Even if they're iffy. Even if we're not really sure. Imagine yourself as Saint Peter at the Pearly Gates, but instead of separating people into good or evil, you had to separate them into man or woman. Everyone, no exceptions. Someone might just squeak into the woman category with a barely passing grade, but ultimately, she's either in or out. That's the way gender operates. When we look at the people around us, our minds put them in one category or the other. It's a snap judgment, and we could very well be wrong a lot of the time, but that doesn't keep us from doing it.

Despite that, there's this niggling feeling that you know what a woman is even if you can't define it. I used to think that not being able to define "woman" might undercut the idea that sexism is real and that oppression against women exists. Unluckily for women everywhere, disappearing sexism and women's oppression is not that easy: All you need to be oppressed as a woman is for someone to decide you are one. The person doesn't have to know what it means to call you a woman, or why he or she decided you are one. I could decide tomorrow that I'm a man if I want to escape sexism, but unless I transition, or move to a deserted island, or otherwise remove myself from human society, there is always the chance that someone will come along and decide I'm not a man. Gender is kind of like that tree falling in the forest. Without someone to observe it, it's just an idea. But to the dismay of naturally androgynous people and nonpassing transsexual people, and to feminists, gender is played out on the ground, where everyone who comes along puts you in one of the two boxes available and has expectations of who you are based on which box he or she put you in. That's why trans people use those obvious markers; they want to pass that "snap judgment" that people are always making.

None of us has much of a choice about which gender other people think we are. When I was a teenager with a shaved head who wore no makeup, a conductor stamped my monthly train ticket M, and I didn't know what to do about it. If I got it changed to F, I might get another conductor who thought I was an M, too, and not honor my ticket. But if I didn't get it changed, a conductor might think I was an F and trying to pass off my brother's ticket as my own, and not honor it. I finally decided to get it changed to F and started carrying a copy of my birth certificate around, just in case. People are trying to make gender less absolute, less either/or: Some people want recognition of more genders; others assert that "male" and "female" are closer to archetypes, or stereotypes, or ideals[19] and that none of us is absolutely one or the other. Feminists, of course, have been trying for years to expand what "woman" means so that more kinds of behavior, attitude, and presentation will be socially acceptable, so that wearing your hair short or wearing pants won't get you tossed into the "man" category. Jamison Green, a trans man and activist, jokes about how young, transitioning trans men complain about getting called "ma'am" in San Francisco, where he lives; he tells them they need to go somewhere other than San Francisco to find out if they're passing as male, because many years of outreach by lesbians have trained locals to call even the most masculine woman "ma'am" for fear of offending her.

The irony of having only two huge, all-encompassing genders is that everyone fits in one or the other or is made to fit.[20] Once you're in, however, you're expected to behave in certain ways, look a certain way, and depending on the time, place, and culture, have only certain kinds of jobs, have sex with only the opposite sex, have the right to vote, own property, be educated, or not. That's kind of a lot to determine by a vagina or a penis, in my opinion, and may explain why, despite parents' attempts at "correctly" socializing their boys to be masculine and their girls to be feminine, and despite the strong cultural taboos against bending gender to your own ends, there's so much gender variance out there.

You've got the tomboys and you've got the kids who engage so persistently in cross-gender behavior they get dragged to shrinks to be diagnosed with gender identity disorder of childhood (GIDC) (a great many of whom seem to grow up to be gender-normative homosexuals[21]). Crossdressers innately know or learn very quickly to keep their mouths shut about donning frocks. But then you've got the more medical models: the women who have XY chromosomes but whose bodies are entirely insensitive to androgens (androgen insensitivity syndrome, or AIS) or are only partially insensitive (partial androgen insensitivity syndrome, or PAIS) but who grow up to be gender-normative women. The larger group of intersex (IS) people includes a lot of different types of people, such as boys who need to sit to pee and girls whose ovaries turn out to be internal testicles and who masculinize at puberty when those internal testicles start producing testosterone. Many of the intersexed people I've talked to struggle though life with "cross-gender" urges while utterly in the dark that they were born in intersexed bodies and that doctors chose them a sex at birth. Some of them choose to identify as trans as well, if they transition from the gender they were assigned at birth to the gender they feel more comfortable in, but not all.

If you count homosexuals in general, because some people consider it "cross-gendered behavior" for a woman to like women or a man to like men, the ranks swell considerably. Then of course there's the trans community: You have the full range of MTF crossdressing and cross-gender behavior, including t-girls[22] and transsexual women and people who identify as transgendered or transvestites or just trans. The FTM spectrum includes genderqueers and bois and trans men and men of trans experience. Then throw in the drag queens, some feminists, and the occasional metrosexual.

But then, where does it end? Who "counts" as gender variant? Aggressive businesswomen? Female architects and engineers? Straight male hairdressers, interior designers, visual artists? Male yogis and pacifists? Female soldiers, presidents, firefighters, and steelworkers? Where you draw the line to define what is and isn't gender variance gets a little tricky. I like to count anyone who might walk into a bar and get called faggot or dyke on the premise that sometimes it's easier to know who's in your gang by knowing who else the people who hate you hate. Or you can count all those who—in their work uniform or out of it—might get mistaken for being the sex they're not. Likewise with anyone whose livelihood is assumed to be the domain of men or women, but not both, such as female bus drivers or boxers, or male hairdressers, nurses, and party planners.

But gender variance is relative and very contextual. If you took a calf-roping, self-respecting cowgirl and put her in a room of blue-blood Connecticut society ladies, the cowgirl would be the gender-variant one, even if she doesn't feel gender variant when she's in a cowboy bar. The working-class woman might find herself amazed at how masculine she felt in a party full of middle-class women. European and Asian men might feel effeminate when it comes to American Midwestern ideas of masculinity.[23] I consistently have the deepest voice in rooms full of lesbians and trans women, and as the het one, I'm "supposed" to be closest to gender normative.

So where do we draw the lines between what is variant and what's within the norm? That would require us to know what the norms are. But whose? Any sociologist could tell you that the norms of acceptable behavior vary greatly within social groups. Subcultures are notorious for having different standards: Think of hippies, beatniks, goths. Even if we were to restrict our norm to "mainstream American," how exactly would we define that? Whose America? Urban or suburban? Red or Blue America? Rural or urban? When I first walked into the Million Dollar Cowboy Bar in Jackson Hole, Wyoming, I assumed that the women in jeans and boots with short hair were dykes and the guys in chaps and cowboy hats were gay; I'd seen Tom of Finland's erotic drawings of homosexual cowboys but hadn't ever met an actual cowboy. After I looked around a while I realized that they were all heterosexual, and I probably would have gotten my ass kicked if I'd said anything about what I'd thought when I first walked in. I felt distinctly effete compared to the women I met out west, even if I met them while I was wearing a leather jacket and checking the car's radiator. That was the first time I noticed that urban can often be considered more feminine than rural, just as the term metrosexual suggests.

I didn't know how to interpret their genders, and they didn't know how to interpret mine. Gender is so contextual; one man's masculine is another man's effete. Around femmy men and feminine women, I'm usually the most masculine without a contest. Around macho guys and butch lesbians and those tough Western women, I'm a delicate flower, which leads me to believe that (1) I'm both masculine and delicate flower, or (2) I'm neither, or (3) the idea of pinning down gender is pretty much useless. That's true even of people who don't think about gender much, at least not consciously. I used to live in a predominantly Dominican neighborhood, where on Saturday nights some of the men put on their best macho, cocks of their walk. But on Sunday I would see those very same men spit-and-polished and docile, ready for Mass. That's contextual gender: when a guy can be one type of man in one place, with certain people, and a very different kind of man elsewhere. Because gender comprises so many things—manners, presentation, language, class, something I'm going to call "vibe"—it's very variable and definitely not connected with genitals. To me, "putting on your church manners" for a boy means he is behaving in a more feminine way. If he acted that way out on the playground, he'd be called a sissy, but in church it's what is expected. Girls are always expected to speak with their "inside voice" (or at least they were when I was growing up), but boys are not.

Gender is the name for what kind of man or woman you are in social spheres, and your gender changes when the social sphere changes. It's all based on comparison and context: The most feminine woman in the world can't be feminine without the idea of masculine existing in the world elsewhere. Even when she's alone, she feels feminine because she doesn't feel masculine. We define our genders often by what they *aren't* more than by what they are, and we think that being masculine or feminine is mutually exclusive when it's not.

Often, ultimately, it's the bigots who decide. They know a sissy when they see one. Mostly. Unless a slender teenage boy with delicate features happens to be holding his mom's purse in the wrong time and place. To "protect" his son from the dangers of gender variance and homosexuality, a father recently killed his own three-year-old by enforcing masculinity on him: He shook him and hit him and taught him to "toughen up," and the child ended up with a concussion. This father didn't want his kid to grow up to be a faggot, and now the kid isn't going to grow up at all. And while a lot of our drive toward gender conformity is deeply embedded in homophobia, heterosexuals are not always stereotypically gendered, either. But gender variance in straight people isn't acknowledged, which makes it a little more difficult for them to live openly gender-variant lives. I didn't know there was a chance to continue being a tomboy or that there was a chance of meeting a feminine man for a romantic and sexual partnership. I had to find the trans community to even know such gender variance existed. Heterosexual gender variance is invisible for a few reasons, some of them practical, some of them historical, some of them a combination of both.

For starters, the dominant belief is that *gender variant = homosexual.* We believe, as a culture, that gender variance belongs to gays and lesbians. It's a tautology: *All gender-variant people are gay and lesbian. She is gender variant. Therefore, she must be a lesbian.* In a sense, there is no way for a heterosexual to be gender variant and still be seen as heterosexual; it's a Catch-22. It's not just heterosexuals who believe this, either; plenty of crossdressers can tell you how difficult it is to convince a gay man that just because they like to wear dresses doesn't mean they don't also like to date women. And older lesbian femmes can tell you how much they weren't accepted as lesbians during the seventies.[24] The belief that *gender normative = heterosexual* (and its inverse, that *gender variant = homosexual*) is so intense that any man who acts feminine is immediately labeled a fag, and so faces the discrimination gay men face, and likewise for any woman who is perceived as masculine. To avoid being discriminated against, gender-variant heterosexuals submerge or hide or repress or closet their gender variance. While hiding gender variance isn't entirely stupid, considering the consequences, it does make heterosexual gender variance disappear from public view. If they don't hide it, they're assumed to be gay, which means that either way, heterosexual gender variance is effectively invisible, which "proves" that only gays and lesbians are gender variant.

That heterosexual gender variance is invisible is one of the things that living with someone trans teaches you very quickly. And yet, no one would have ever guessed that Betty was gender variant, because she hid hers for the same reason that I did: to date. Because *feminine man = gay man* in this culture, there is no way for a heterosexual man to both date women and express his femininity. Shoot, we're so obsessed with men being masculine it's hard for gay men to express their femininity if they want to date; in a story that appeared in *The Advocate,* one gay man is quoted as saying, "I don't like it when a guy opens his mouth and a purse falls out."[25] But at least there's some kind of acknowledgment that it's possible for a man to be a femme, even if no one wants to date him. (Your average het crossdresser would probably have as much luck if he were open about *his* femininity, too.)

Because we pretend there is no heterosexual gender variance, there really are no alternate models of heterosexuality out there at all. We're all supposed to do our best at fitting ourselves into the preordained boxes. The lesbian community may have butches and soft butches and femmes and bulldaggers and stone butches, and the gay community has queens and bears and "straight-acting" gay men (which means, of course, heteronormatively gendered men), but in the heterosexual universe there are just men and women. There are no other names for "types" of men and women; there is little acknowledgment that there are types of heterosexual men and women at all, at least not in the language we use. "Sissy" implies an effeminate gay man or a young feminine male child, tomboy a masculine female child. I know I always felt ridiculous calling myself a tomboy as an adult, no matter how much I was one at age twelve. There is no such thing as a tom-man, no matter how much I am one now.

To me that's just another good reason for heterosexual crossdressers to come out of the closet already.

Homophobic reasons underpin why gender-variant people who like the opposite sex learn how to hide their gender variance. Gender-variant people can be especially homophobic because they feel discriminated against for something that they aren't, and they end up feeling that their lives wouldn't be so complicated if there weren't gays and lesbians for them to be compared to. The homophobia can be more of a self-hating instinct; that is, gender-variant people[26] might hate that part of themselves that they don't think is "normal," much in the way some gays and lesbians and trans people can be self-hating. Gays and lesbians might hate having same-sex attraction, and trans people may hate being trans; in other words, people can hate the thing that's causing their lives to be difficult, or estranging them from their families, and they take that self-hate out on others who have adjusted to their "deviance."

But homophobia isn't the whole reason, either.

First, there's plain old confusion. I was told so often and so regularly that I must be a lesbian that I doubted my own sexual orientation. Crossdressers guess and second-guess their own sexualities as well, and while some do discover they're more bisexual than they would have expected—especially when crossdressed and treated "like a lady" by a man—a lot realize that the crossdressing has little to do with their orientation. A person who is assumed to be gay can spend years trying to figure that out. Even when I did figure out I didn't want to have sex with women, I still assumed that I couldn't be gender variant *and* heterosexual—well, at least not actively heterosexual, and what's the point of having a sexual orientation if you're not actually having sex with anyone?

There's also the simple fact of trying to get laid and/or fall in love. People want to fall in love with the sex they like; het women want to get hit on by guys and het guys want to be flirted with by women. Since *gender variant = gay or lesbian*, letting your gender variance "show" as a het means you get hit on by the wrong people. For me, being with a woman was too much sameness; it was disorienting because I couldn't feel where I ended and where she started, and I wanted to feel a body that was hard where I was soft, straight where I was curved. (That's the only really visceral sense of my own "opposite sex" attraction I can articulate.) Since Betty is also an actor, and there are plenty of gay men involved in theater, and plenty of stage door Johnnies who appreciate a good-looking young actor, he tried finding some interest in men, but every time he thought about it, it was *stubble and muscles and hair—oh my!* And that was the end of that.

The other funny thing that happens as a result of this foregone conclusion that *gender variant = homosexual* is that heterosexual people who actually are gender variant are pardoned, or their gender variance is kind of ignored. If a married couple are both a little gender variant—she's more aggressive in business, and he's better with children—everyone will gloss over it, because both their marriage and their children "confirm" their heterosexuality. Single women with cats, or "crazy cat ladies," tend to be assumed to be lesbian, but often aren't. Those older male bachelors who collect things tend to be assumed to be gay. My brother-in-law collects both neckties and fiestaware and knew for years that plenty of people assumed he was gay. The tautology works both ways: *Heterosexuals are gender normative; she is married to a man, therefore she is gender normative.*

And so, gender variance in heterosexual people simply doesn't, and can't, exist.

Except it does.

Gender-variant heterosexuals often are the people others gossip about. Those slightly feminine older bachelors who everyone assumes are gay are probably at least occasionally crossdressers. Some of them are perhaps surprisingly het—as Betty and I both were to many people who knew us, including our families. But we exist. (I like to joke that Betty's parents didn't care so much that I was a liberal because they were so relieved I was a woman.) Quite a few of us just learn how to get by; Betty hid her gender variance from a young age because of how huge the taboo against being a sissy is, and I was free to be a tomboy until puberty. We both got a slight break in the androgynous eighties, and we're both very thankful for that bit of cultural good timing. But once we were both in our twenties, we tried very hard to perform our respective gender roles properly. For Betty that meant pretty much avoiding relationships, and for me, it always felt like playing a part. My guess is that we have both now begun to acknowledge our gender variance because we have found a place to do so: the larger LGBT community. Since the T has been added, we have effectively been welcomed into the only subset of American culture that acknowledges gender variance. We are those mysterious "queer heterosexuals" that are starting to get mentioned in academic journals and LGBT papers.

For us, the T getting added to the LGB not only made perfect sense, but it opened new doors; had we remained "heterosexual," we would have floundered much longer. Why we needed a space to be able to explore this stuff doesn't need explaining, but just in case: Bucking gender roles is huge. Monumentally, backbreakingly huge. The overwhelming pressure to conform to masculine and feminine ideals—or die trying—is constant. The obligation to conform is also somewhat invisible and harder to put your finger on. It comes out in the funny looks people give me if I open a door for Betty when she's in guy mode. Or the funny looks I get pushing an elevator button myself instead of waiting for the guy nearest the panel to ask me where I'm going. Or the way a man might tell a woman he doesn't even know to smile, as if it's a woman's job to keep up that cheery countenance for his sake. It comes in the form of subtle reactions, jokes you hear, ideas about what men and women are. And if you start breaking the rules, you start to feel cut loose, a little adrift; you don't know why all the jokes other people are laughing at make you uncomfortable. The experience of being differently gendered in America is a little like being a stranger in a strange land, where you're constantly trying to pretend to be native, but you're not. You start to speak gender with an accent, an accent that lets people know right away that you're not the same as they are. But Betty and I really had no choice. When your husband's name changes depending on what clothes he's wearing and how he's styled his hair, you're pretty much tossed out of the "normal" category.

Most of the couples I've known who were variations on typically gendered people got accused of being closet cases, and often in cruel ways (by both gay and straight folks). Sometimes there'd be nervous jokes about her being a ballbuster or his being whipped, but *if* any gender variance was noticed, it was either (1) gossiped about in whispers, or (2) joked into invisibility. In either case, what I heard was never anything the people being talked about would take as a compliment. It's insulting to have your own sense of self and sexuality questioned by others; bisexuals and queer women[27] often have similar experiences of not having their own realities "believed" because everybody likes the little boxes.

How a person's gender variance is perceived falls along the same lines as that old saw about how poor people are considered crazy but rich people only eccentric. If you're homosexual and gender variant, it's an explanation for what makes you homosexual. If you're heterosexual and gender variant, everyone tries to politely ignore it. Granted, if you're a transvestite, you have to be Eddie Izzard, and even he has a hard time getting interviewers to ask him about his comedy and his movie roles rather than his clothes. I've started to think you accumulate demerits, and once you gather more than a certain amount, you're thrown out of "gender normative"—even if it's lots of tiny infringements, or one big one. For gay folks, it's often just the "one big one" of desiring someone of the same sex and actually wanting to bring that person to parties and bars and raise children together. With us, I'm not so sure which gender markers get us thrown out, whether it is the dynamic between us in general, or whether it really is that unusual for me to give Betty money so she can buy herself a drink, or whether the weird part is that I took the money out of a wallet I keep in my back pocket. I don't know. We're considered gender variant enough for drunken friends of friends at parties to ask us questions they wouldn't ask a couple who registered as normal. I know another couple in which the woman doles out the money as needed, and they hear about how she "wears the pants," too, and they couldn't care less what people think. But then again they're actors, and the white adoptive parents of three Ethiopian children, so it's best that they live their lives without caring what judgments people might or might not be making about their lives.

Every one of us has felt restricted by gender or locked into a gender role. Every time a woman goes to work and can't decide if a dropped neckline will help or hurt her chances at a promotion, she's struggling with gender. Every time a man is reluctant to hold or hug a male friend, even when he wants to, it's gender that hems him in. People wonder all the time whether or not they "measure up" to being men and women. If a man is worried about whether he's hard enough, long enough, he's worried about being a "real man." When a woman wants breast implants that may be dangerous to her health, she's seeking a more secure place in the box marked WOMAN. Considering the enormous biases on the parts of parents and teachers and older siblings and television and movies and our culture as a whole, it's amazing we have gotten to see any so-called "cross-gender" behavior at all.

For me, playing what's traditionally considered the male role in a relationship has unleashed something I'd long left behind. I had to figure out (again) who exactly I am, and why I seem to love Betty so much and so easily when she is flirtatious and femme but still feel so reluctant to give up having a male lover with a male body. A part of me that had gone underground long ago understood that I was her boyfriend sometimes, even if she was my husband. Getting that person to come back out was one of the trickiest things I've ever tried to do, and I'm still trying. Sometimes

I'm convinced I'm making progress, getting back to who I really am; other times I feel as if I'm regressing into a state I left behind with good reason. As with so much else in our relationship, I'm convinced that embracing my tomboy self now, for the sake of our relationship, is a positive evolution, and on other days I'm wholly convinced it isn't. Our relationship has definitely opened up an opportunity for me to explore my masculinity in ways I hadn't thought possible as an adult, and my experience figuring out how to recall those parts of myself reminded me of how gendered I had let myself become.

wearing
the
pants.

One of my first moments of *Wow, has my life gotten weird* happened on Betty's and my first Valentine's Day together. I went to Macy's to buy her a present. As I traveled up the escalator, bypassing all the women who were shopping in the men's department for their boyfriends, I momentarily thought I should get her something a guy would wear. A vision of Betty's face if she opened a clothes box to find a pair of boxer shorts and a tie flashed through my head. I stayed put on the escalator. I was going to Women's Lingerie, Sixth Floor.

I've been there a few times since, and I'm not quite used to it yet. A friend who was coming out as lesbian told me years ago that when you check *Rubyfruit Jungle*[1] out at the library, the librarian stamps the due date in your book and LESBIAN on your forehead. But buying a handful of panties for Betty—and I mean a handful, precisely—causes Macy's sales clerks to look at my ass. Maybe she was trying to be helpful, but the cogs were turning in her head as she scanned tags—SM, SM, and SM—and again looked at my butt. No joke can lighten the mood while she's figuring out whether I'm delusional or a lesbian, and saying "They're for my husband" wouldn't help anything at all. I don't want to know what name she'd ring up for me in that register in her head if I said that.

The one perk was that I felt like the only "guy" shopping in the lingerie department who had any idea what to buy; I know what my girlfriend's size is, and what goes with what (though that's assuming there were no crossdressers there passing as boyfriends buying Valentine's Day presents, because they know way more than I do). I was a sensitive New Age guy, and I gave myself a pat on the back not just for knowing Betty is a SM, but for knowing what colors and fabrics and cuts she likes, too. And also because—unlike all those other guys who'd get an erection once their girlfriends put the gift lingerie on—all I would get is a Macy's bill and a happy Betty. A gift of lingerie usually benefits the wearer—who feels sexy and desirable—and the giver—who is turned on by seeing it on the woman he loves, and rightfully so. But once again, a simple, loving transaction for a heterosexual couple can be, for me, a source of confusion. If your average straight guy buys his girlfriend lingerie because he likes the way she looks in it, then why was I buying any for Betty? I preferred him naked.

I learned how to get my own "girl wood" over Betty in lingerie eventually, but it took a while, a lot of creativity, and my willingness to embrace that being a top was a lot more fun than I'd imagined, and topping a very coy, undersexed Betty was a challenge. I like challenges, and this was another way that I was better suited to the "guy's role." It's more direct, more about asking than vetoing, more about being in charge. Even now I blanch at admitting such a thing, because I worry that people will assume the worst possible other names for me, the ones I'm not using for myself: control freak, bossy, emasculating. The words we use to describe women who use kinds of power that are traditionally reserved for men are almost always negative. But men themselves also have a very fine line to walk between making decisions and being steadfast and "taking charge" or being an asshole. It's a line I've flirted with way more often than I expected as a result of wearing the pants in our relationship. And because of it I have a lot more sympathy for men who are trying to be decisive and come off as arrogant instead, or who err in the other direction and are judged as not manly enough.

Men complain about how horrible it can be to be the guy: to be the one who crosses the room to start the conversation, to make the initial phone call, to make the plans and hope they make your date happy. MTFs find those expectations especially frustrating while they're still living as men, but for me, these things are much easier than their opposites: anxiously scanning the room to see if someone's crossing it, waiting for the phone call, having to go where your date chooses to go. While this picture of dating may be more traditional than the way some people date, it still seems to be the assumed way to go about things. One of the things I love the most about knowing crossdressers and transsexuals is that they know that the too-rigidly-enforced roles aren't much fun from either side; a newly single crossdresser named Shelly recently told me that waiting for the phone to ring is at least as bad as making that initial phone call. Both gender roles in relationships have their downsides, which is one of the reasons that we should be able to choose which role we want and to make that choice based on our overall personalities rather than on which genitals we have. If you're more the type to bite the bullet and get the worrying over with and just make the call, you get to play the "guy role," whether you have a vagina or not. Who knows how many female gentlemen there are out there? I, for one, would love to watch a few guys bite their nails while they wait by the phone. I love playing *The Sims²* because the women can do the wooing, and it tickles me no end to see the male being wooed put his hand to his forehead, swoon slightly, and giggle in response while my female seducer, down on one knee, serenades his pretty self.

That said, feeling like the guy is not everything it's cracked up to be, either. Sometimes I wind up in situations with Betty where I become aware of the pressures of being "the guy." There's the easy, enjoyable stuff—buying drinks, opening doors, holding both our jackets; but then there's the scary stuff, as when a guy is hovering a little too close or she gets clocked by someone who isn't hip to trannies. Then I feel the pressure of knowing it's my responsibility to radiate a "don't fuck with me and mine" vibe, and when I'm not feeling confident, it can be difficult to look a little bigger and a little tougher than I am. I look around at guys much bigger than I am and know I had better be able to disarm a potentially bad situation with my brain, because my brawn is not going to do the trick—and that's even knowing that Betty knows how to throw a punch and can take care of herself.

But I wonder about all the gentle guys I've known over the years—and even the not-so-gentle ones—and how they manage. I think about the trans men I know and I'm impressed. When I think of the butches I see on the subway in their army jackets and tattoos, who look out at the world with a kind of defiance and sadness in their eyes, I'm awed. I can't imagine existing in a male world of physical power as someone born female but masculine; no matter how masculine I feel some days, I'm a powder puff in comparison. Those are days that make me thankful I can exist in a more androgynous space, or register as genderless-but-female-by-default, even if existing as female in a man's world comes with its downsides, too. But still, I feel protective of Betty. I often feel like Thelma, warning my Louise[3] that walking down to the corner bodega to get a beer in really tight jeans at 2:00 AM really isn't a good idea. In an essay written for the now-defunct magazine *Anything That Moves,* the bisexual girlfriend of a pre-op MTF trans woman mentioned the kind of fear you can experience as the partner of a trans person: She and her girlfriend were waiting at a bus stop when some men only stared at them. She found herself hoping her girlfriend would get her genital surgery soon, because then "they'll only rape her, not murder her."[4] And unfortunately, that's the reality of living with someone who is trans, which is maybe part of the reason I feel I come up short in terms of playing the male role. What can anyone do against that kind of ignorance and hate?

The notion that it's difficult to be male isn't news to me.

Whenever I've read or heard jokes by women about men, something in me has felt a little sad because those jokes seem unfair—at least as inaccurate as the ones about women. Many of my closest friends have been guys through the years. I've had consecutive sets of adoptive older brothers, such as my two punk rock friends, Marc and Peter; later there were Doug and Maurice, my roommates during my early twenties. I've had guys in my life who were mentors, who challenged me intellectually, men who related to me as an equal, who admired me and whom I admired in return. I've had guy friends I talked to about sex and dating and love, and guys I talked to about politics and history. Some of my guy friends are gay, but a lot of them are heterosexual.

It would be easy to assume that I related to guys because I was a tomboy, but actually my friendships with men often made me feel more female, and more aware of being female, than I might have otherwise felt—but not in a sexualized way. A lot of the time I felt more like a sister, or a cousin—older or younger depending on the guy in question. They talked to me about music and actually listened if I had an opinion, but they also teased me for having crushes on musicians exactly because it was such a "girly" thing to do. My former roomies, especially, took care of me as if we were siblings, and I did my best to return the favor. It was quite useful having male roommates, even if the Dominican ladies called me *puta*[5] on the elevator, because I could bring home a date if I wanted and not have to worry much about my safety. Doug and Maurice were the ones who organized my bachelorette party, and while we all recognized that maybe that wasn't typical, none of us thought it was weird, either. I was just a woman who got along well with guys, and they were guys who liked having a female friend.

Sometimes I wonder if my own internalized sense of maleness, and my ease in being friends with men, is simply the imprint of having been the youngest daughter in a family where men were highly valued.[6] I've often joked that my brothers behave like crown princes. But I also always admired their life, their independence, their surety, and their vulnerability. I admired the way their charming selves could make women such as my mother and grandmother happy in simple, stupid ways, by telling jokes or doing impersonations or being otherwise larger than life. Betty has a similar skill with women no matter how he's presenting. My mom was quite relieved when we met because he was an oldest son and I was a youngest daughter. She puts great stock in the way birth order determines the way people communicate; in other words, Betty would know how to tell me I was being a spoiled brat, and I would know how to tell Betty to stop being an arrogant prig. Like mutual parenting, that kind of dynamic is part of a romantic relationship, because how you're taught to treat a sister or brother has a lot to do with how you think of gender and how you relate to the opposite sex. (A close cousin might stand in if you don't have a sibling.)

I was never like my father or my brothers in that gregariousness; I'm an introvert and naturally kind of serious—much like the other women in my family. But I did manage to use men as role models in a way; I wanted to feel like Indiana Jones felt in his clothes, sweaty fedora, bullwhip on his hip, or like Sting in his organic cotton sweaters, or the way Adam Ant did in his leather pants. The thing is, I like guys. I grok them at a level many other women don't seem to. I recently tried to explain to a friend that I didn't much like Norah Vincent's *Self-Made Man*[7] because the whole point of the book seemed to be that she discovered that men aren't assholes, which I've always known; not only that, but it struck me that her discovery was a shocking, life-changing revelation for her, which I didn't understand. It never occurred to me that a woman could go through a couple of decades without noticing that men were human. I was even more surprised when my friend retorted that that was exactly the reason she liked the book, because it was a shocking, life-changing revelation for her, too, that guys aren't assholes. Later, I wondered out loud to another friend about how many women would think this was a revelation, when a feminine gay friend of mine agreed that for him, too, it was a revelation. It made me wonder where I learned to appreciate men and why they didn't, and whether my appreciation had something to do with my own masculinity and my ability to relate to men because of it.

I had an experience with a therapist not long ago, in which I was talking and talking and talking, the way you do in therapy, and at some point she just said, "I'm pretty sure your feelings are in this room somewhere, maybe up there near the ceiling. Maybe we should try to work on pulling them down here, where we can look at them." My therapist was wearing a tie. It took a woman who wore a tie—a woman who was at peace with her own masculinity—to see that what I really wanted to do was run out of the room. I have been intellectualizing my feelings for a very long time, and maybe the joke is on me that this habit of mind is stereotypically male. My guess is that I've always known how men are and how they don't allow themselves to feel things and how troubling that can be—and how difficult it is to break that cycle and engage a more emotional, vulnerable self.

Had I not been born female I would have had no excuse or ability to connect to my emotions at all,[8] and I wonder what kind of asshole I would have been as a result. As much as having been born female seems neither here nor there, being female afforded me cultural space to even consider connecting with how I feel, and not just with how I think. In that sense, I have always been glad I'm female, because men aren't given much room to explore how they feel, and when they do, they're called "navel gazing" or "sensitive" or other things that are pejorative in the same way that calling a woman "bossy" is. For me, there has never been anything more beautiful than a man who is trying to be impressive but who is trembling or stuttering or bumping into things at the same time; I fell in love instantly with one guy because of the way he dropped his glasses when he was telling me about a short story he'd written. That's the kind of masculinity I like to emulate—one that's always trying to be impressive but is obviously and awkwardly gentle. It comes a little too naturally to a geek girl like me. Even when I called Betty to ask her out I had to make up an excuse so I wouldn't stutter through the call.

I told him—and myself—that I was calling only to make sure I had his correct address so that he'd continue to get updates about our reading group meetings. It would have been a reasonable reason to call if I really weren't sure I had it, but the very first words he ever said to me that night in Peter's kitchen were, "So you're the woman who does the mailings." I remember panicking and mumbling and walking away and talking to another person I knew. I really am bad at being the girl, really bad, and when you combine *girl + introvert* you get *panic-stricken + dateless*. But of course it did turn out well in the end; after I'd gathered my nerve and come up with that ridiculous excuse, I called, and he said yes, and the rest, as they say, is history.

We've stumbled our way through eight Valentine's Days so far. Only a few years ago, we decided that Betty would plan a Valentine's Day date for us. We came up with the idea because Betty had been gradually increasing how often she presented as female, and I was missing the guy I'd married. Even though I was supposed to stay out of the planning completely, I requested we go see Almodóvar's *Talk to Her*[9] because I'm a fan and it was playing. And Betty did all the "right" things: There were chocolates and roses and tickets to the movie and reservations at an Italian restaurant downtown.

It was a peerless disaster. I loved the roses and the chocolate and we both loved the movie. The problem was my coat. I took it off myself. Then I tried to seat myself after the waiter had pulled out my chair for me. My discomfort grew through dinner. A half hour after we left the restaurant, I snapped at Betty about something minuscule, and when I saw the wounded look on his face, I apologized and reviewed the evening to figure out what was bothering me. At first I thought I'd been uncomfortable being seated at a tiny café-size table packed into a room with fifty more like it because I'd recently gained weight. I hadn't liked the way everyone looked up when we came in because I'm so introverted, and then I remembered that I took off my coat before my husband even thought to, which made me feel that I had no class whatsoever. I don't know how you're supposed to just stand there as if your arms are broken and have someone else take your coat off; it just doesn't make sense to me. Still, I felt like a failure; we were trying to be "normally" gendered, and I had tried to play the girl, but I had failed the Coat Test.

We watched *Talk to Her*. We both cried, and afterward we talked about men and communication and the dance sequences, but especially about the odd way the movie suggested that it's much easier for men to be in love with women when they're in comas—the ultimate in female passivity. That was when it hit me: I didn't want doors opened or chairs pulled out, not because I felt chubby, but because I don't like having things done for me; it makes me feel uncomfortable. I feel as if I'm being insulted.

I'm not so stubborn about it that I won't ask for help if I really need it, but I don't like guys to do things for me that I'm perfectly capable of doing myself. I can take my own coat off, for instance.

What amazed me the most is that I'd made it to the age of thirty-four before understanding this about myself. Perhaps I've just always had maybe lazy, maybe egalitarian boyfriends who never pulled out chairs, but honestly I'd never thought about it. I open doors if I reach them first, for men and women, and always have; that's how I earned the nickname "The Gentleman" in high school. I am capable of going through a door that's opened for me, though it does often make me feel awkward. I'll happily hold a door for a man or a woman, or give up my seat to someone older or pregnant; I find good manners polite and charming. I just don't like to accept the offer of help when that offer is made because I'm a woman, because then I feel as if I'm being told I'm incompetent.

Early on in our relationship, I remember trying to explain to Betty that going around in the world as a woman is an odd thing, because how or where you might feel safe or threatened isn't always predictable. I described the difference between the way that one man can stop dead in his tracks, undress you with his eyes, and announce that he'd like to make love with you all night, and you can take it as a compliment and not feel threatened by it, while another man will simply shake your hand and give you the heebie-jeebies. I'm not sure what causes the difference, although I'm pretty sure it's not looks, or desire, or lack of it on the woman's part. What comes across is that some guys like women because they're attracted to them, and some men resent women who turn them on, because their own desire makes them feel needy, and men aren't supposed to feel needy. It makes them—well, womanish. For me, the opening-the-door and pulling-the-chair-out stuff feels similar: Sometimes it feels like an insult, and other times it just comes off as polite. Again, I can't tell what's behind the difference, but I'm sure—because of that Valentine's Day—that I don't like "chivalrous" behavior because it forces me to feel this weird social pressure to be the woman, or the girlfriend, or the *{insert traditional feminine gender role here}*. It requires me to be those things, and without asking me if I'm okay with it, which doesn't strike me as polite at all.

My discomfort with this ladylike behavior dovetails quite nicely with certain aspects of my own masculinity, and it certainly works well with Betty's desired gender role. We've reversed things on many occasions: I got to buy the flowers and pull chairs and open doors. I can play the butch[10] to her femme when we're in a situation where we want to enjoy the tension—and even the predictability—of more traditional romantic gender roles. All we're doing is something a bit Shakespearean; I'm doing the trouser role,[11] and Betty's playing Juliet to my Romeo. Luckily, we don't die at the end.

But reversing roles didn't quite work either, because I'm still the one who likes chocolates, and we both like silk lingerie, and I'm not quite cool and groovy with playing that part—yet, or maybe I won't ever be. While it comes naturally, I've also repressed it a long time. But I'm also just plainly bothered by how gendered it feels; I don't want rules or myths or traditions to tell me how to behave. Betty, likewise, will occasionally act the gentleman no matter how girlish her exterior. Either both of us are standing there waiting for someone to open the door, or we run into each other while we're both going to open it. We have no idea what we're doing in this gender-nebulous space, but I like it that way. We're always guessing and second-guessing what the "correctly gendered" role is, and what we actually feel naturally, and then trying to figure out if those two things align or don't. It can be a lot of fun as long as you keep your sense of humor intact. Now we occasionally check in with each other before we leave the apartment. "Do you want to be the guy tonight?" works wonders, but most of the time we don't bother and end up being mutually considerate—getting each other drinks depending on who wants one first or who's nearer to the wine bottle, much like the way the person who wears more Dry Clean Only clothes is the one who drops them off at the dry cleaners. We've both pushed ourselves not to fall into the stereotypes no matter how we're dressed; I don't expect Betty to light my cigarette when she's in guy mode, and she doesn't expect me to light hers when she's her female self, though we occasionally surprise each other. Gender has become a little more playful as a result, and has helped declaw Betty's transness.

Now we have much better Valentine's Days. I get the truffles I love and Betty gets the handful of underwear, and we go shopping in the rain or watch an entire season of an HBO show in one night or get manicures together. It took us a long time to figure that out. Maybe other couples are much cooler about this stuff and don't feel this tremendous pressure to play out these traditional roles. Maybe we had difficulty with them because of our gender stuff. But people buy books such as *How to Get That Lunkhead to Call You Back* and *The Rules* and *What He Won't Tell You but Your Gay Friends Will*,[12] and lots of people are trying to figure out how to be the right kind of woman or the right kind of man. Those books often remind me of that faked old home economics textbook entry of 1954, *How to Be a Good Wife*,[13] just new and improved and updated for the 21st century. I often hope that those books are bought only by crossdressers who want to feel girly, but I fear they aren't. What I fear is a whole new generation of women gendering themselves to be acceptable marriage prospects, and a whole new generation of men pretending they don't feel scared or sad or hurt—ever.

The irony of my situation is that what most people fear would happen if they were to disregard gender roles is actually my life: when gender becomes so fluid that it is no longer clear which partner in a relationship is the man or husband and which is the woman or wife. People feel more assured when they know what role they play, whether it's as a spouse or a parent, because then they know what's expected of them and in a sense, what kinds of traits make their loved ones happy. But both women and men seem to want to have their cake and eat it, too: Women want male partners who listen, who will watch chick flicks, and who share the remote, but they also don't feel desired if a man doesn't get hard when they take their clothes off. Women want men to break some of the rules of masculinity, but only certain ones, and only at appropriate times. I know a woman who loves that her husband is kind and nurturing with their disabled son, but it still bothers her if he wants to wear flowered shirts or perfume. We can accept some femininity in men, but not too much.[14] The reverse is also true: Some men love women who are strong, smart, and independent, but they might also feel unnerved by a wife who makes more money than they do. People seem to think that if they let go of gender markers, there's not going to be any fun, or sex, or frisson in a relationship, but for us it's been just the opposite. It's freed us to love each other in new ways and to get to know each other and ourselves better. Frankly, it's made our partnership work. Clearly, most couples are not going to break one little rule about who brings whom breakfast in bed and end up like us. We had the issue of transsexualism to deal with, and most couples don't need to fear becoming the multiply gendered types we've become because they want to push the boundaries of traditional gender roles here and there.

It is fun, after all. It's like four relationships built into one. There's the het one we started out with, the lesbian one we're clocked as, the old-school butch-femme[15] one that reverses and queers our heterosexuality, and then—most rarely—the one where we're more like an older gay male couple who prefer quiet parties, drinking and talking with friends, or sometimes with just each other. We talk about what we might have been like as a couple if we'd met when we were seventeen, or if we'd met after Betty had already started exploring her gender. We don't know what we would actually be like, but exploring the ways we connect and the ways we don't by trying on other manifestations of couplehood has been a way of extending our romantic reach out of the world of damsels and knights and even beyond the dysfunctional sitcom version of those roles. We get to draw on a much larger legacy of loving. Relationships are hard work, after all, so why limit what tools you allow yourself to use?

Most people don't even recognize how few of the tools they do use; our socialization, and a lifetime of habit, lock us into ways of being and behaving with a partner. I can't emphasize enough how much I had to push against the walls of gender before I was really okay stepping into other kinds of behavior; the taboos are much stronger than people give them credit for being. We are the most vulnerable when it comes to romantic relationships, so the taboos can be even more overwhelming. We don't want to be judged as unlovable, or weird. We want to fit with our partner like one puzzle piece into another, but you have to play around even with a puzzle piece for a while until you figure out where it goes. That is, there is no "correct" way to be gendered in a relationship—there's only the way that suits you and your partner best and most comfortably—and figuring it out can take a while.

Of course, a lot of women would say that they're comfortable with him being the man and her being the woman. But what "being the man" is and what "being the woman" is isn't always clear. We've all got assumptions about what those things mean, some of them cultural, others familial, others largely individual. Some women love little gifts of knickknacks and others see them as more things to clean. Is either sentiment a "more female" response to receiving a tiny crystal elephant? For some women, receiving a kitchen appliance as a present is decidedly unromantic, a sign that their guy doesn't think they're sexy anymore, or they might feel demeaned, as if they're being told that their place is the kitchen. For me, Betty's gift of a teakettle was the most romantic thing I could have gotten because I drink tea by the gallon and mine had just broken. (Though I suppose it is awfully girly to think *Wow, he really knows me* when your husband gives you a teakettle for a present, which I will admit I did.) Some men will genuinely appreciate a woman's attempt to get into a sport they love, and others don't want to talk and explain plays while they're watching and would rather their love of sports be something they share with their guy friends.

When I've talked to women in workshops I've given, at least one person always says something along the lines of "He should be the man, and I should be the woman," but saying that she is comfortable "being the woman" doesn't mean much, because all of us have had different mothers, sisters, women we admire; we even like different models. If someone can prefer Christy Turlington to Linda Evangelista or Tyra Banks to Cindy Crawford, then there's obviously an issue of personal taste involved, since all of these women occupy a kind of rarefied status as "perfectly beautiful" women, and they all have similar measurements and hairstyles and beautiful faces. But if we do still have a preference for one supermodel more than another for reasons that we might not even be able to identify, then how can we agree about what might make a great wife or girlfriend? It's kind of like saying you want someone with a "sense of humor," when humor is highly individual; pratfalls always make me laugh, but other people prefer snark or sarcasm or clever references to obscure books. Two people who both think they have a great sense of humor might not even once make each other laugh on a date, and they'll both go back to their friends and complain about the other person.

One of the things that amazes me about all the articles about gender and gender roles, and especially the ones about career women and babies, or the ones about the crisis of masculinity (*there sure is a crisis of masculinity, but it's not now and never has been what you guys are complaining about*),[16] is that they see gender-role change as a problem. Where is the problem if gender roles have changed enough so that women have a choice between having a career or motherhood, or finding a way to have both? Where is the problem if men decide it's okay to cry?[17] It's especially funny to hear Americans complaining that too many gender choices are confusing, or too complicated, when in every other aspect of our lives we have a tendency to demand umpteen options. Which kind of ketchup you use or car you buy is apparently vitally important, but if we actually decide what kind of men or women we're going to be, the world is going to hell in a handbasket.

Somehow, I don't think so.

What I've seen instead is guys opening up whole new parts of themselves, learning—or trying to learn—how to bond with their own children; I've seen women decide whether they want to be housewives and full-time mothers or if they want to be career physicists. It's all pretty great, actually, and I wonder about the people who write these teeth-gnashing op-ed pieces about how everything was much better in the past when everyone knew his or her proper role. I always wonder if they mean "The Yellow Wallpaper" past, or the "Mother's Little Helper"[18] past. I really enjoy living in a world where a geeky guy such as Mark Mothersbaugh is cool, but so are Prince and Henry Rollins. Women can be geeks, too, like Tina Fey, or kind of gender neutral like Ellen DeGeneres, or they can be Julia Roberts[19]—and all of them are still feminine in their own individual ways. Apparently not enough people watched *The Twilight Zone*,[20] because too many have missed the bit about how being a conforming automaton is a bleak, boring way to live.

People think of masculine and feminine as being like hot or cold: When you make something hot, it stops being cold. But masculinity and femininity are not like that at all. My femininity didn't go away because I was exploring my masculine side, and my masculinity—even the innate bits of it—does not cancel out my feminine side. What exploring gender roles does is give you more tools. It gave me back things that I had repressed to fit in better, and I like having those things back. I don't feel as lopsided as I once did. And exploring gender doesn't mean that anyone or everyone should feel androgynous, or look gender neutral; those are just choices among the many we have. We give gender way more power in explaining who we are and how we are and how we should be than makes sense. Sure, there are true things you can say about women in general, and true things you can say about men. But if we divided the world into left-handed and right-handed people, surely we'd find that there were true things you could say about left-handed people, too.[21] We could split the world into blonds and brunets, and redheads would have to decide if they were more blond or more brunet, as would streaky-haired types like myself. We could find things that were true about a lot of blond people that were in opposition to what most brunets do. Or, we could categorize by blood type like they do in Japan.[22] There are all sorts of ways we could divide up human beings, and no matter how we did it, we would find commonalities within groups and differences between groups. Categorizing people with the labels of "male" and "female" is about as arbitrary.

I'm not trying to argue that there are no important innate differences between women and men—probably there are. But we don't socialize people differently if they're blond and not brunet, and we do socialize people differently if they are men or women. It's nearly impossible to sift out which differences between men and women are the result of the biology we're born with and which result from the difference in how we're trained to be men and women. Acknowledging gender difference based on socialization is passé, but my own recent experience in trying to allow my masculinity some expression has drawn attention to exactly how intense socialization is. What concerns me the most is the way we restrict the way people can be, and then point to the successful self-repression as if it were natural, and then argue that people are supposed to behave that way because that's the way people behave.

I saw a couple on the subway not long ago; they were sitting together in the double seats way at the end of the car. She was sitting bolt upright, maybe angry, maybe tense, but not what I'd call happy. He sat curled into the space between her shoulder and her head, maybe sorry, maybe sad. It struck me as both sweet and troubled, but mostly I noticed them because their postures, and the way they were physically relating to each other, was unusual. He may have just been tired and resting his head on her, or he might have been in the doghouse, acting coy and sweet to win back her favor. His posture gave him a kind of feminine air, his long thin form draped into the small space he made for himself; I wondered if this dynamic was typical for them, or exceptional. It made me wonder if other couples have similar moments that we don't see because they happen only in private. The pressure I feel to refrain from telling people that I'm the one who wears the pants in the relationship is felt by most of us, is my guess, so maybe we hide away those dynamics in the private spaces of our lives. I've known men who store up their vulnerabilities and find solace only in having sex with a woman, or kissing her while she's asleep. But I'm not sure why men have to express intimacy and vulnerability on the sly. Again, I think it goes back to thinking that masculine and feminine are on a kind of dimmer switch: that any feminine expression of tenderness means a man isn't masculine. We seem to want to allow men to be tender only up to a point, beyond which we might perceive them as weak instead. We also restrict what kinds of things it's okay for men to express sadness or vulnerability about: A man who can't get past feeling scared after being mugged is not going to get the same approval as he might if he's brokenhearted after a romantic breakup. Women can go weak in the knees if a man cries watching a romantic movie, but they definitely won't appreciate a man if he cries when he gets laid off.

A doctor friend of mine recently told her patients that he would be transitioning to female. One patient explained that the transition made sense to her, because throughout the years "he" had nurtured and cared for her children, and she had perceived the care as feminine and maternal. Another patient noted that my friend's quiet knowledge and gentle diagnoses had seemed more masculine to him, in a very paternal, masterful way. Both patients are probably right; being a good doctor, like being a good partner (or a good anything, in my opinion), requires that you use all the skills at your disposal. Some of those skills will be perceived as feminine, others masculine. It may be okay for Dr. House[23] to be a macho prick with no "people skills" because he's a diagnostician for unusual cases (and he's also only a character on a television show), but no one would want that in a family doctor, or in a gynecologist, proctologist, or a pediatrician. Yet, when it comes to relationships, everyone seems to want the Knight in Shining Armor, or the Princess in Distress, and when our knights come a little gentle or our princesses a little empowered, people get nervous—as if they're onstage without a script.

Partners of trans women and crossdressers often say things along the lines of, "I want to feel like the woman in our relationship." Their crossdressing or transgender partner is often fantasizing about the very same thing, and I've certainly felt pressure—maybe from within, maybe from without—to butch up so that Betty can feel "like the woman." I didn't mind so much when it was occasional, a kind of role play, but when it started to seem that I might be expected to keep it up all the time, I objected, as do many partners of trans women.

Women in relationships with trans people often already feel forced to accept change they're not excited about, and so they dig in their heels. But one of the things I ask partners to do when I'm giving workshops or lending an ear privately is to define what "feeling like the woman" in the relationship means to them and what it would take for them to feel that way. "Feeling like the woman" is not about the natural order of things but about how you feel about the person you love, and how the person you love makes you feel about you. When we partners say such things, we usually mean some specific things: Some women mean they want to be seduced; others really like the little mash notes[24] or presents their husbands have left for them; still others want the sense of security that having a provider-husband gives them. For me, it was Betty's love and attention, her pride in our relationship, that always made me feel "like the woman." It was the little things he did that made me feel prized; he always kissed me before he went to the restroom, even if I was engaged in a conversation and might not have noticed he'd gone and come back. Identifying those things that make you feel the way you want to in a relationship helps you preserve what makes you feel valued and special. For us, it provided the chance to work things out despite these seismic shifts in our lives.

Sometimes the inexact way we use language gives rise to the problems we encounter when we talk about gender roles. Imagine having only black and white, or red and blue, to describe the colors you can see.

That we try to describe gender roles with just two words is problematic. They're not enough. As a writer, I'm often offended by how inaccurate our language is when it comes to gender. "Feminine" is used to stand in for all kinds of other words—like gentle, permissive, empathetic, kind, nurturing. Those are also the traits people imply when they say "woman." "Masculine," likewise, is used to mean strong, athletic, protective, gruff, or authoritative. Sometimes I feel like a writing teacher walking through the world—and the trans community—because I want to stop all the time to explain, "Say what you mean, because 'feminine' doesn't *mean* anything." (I guess that makes me schoolmarmish, doesn't it? Unless I raise my voice when I say it, and then I'm stentorian. I'd prefer to be pedantic or exacting, since those words don't come as heavily gendered, but at the end of the day, I'd really rather be considered whatever the female form of avuncular is.)[25]

Plenty of women are nurturing. Sometimes people seem to think being nurturing makes women innately better than men, and others think it makes them kind of doughy. But tell me, which of these people is nurturing?

1. The woman who has a special spray bottle to water her plants, who every day sprays them just the right amount according to the little planter tag, and who sings while doing so. She dusts the leaves off, prunes any dead leaves, and sweeps up any soil that might have fallen out of the pot as a result of watering.

2. The man who, while drinking a glass of water when he gets home, stops midway and pours the rest of the water on the plant. He looks at it, prunes the dead leaves brusquely and distractedly while turning on the TV, and then turns it a quarter way around because he read somewhere

you should do that to plants. He leaves the extra water droplets on the windowsill and changes the channel so he can watch the news.

Effectively, these two people have both just watered a plant. That's all they've done. But the style in which the woman does it would be considered nurturing, and the style in which the man does it wouldn't. So isn't nurturing, in this case, more a word that describes the *style* of the person rather than the actual accomplishment? When we say, "Women are more nurturing than men," what do we mean, exactly? That generally speaking they are more responsible for child rearing? That they pat their child's head after giving them the lunch money? Is a man who goes to work for that same lunch money less nurturing than the woman who doles it out? Nurturing is enabling something to grow. There are a lot of ways to do that.

If the inadequacy of the language of gender didn't mean much except that a woman might be surprised to find out that her guy defined "being a man" as being an arrogant prick who thought it was his right to sleep with anyone in a skirt, that would be her personal problem. The same could be said for a man who discovered his new girlfriend felt that "being a woman" meant she never had the heart to deny her ex sex because of her innate empathy for him. But the inaccuracy of the language doesn't stop there. I wish it did.

Researchers use terms such as "nurturing" when they publish their findings, and so do journalists when they report said findings. One of the most frustrating recent examples concerned (vervet) monkeys and (human) toys.[26] The researchers observed that the female monkeys gravitated to dolls and pots, while the male monkeys seemed to prefer toy cars. The researchers came to the whopping conclusion that gender roles in humans must be innate. I'm still trying to figure out how many vervet monkeys actually cook with pots. My guess? None. My own conclusions from this study are that cooking pots can't be female or male to monkeys, because *monkeys don't cook*. When I read such profoundly idiotic presumptions being made about innate differences between men and women, I find myself wanting to know why on earth I should trust a study—the kind of study that makes headlines—in which the people involved haven't worked out such basic facts as the ones that often seem to jump off the page (that no female *or male* monkey has ever stood in a kitchen and cooked anything in a pot, for instance). A study like this one is loaded with cultural stereotypes about what is female or male, what is masculine and feminine, and yet by the time we read about them, the details are conveniently taken out so that the headline reads, "Gender Roles Innate in Humans."

Maybe gender differentiation is determined by sex. Maybe it isn't. I don't know. But I'm not convinced that the people who say they *do* know actually know for sure, either. Sometimes their ideas about "girls" seem so old-fashioned that I'm expecting diagrams of girls in pinafores rolling hoops. I'd prefer to believe that gender is not wholly determined by chromosomes, because I can't account for why I'm masculine and Betty is feminine. Some of the physical attributes of the body—biological issues such as hormone levels—help determine gender. My PCOS has always been one way I've understood or explained my own masculinity as a teenager, even if other women with PCOS don't act in masculine ways at all. People who research gender and sex differences should talk more about their own biases, because it'd give everyone a better way of judging what exactly they're saying and how limited their "conclusions" might be.

The other problem with gender vis-à-vis roles is this issue of opposites. Living in a gender binary means the opposite sex of "man" is "woman." But what's the opposite of a feminine man? Once you put that qualifier in front of man, you have a whole other problem. Is the opposite of a feminine man a masculine man? A masculine woman? A feminine woman? Which parts are you supposed to be "same-ing" and "opposite-ing" exactly? It might prove useful for someone to design an elaborate wheel, like the color wheels art students use, so that you could run your finger across from indigo to find its best contrast. Because when we talk about same/opposite what we're talking about is no contrast/contrast. The opposite of something is the thing it is most different from. Not knowing what your opposite is could make this whole heterosexual thing quite complicated. My friend Johanna tells me it makes the homosexual thing kind of complicated, too; once, while traveling on the subway with her girlfriend, a drunken straight couple across the way noticed there were lesbians on the train with them. And as drunken people will, the woman started talking about them rather loudly, wondering which one of the women was "the boy one" and which was "the girl one." (Quite hilariously, Johanna and her girlfriend made T-shirts for themselves afterward that both read: I'M THE GIRL ONE.)

Every time I visit with a lesbian couple I recall all those years I lived with my roommates Doug and Maurice and wonder how a woman could ever live with another woman. Sometimes, too, I wonder how exactly I'm managing to live with someone as feminine as Betty is now, and I long to live with a gender-neutral lesbian who won't come with as many hair dryers and flatirons and the other "tools" of femininity that Betty clutters our bathroom with. My natural instinct as a heterosexual woman is to be wary of the smell of competition and the unspoken beauty contest when there are other women around. It makes me cranky. I worry that the shoe issue is going to come up. I worry that I'm going to be expected to male-bash (which, by the way, is far more expertly done by heterosexual women than it's ever been done by so-called man-hating lesbians, in my experience).

One of the observations that comes up when sexologists ponder the differences between heterosexual and homosexual sexualities[27] is that the latter is like a "pure" form of the gender of the couple—that gay male sexuality is something like a distilled, 180-proof version of masculine sexual energy, consisting of indiscriminate anonymous hand jobs, while lesbian sexuality is a kind of stabilized cuddle fest. While some of those things are sometimes true, I'm also baffled by: (1) How prejudiced by gender stereotypes they are, and (2) how the exact same things can be said about heterosexual social groups, or what I like to refer to as "Thanksgiving self-segregation." The guys are watching football and eating nuts, and the women are setting the table and washing dishes and basting the turkey. As a child and young adult, my chosen "place" tended to be hanging out in the doorway that separated the kitchen from the living room. I found both groups pretty boring and often disappeared to my bedroom to read between courses instead.

Gender stereotypes are emphasized and studied and usually found to be wanting, one way or another, when groups of homosexuals get together, yet when groups of heterosexuals get together, words like "natural" and "comforting" and "innate" get thrown around, especially in articles about evolutionary biology. Ah, researchers. The irony is that, in my experience, groups of gay men express more gender variance than groups of straight men of about the same size. That's one of the myriad reasons I'm comfortable in a room full of lesbians in a way I am not comfortable in a room full of straight women; in a room full of lesbians, there will be other women, with short hair and masculine gaits, one in a backward baseball cap and another in heels and jeans. But in a group of heterosexual women the gender variance is skewed toward the feminine end of female gender expression; all of a sudden, I'm the masculine one. In an all-female group it's the tomboy who is called upon to be the "honorary man" and unscrew a difficult jar or get rid of a spider. But there are times when I'm in a group of women complaining about their husbands that I'm glad for the distraction, because when a group of partnered heterosexual women gathers, something else happens that anyone in a relationship should avoid at all costs: misery loving company. One of the best pieces of advice I ever got was when my mother told me to avoid hanging out with other married women.

Women get together to blow off a little steam and bitch about their husbands. That's all well and good if that's what works for them. But here's my problem: If everyone's doing it, then everyone who joins the group is going to do it, too. A pack mentality develops. If you're there, you don't have a choice. A room full of women who believe that all women are one gender and all men are another quickly becomes a rarefied wife-o-sphere, where women suffer their husbands' idiocies and faults just because that's what wives do. For me it feels like walking into an anachronism. The worst of it is that you often end up borrowing trouble and starting to think that your husband will never change because he's just a man, after all. Complaining to other women is not going to resolve anything, either; if you have a problem with something your husband is doing, tell your husband: That's the only chance you have of airing your grievances in a way that will fix anything.

My mother was right. What you wind up forgetting is that meeting someone you like and who wants to spend the rest of his life with you is a simple matter of luck and timing. Staying with that someone is what requires effort: It's not a time to get complacent or lazy. Your husband shouldn't treat you any worse than your best friend does, and honestly, he shouldn't understand you any less, either. It's hard to not feel as if you've leaped off a cliff when the "honeymoon" period ends, and you can't expect sex to be like it was when you met, but that doesn't mean it has to be boring or predictable, either. Sometimes it's just about not wanting more than you're getting and knowing if what you're getting is what you want. But mostly it's luck, and after you meet that person, it's about never deluding yourself into thinking that relationships aren't brutally hard work, because they are, almost all the time, and what makes it worth it is that the payback is fantastic.

When women say, "I just want a regular guy," it's about the same as someone talking about that mythical "typical woman." He doesn't exist. And no matter how many times women say they want "regular guys," I'm pretty sure they don't. What they want is their perfect guy, which is very, very different. He doesn't exist either, of course, just like the perfect woman doesn't, which is why so many people in reasonably happy relationships advise, "Just be who you are." It's true. I had finally let myself "be who I was" a couple of months before I met Betty. I'd given up entirely on meeting someone I wanted to live with. I'd made up my mind to date enough to have sex, and I vowed not to get into a long, drawn-out miscommunication of a relationship again. I'm still kind of astonished at having met him, still astonished that I asked him out, still astonished he said yes, and still astonished that I can sit with him for hours in a room, saying mostly nothing, and yet I am just happy to be there, with him. I am still surprised when I meet him on the street, and she is all in denim, wearing dangly earrings, and we both get that shock of recognition, the thrill of having met. Sometimes, walking down the street to meet her, I still feel I'm meeting him for the first time. It's not like that all the time, but I'm amazed it ever is.

These days that moment is often followed by the hope that Betty's transsexualism won't make that flash of recognition go away. People can go ahead and think we're freakish and ask indelicate questions about our sex life. They can think I'm a lesbian or that we are. I can even live with hearing her gorgeous baritone only in the privacy of our own home, as long as that little shock hits me when I see him, or her, walking toward me on a crowded Fourteenth Street, and knowing she's just felt it, too.

Sometimes it amazes me how corny I am about my love for my partner, but it really is the best drug ever.

But those moments are just moments. They're reminders or flashbacks to when you first fell in love. But it's not a relationship. Those moments might happen once in a day if you're lucky; they might come far less often when you're arguing about money or children or sex or the other eight million things people argue about with their lovers. You just get busy sometimes, too, and forget to tell your partner how much you love him or her because your head is otherwise occupied with a deadline or a potential raise or how much your tooth hurts. Other times you just out-and-out take the person you love for granted; you forget what it was like to be single, and alone, and wishing you had someone to see the world with, to ask you how your day went (even if he or she doesn't always remember to). Sometimes I want to tell my single friends that they don't want to be married, that the sacrifices are pretty huge, and that it takes up a hell of a lot of time to talk things out with someone in a way that means you're actually communicating. Listening is especially hard; I've always got an answer for all of Betty's problems when all she wants to do is talk, which is yet another case where we are "wrongly" gendered, because I'm the one who's supposed to want to talk about my feelings while he gives me solid, sound, practical advice. But in my family, it was the women who stopped worrying and made a decision or got something done when there was a problem, so I don't think I'm being "the man" and he's being "the woman": Instead I'd say that he's being indecisive and I'm being practical.[28]

I wonder if people actually think about why they want to get married, or why they want to be in love. I'm not talking about health insurance and hospital visitation rights, but more about what people think they're looking for when they're looking for a partner. Watching reruns of *Sex and the City*[29] late at night, I'm struck by how desperate the narrative is, how full of longing. But longing for what? Have I just forgotten what it's like to be single, even though I've been married for only five years? Betty and I have been together for nine, and happy but captious all that time. I wonder now what exactly I was longing for, and whether or not it's even useful to remember what that was, because I'd probably be safe in guessing that I'm not getting what I thought I wanted back then. Yet the disappointment I've felt in dealing with Betty's transness is always offset by the love between us and the profound way we've gotten to know each other, which makes me wonder if Betty's transness ended up being one of many ways in which we've found what we were both longing for when we met. If Betty weren't trans, and we were just a gender-normative heterosexual couple, we might have split up by now for completely different reasons. I can't know, and honestly, I don't really want to. Seeing happy couples on the street who can hold each other's hands and kiss in public without attracting dirty looks and outright stares is quite enough for me to wish we could have that back, but I'm not going to hold my breath.

That's yet another instance of how the Knights in Shining Armor stories fail us, how the romantic comedies leave us with nothing but hope. They always end after the couple manages to get together, but we don't know anything about how they cope after that, or what exactly "happily ever after" means.

The one thing about Betty and me as a couple that is pretty different from most heterosexual couples is that we stopped being het. Not because I stopped liking boys or Betty stopped liking girls, but because we stopped assuming anything based on the "Me Tarzan, You Jane" philosophy that straight couples have a tendency to default to. Straight people don't think so much about gender, and one of the chief issues of our relationship was gender, so I found other people to talk to about it. I sought out our gay and lesbian friends because they had thought about these things in the context of their relationships. Gay and lesbian folks don't have a corner on the market—of course there are straight people who think about gender—but odds were better that our gay and lesbian friends were going to be a little more postgender in their thinking, having long ago thrown out who was "the girl one" and who was "the boy one." And yet, friends of ours who were planning to have a baby realized that maybe they hadn't thought about gender quite enough either, because it became clear that each woman assumed she would be the one to become pregnant, carry, and give birth to their child. Because as much as people want to believe that "there's a boy one," the shocking truth of lesbian relationships is that there isn't, even in butch/femme relationships. They're both women, after all. My mind must be too heterosexually programmed, because I can't figure out what you do when both people in a relationship want to "feel like the woman." Part of the problem is that I can't figure out who's supposed to come along and make them feel that way. I was raised to believe that only a man can make a woman feel like a woman, and yet lesbians manage to feel special, valued, and cherished in their relationships (at least as much as anyone does), and presumably made to feel like a woman by their partners if that's what they're looking for.

George Saunders wrote a satirical piece for *The New Yorker*[30] about what he called "The Same-ish Sex Marriage," which he defined as existing when a slightly fey man with long hair and small stature marries a woman with a deep voice who knows how to fix cars. He suggests that if we're going to ban same-sex marriages then we should also ban the Same-ish Sex Marriage, because for the fey man "it is only a short stroll down a slippery slope before he is completely happy being the 'girl' in their relationship," and as a result he will eventually end up married to a masculine man rather than to a woman at all. Saunders makes a nice point about the natural variation of gender and the mysteries of attraction.

But while there's humor to be found in all this same-ing and opposite-ing, we do live in a country where some people find the idea of same-sex coupling so horrendous that they are passing laws and changing state constitutions to prevent it. My proposal is that we should tell them they can have their amendment as soon as someone can tell me categorically and with no exceptions what the opposite of a feminine man is, and whom exactly he's supposed to marry. My guess is that these gatekeepers of puritan values would get so caught up in discussing the impossible existence of such a thing as a feminine heterosexual man that we would be free of their amendment for as long as it takes to find the Loch Ness Monster. People who are that worked up about homosexuality in men lose their ability to see finer distinctions, and can't see the differences between gender, gender role, and sexual orientation.

The thing that has given me the most freedom was moving away from such a categorical identity altogether. "Confirmed" identities such as "lesbian" or "heterosexual," and sometimes even "wife," come with gigantic assumptions attached. People know what those words mean, or they think they do. After years of answering questions about who I am and what's with my husband and what we do or don't do in bed, I've found it's much easier to answer questions with what we do rather than with labels that attempt to explain what we are, because . . . *Slightly masculine heterosexual woman who likes makeup and corsets but also trousers and neckties who is legally married to a trans person who was raised male but most often presents as female and who likes sex with alpha females* . . . is way too long and doesn't actually get at the whole of it. Just using the term "masculine woman" causes problems, as people think of Janet Reno or Margaret Thatcher when I'm thinking more along the lines of Marlene Dietrich. At least "feminine man" conjures David Bowie.[31]

The code words that I might use to describe us in the trans

community don't help the world at large because it's jargon, shorthand within a subculture, but also because what we are is not very typical even within the trans community: *I am a trans-amorous woman-raised-female partner of a non-op, noho MTF, not-currently-socially-transitioning trans person who is lesbian-identified.*[32]

If I explain what we do it eliminates the need to discover what assumptions someone has about the word "lesbian" or "queer" or "heterosexual." Taking that stuff apart takes so much time, and I don't want to have to redefine every term before I can actually explain who we are.

We were/are a legally married couple.
We were/are a queer couple.
We were/are a genderqueer couple.
We were/are a heterosexual couple.

Dumping labels altogether allowed me to stop disappointing people by simply being myself. When I show up somewhere in a skirt I don't want it to be a big deal, and when I show up in a suit I don't want it to be, either. What I wanted to do was eliminate the possibility that anyone should be able to predict how I should behave, or how I would. It was to loosen the ties that bound me to what others thought and what they wanted from me. Betty chooses the label "trans" for similar reasons, since transvestite implies pervert, transsexual implies transition, and transgender implies nothing and everything because the usage is all over the map.[33]

I'd love to be able to say that you can free yourself from these expectations from within recognized identity labels. Maybe some people can. Unfortunately, most people don't know my identity even exists, so opting for the largest possible categories gives me a little legroom. Maybe there are people who don't build as many expectations of self into identity, but for me it was vital to throw out the idea of *being* anything. Kinsey[34] thought that a person couldn't *be* a sexual orientation—that is, you couldn't be a homosexual but you could engage in homosexual acts. But even if we're defining only sex acts, that's a little blurry for us. I'm not sure anyone would call what we do heterosexual. They might call it homosexual. Although I'm sure Kinsey was right when he said that you can't be a sexual orientation, I'm not sure he would make the same statement now. A homosexual identity does exist today in a way that it didn't when he was writing. For us, the "homo" and "hetero" categories were utterly useless. I needed a way to understand myself outside of same/opposite because I'm not sure what gender either of us is all the time, and I'm absolutely sure that neither of us is "correctly gendered" in terms of our roles, sexual and otherwise.

My friend Tom mentioned that he likes to think of himself as dating "people who are femmier than him." As he explains it, that's usually women, but it doesn't rule out the occasionally feminine man. Since relationships are about relating, it strikes me that Tom is onto something, that maybe defining how we want to relate to another person might be more useful in the long run. You can use any kind of language you want to describe how you want to relate: Maybe you date only people who are more submissive than you, or more dominant; maybe you like someone more dependent, or less. Maybe it's time for someone to design that gender color wheel so we can all figure out what range of what kind of behaviors and characteristics we like in a partner. Or we could just keep trying to fit that puzzle piece into various spaces. It may be too that some of us want a partner who picks a gender and sticks to it—which seems a completely foreign idea to me these days—or we might want someone who doesn't take gender very seriously at all, or someone who seriously plays with gender.

At the very least it would be helpful if more people started reminding themselves that what genitals you have doesn't necessarily determine how you are as a person. Gender is a vital part of identity, and yet people don't seem to figure out who they are or what they want their partner to be. They may know they prefer something as specific as lit candles, or silk sheets, or the smell of sandalwood, but often they assume that they want to be seduced (because they're female) or the seducer (because they're male), and they make that assumption without even trying to relate to each other in another way. Some women might like to be on top—this time, sometimes, every time—and don't know it because they won't let themselves try it for fear of being seen as masculine, or weird, or perverted, or out of control. Most everyone wants to have a fulfilling sex life, and perhaps people don't have the sex they want because they don't do—or even think about doing—anything but what they're "supposed" to do in the bedroom.

Necessity, as they say, is the mother of invention, and for us, the need to have a satisfying sex life meant we had to stop listening to the things that told us we couldn't play in ways that made us both happy. I expected my inner rebel to have no trouble dismantling those taboos and restrictions, but in actual practice, it proved much harder than I would have ever predicted.

genitals are the least of it.

I learned a lot about sex before I had any. I used to hang out in the public library when I was in high school, usually with my best friend, Lara, and together we'd read sex books that we didn't have the nerve to check out, books by turn-of-the-20th-century sex researchers Havelock Ellis and Krafft-Ebing, books titled *Studies in the Psychology of Sex* and *Psychopathia Sexualis.*[1] It was like having a publicly accessible, slightly exotic porn stash—esoteric, literary, and pervy. We often sat in the loft where they were shelved for hours, pointing out particularly intriguing entries. They were irresistible, full of case studies of people with fetishes or who otherwise engaged in unusual sexual practices. My favorite case study was Case 34 in *Psychopathia Sexualis,* and it described a man who liked to see women dirtied in a very specific way. [2] All the woman had to do was sit in front of a mirror, in a negligee, with her hands blackened with soot, for him to get off.

I was fascinated, and intrigued, and often wondered what was happening in the man's head if after a long conversation with the woman—and never once touching her—he could leave, as Krafft-Ebing put it, "fully satisfied." Maybe reading those books wasn't the normal way to learn about sex, but I was brought up Catholic. I assume it was odd, and ask Lara, and she sighs, "I read them too, so I guess that makes me odd as well," a conclusion she'd really already come to and is always hoping to see disproved.

Because I didn't quite understand what exactly was going on, I tried to picture the scene, and the picture I formed then has stayed with me since. I still don't understand how there could be anything erotic about a woman's dirty hands reflected in a mirror. This scenario was someone else's orgasm, and though I didn't understand the why, I understood the fact of it. The man whose turn-on it was had no idea why this particular scenario was hot for him, but it was; it was the first in many lessons that told me there's no point in trying to understand anyone's sexuality. I was fascinated by the descriptions of people's unusual turn-ons: descriptions of tightly laced high-heeled boots, corset-lovers, rubber people.

Back when I was reading those sexologists and their empirical books, I hadn't really begun thinking about my own sexuality. Like most teenagers, I did think about sex a lot, but I didn't have the language, experience, or confidence to think about how I wanted to be a sexual person, even though I wrote my own erotica, even at age sixteen, that involved various pretty boys, mostly famous musicians but occasionally someone I knew. Chairs were always featured in my stories, though for the life of me I can't remember one instance in my actual sex life that involved a chair. (Note to self: *Must try to get a chair involved in future and see if it has any special charge.*) My stories back then were always full of expectation, tension, buildup, more tension, kissing, suggestion, but no one was having sex per se: no exchanges of bodily fluids, no orgasms, and no condoms or anything practical, for that matter. But then again, I hadn't had sex yet. What did I know, besides Havelock Ellis and song lyrics and urges? Nothing.

What I did get from those case studies was a testament to how variable and delicate human sexuality is. I was also profoundly impressed with the infinite ways we are capable of being turned on and with how much of that destination is out of our control. One day while Betty was reading Neal Stephenson's *Cryptonomicon*, I peeked over her shoulder and happened to catch a few pages where the narrator is trying to make peace with a fetish for black stockings. He'd finally forgiven himself for it because he'd read somewhere that kinks are set at a very early age and that "no therapy will unkink the brain once it has kinked. . . . So, all things considered, being turned on by black stockings wasn't such a bad sexual card to have been dealt."[3] He comes to that conclusion once he realizes that he could have ended up an ill-fated pedophile instead. Of course, he wasn't talking about wearing the stockings himself, only requesting that his lovers wear them.

But of course there were transvestites in those turn-of-the-last-century sex books, too, who wanted to wear those black stockings themselves. Long before Betty realized the full extent of her transness, back when we were first dating, I found myself needing to come up with a name for my new boyfriend's predilection for dressing like a woman, and I knew I could tell Lara, because she'd know what a transvestite was. She did. She was not wholly surprised that I was dating one, either.

Those retrograde sex books that painted transvestites as pervs who stole knickers from clotheslines in the dead of night taught me that no one really understood anyone else's desire, where it came from, or what it meant. Those books certainly didn't teach me to think that transvestites were wrong or bad, or that having a kink was. Ellis and Freud and sexologists since then have made some really good guesses[4] as to why some people are turned on by things that others don't find erotic at all, and some of their guesses make sense, such as oral fixation and taboos. Despite how bad a rap sexologists get for pathologizing desire, they were actually the ones responsible for my being familiar with transvestism. Those wacky, sex-obsessed pre-Weimar guys might have been paternalistic, but they were also compassionate. (Well, Krafft-Ebing not so much so, but Ellis and Hirschfeld were, though there is a rumor that Hirschfeld himself liked to wear dresses,[5] which in his case might explain why, but he might have also just been empathetic.) They helped me come to the conclusion that no one really knows why the things that turn us on turn us on, but that narrator in *Cryptonomicon* is correct in concluding that nothing is likely to undo it and you should be thankful if whatever turns you on is only a little odd and not illegal, or fatal for that matter.

It was with that attitude that I received Betty's admission that he liked to wear women's clothes, which he told me about ten days after we'd started dating, on maybe the fourth or fifth date. As a result I put Betty's crossdressing into the "sex" box, and she didn't object to my putting it there. For her, it was sexual, and that made sense to me in a way that maybe it doesn't make sense to other people, or they conflate the trans stuff with sexual orientation. One time, at Lee's Mardi Gras Boutique,[6] one of the guys who worked in the store was quite surprised to see a woman buying women's clothes for her boyfriend, and he joked with us about how he had never believed the men shopping for women's clothes who said they were straight. Laughing, he explained, "They sure don't seem straight when I'm putting a corset on them," to which Betty and I both smiled. He didn't realize it was being tied into a corset that turned those guys on, not who did the tying. I responded that he was very handsome and all, but who was putting them in the corset didn't matter one whit. He looked a little crestfallen and I joked that I knew how he felt, and he asked a little more about us and told us stories about other customers. It was a conversation we had long before we were intentionally doing outreach. Apparently more people should have spent their teen years reading sexology books in the public library, or I wouldn't have to explain so often that crossdressers sometimes like women, and sometimes like men, and often just like the corset.

What I "knew" was that Betty's crossdressing was sexual. For me it had the ring of taboo (exciting), the air of odd (interesting), and something more than that, something authentically sexual in that deep, impossible-to-understand, innately complex kind of way. My own libido had proved remarkably unkinky: I still prefer what one partner in an online support group referred to as "naked sex"—by which she meant sex that didn't require props or special costumes—and perhaps Betty's crossdressing was a kink I might participate in. Before I met Betty my boyfriends liked me best makeupless and naked. I got no requests for high heels, corsets, or stockings from my lovers, which was something of a disappointment. Perhaps it was a good Catholic girl's urge to be a Magdalene, but I bought fetishy lingerie anyway, only to be told, "I prefer you naked."

I kept the lingerie and ditched the boring boyfriends instead, which is why when I met Betty I owned a black corset. Our first months together, our first times having sex, were spent poking through my underwear drawer and his duffel bag of Bettyness,[7] which contained a "borrowed" dress, a wig, a few pairs of shoes, bras, makeup, and breast forms. She was lucky to have been an actor while a closeted CD; there was always an excuse for why a pair of shoes had gone missing. But we didn't have much, and we didn't need much. Our props were worn or borrowed, but we were new to each other, and that was all that was needed, at least for a while.

After Lara took the news well, I told both my sisters. I started to tell a lot of other friends: first gay and lesbian friends, then a good many of my straight female friends, and slowly, very slowly, my straight guy friends, too. Betty was always the most twitchy about straight guys' knowing, no matter that my straight guy friends weren't quite gender normative. But still, Betty was reticent, convinced that straight guys would be the most judgmental. When I introduced Betty to my friend Doug, my old roomie, he pulled me aside to express his surprise that I was dating such a "frat boy." Betty had apparently overcompensated a little too much and had convinced my blond, blue-eyed, farm-raised, regularly-hit-on-by-older-men friend that he was ubermasculine. It was a funny story afterward, but at the time I told Betty she had to cut that out; after all, my friends could understand my dating a transvestite—but a frat boy? They'd think I'd lost my mind.

So while I knew that Betty was a little sexually unusual and not your typical guy, I didn't have any idea early on that his crossdressing meant anything but that he would prefer to be a little prettier than most men when we made love. But that wasn't the whole story, and after subsequent conversations and discoveries about his transness, we both started to realize that the male sexual role was not his favorite. While some might say that his crossdressing should have been a huge road sign, plenty of crossdressers are very happy with a traditional gender role in the bedroom: They want to be on top, just in panties. I realized that not only did Betty's eyes light up when I took the lead in some way—in any way, really—but I was having way better sex, too. It was terrifying. All along I'd thought I was terrifically liberated about this stuff; other boyfriends had preferred nonmissionary positions—who doesn't?—but I'd never been in a situation before where I had to acknowledge that taking the lead felt good for both me and my partner. That is, I had to own it. If I "ended up" on top, in the dark, in those moments of sexuality when no one talks about what just happened, or is about to happen, it seemed okay. But if I were to say out loud, "Hey, I like this," all hell would break loose emotionally.

When you violate a taboo in a secret, private way, and you don't have to talk about what you like, it can just make sex a little sexier.

But when you do have to talk about sex—say, if things aren't going quite right between you and a partner—then it can be terrifying to admit what feels good. Like just about everyone else, I had messages in my head that being aggressive sexually as a woman made me a slut, or a pervert, or another socially awful thing I wasn't supposed to be. But for Betty and me, the choice was between acknowledging these feelings and desires and their taboos, or arguing about sex indefinitely and eventually breaking up over it. The latter wasn't an option.

What was happening in a very private, intimate space between me and Betty involved whole hordes of people: boyfriends who'd called me a nympho, my mother's implied reminders to be a "Christian lady," my years of being called or assumed to be lesbian. I was worried about all the labels I wasn't fitting, and I was even more worried about which ones really could be applied. Betty brought her own horde as well: her guy friends who bedded any woman who was willing, ex-girlfriends who expected her to play the male role, and even one ex who left her for a woman. Then throw in all the cultural voices of religion, morality, and gender correctness. One of the most difficult tasks we had was asking all those people to leave our bedroom and kicking them out when they didn't want to go.

One time, after I presented a workshop on transsexuality, a lesbian came up to me and said simply, "You seem to be worried about what you call what you do, but what you and a partner do together, in private, has no labels. The labels are just what other people call you." That incident became one of many times when someone who had already been labeled "queer" by society put me wise. There's a reason that a gay sex adviser such as Dan Savage gets so many letters from straight people, and why Tristan Taormino similarly has hetero fans.[8] Dan Savage once explained at a reading in Brooklyn that by the time gay men climb the mountain of admitting that they have homosexual desires, any other kink seems a molehill in comparison. Straight folks have no mountain, so their own kinks—such as a simple desire for a lover to wear leather gloves—can seem gigantic to admit.

Admitting to not being heterosexual is one hell of a mountain. Betty and I were both worried about losing all the implications of being "heterosexual," which in terms of sexuality is code for "normal." Not only were we going to lose being heterosexual, but we'd both examined our potential for homosexuality and found ourselves lacking. We finally decided that since what we did with each other didn't seem to have a name, we would describe ourselves as queer, which allowed even more voices to fall away. My brother used to joke, when I was much younger and very much a punk rocker, that my future children, when taunted with the old saw, "Your mother wears army boots!" would reply, "Yeah? So? Doesn't yours?" And that's kind of what it felt like to acknowledge our sexuality as a couple. If people say to me, "You're queer!" my impulse is to say, "Yeah? So?" I'd challenge them to try having sex as three different genders with a lover who has a couple too and let me know how heterosexual they feel afterward. For me, being queer has come to mean that no one gets to tell me what to call what Betty and I do. No one gets to tell me I'm doing it wrong, because queer is already "wrong." It takes us outside of categories that restrict and define us, and that—if we heeded those restrictions—would ruin us as a couple and would definitely ruin our sex life.

Do I wish that Betty and I were perfectly regular about our gender roles and our sexuality? Of course. It would be reassuring to know that I fit in, that who I am and who we are wouldn't raise eyebrows. But so many couples I've known were so perfectly gendered, and are so perfectly not together anymore, that I wonder how much of a prize that really is. That's not to say that being normal is what causes couples to split, even if delimiting who you can be and how you can be might restrict a couple unnecessarily. There's another problem, too, in trying to be normal about desire by stuffing those fantasies that seem troublesome to the back of your mind. They come out in other ways. *Not* playing out roles sexually that you fantasize about can lead to those dynamics' entering the emotional or psychological parts of your relationship instead. Cherríe Moraga once said in an interview, "If the desire for power is so hidden and unacknowledged, it will inevitably surface through manipulation or what-have-you. If you couldn't *play* capturer, you'd be it."[9] She was talking about the way feminism had made this particular fantasy of being a woman who identifies with the male role verboten. It's yet another way that a "supposed to" can interfere not just with your own sexual fulfillment but can screw up the emotional part of the relationship as well. That's one of the reasons Betty and I stopped trying to play the roles we were supposed to be playing and decided that if queering our relationship and our sex life helped, then so be it.

Just acknowledging desires that are uncomfortable is a huge task— and that's even if you have no intention of acting on them. A lot of people could take a lifetime just to be at peace with things they want to do to others, or want done to them. And that means never actually getting around to doing much of it. There's always a first stage of accepting what your desires are and then maybe telling someone else who you think wouldn't be judgmental, like a therapist or maybe an open-minded lover, and then perhaps using that fantasy during sex. A few wives I've known who are uncomfortable making love with crossdressed partners, for instance, can tell their husbands erotic stories about the husband's being crossdressed if the wife can't actually handle seeing her husband *en femme* or in making love to him when he's in nylons. It's not always a perfect solution, but it helps. You should be willing to try just about anything your partner wants to try while also respecting anything your partner can't or won't do. If everyone kept those two things in mind simultaneously, we'd have far fewer letters to sex advice columnists about guys who won't go down and women who won't give blow jobs.

Interestingly, even oral sex was considered outside the domain of people who were "normally" gendered; guys who liked going down on women were considered "soft" (even if they were Mafiosi, as per one *Sopranos*[10] episode), and women who'd do oral were considered unladylike. Now, at least, there's less taboo on those forms of heterosexual sex, but we've still got a long way to go. "Normal" genders still come with a lot of strings attached, and "normal" sexuality does, too, but at the same time, we assume a lot of things about "normal" that aren't always true.

For instance, as a culture we have started to make more distinctions between types of male sexualities. We used to assume that "male" meant "heterosexual male," but now we don't—at least not all of us, and not all the time. A woman who is attracted to a man she's just met should know there's a chance that that man could be gay, which would mean that he wouldn't want a romantic or sexual partnership with her.

But that's not quite enough. A label like "heterosexual" is almost as inexact as "being a man" is. Gigantic codes are still written into the word. The only thing that "heterosexual man" actually means is that the man in question is one who has sex and forms emotional, romantic bonds with women. But that's hardly *all* we mean when we talk about "heterosexual men." Women who date men have a whole other raft of expectations and assumptions about what a heterosexual man is, and does. For starters, a man is supposed to be masculine in appearance, clothing, and attitude. In relation to dating women, they

- are supposed to do the asking (for a dance, a date, marriage)
- take the lead
- initiate seduction, are the seducers

And that's just the basics. If we add to that what we expect of your average heterosexual man, and what he might desire, they

- are supposed to use love to get sex
- prefer sex over tenderness and cuddling

• are likely to prefer blow jobs and quickies more than a
   female partner

In terms of sexual orientation and his sexual relationship to his
own body:

• He's supposed to be offended by any sexual overture coming
   from a man.
• He's "really" gay if he likes any anal stimulation, much less
   penetration.
• It's all about his penis, and specifically, his erection.

Some of these things are true some of the time, but I'm not sure if
they're true because men are "born that way," or because they come to be
that way by following cues and signals and paying attention to feedback
from parents, friends, and even strangers. But it seems unrealistic for
anyone to expect these things to be true if all they know about a guy is
that he's heterosexual. Because what about when these things aren't true?
Most people would probably agree that a man isn't any less heterosexual
if his wife asked him to marry her. They would probably even agree that
he isn't any less heterosexual if he prefers to be sexually submissive as long
as he wants to submit to a woman, too. He's skating closer to thin ice if he
doesn't like getting blow jobs because they feel impersonal to him. But if he
enjoys flirting with other men, he's out of "heterosexual." And he definitely
can't admit to getting turned on anally. In those recent "Man Rule" Miller
Lite commercials, a bunch of certifiably manly men sit around a table
writing up a list of "Man Rules" to be followed by men everywhere. One

genitals are the least of it. **209**

of the rules they come up with is to clink beer bottles toward the bottom instead of the top, because clinking bottles toward the top might result in an exchange of saliva, which would technically count as a kiss. One of the guys obviously misinterprets "clinking bottoms" as code for anal sex and objects that he's "not into that kind of thing," until the rest all clarify that they're talking about the bottoms of their bottles. It's supposed to be funny, but it's really just homophobic. I'm never going to understand why homophobia seems to be a requirement of male heterosexuality, especially since so many men fantasize about lesbian sex. One day women should stand up and demand their boyfriends kiss other men to turn the women on, or maybe we should just have them mud wrestle in Speedos like the women do in yet another Miller Lite commercial.[11] A friend of mine says that heterosexual men are the only ones who define themselves by what they're not: They're not women and they're not gay. The men who beat Kevin Aviance[12] so badly they broke his jaw tried to pull the usual "gay panic" defense, which brings up the double standard brought to light by the New York City Gay and Lesbian Anti-Violence Project (AVP), which pointed out that if women killed or violently beat men who had made an unwelcome advance, there wouldn't be any men left on the planet.

A man's heterosexuality doesn't rule out his being submissive, or tender, or sensitive, or shy. It's supposed to, if he wants to be a man's man. All his sexual orientation means is that he likes to have sex with women and *tends to have* emotional and romantic relationships with women. When we talk about heterosexual sex, what we're talking about is only *who* a person has sex with—not *how*. What I'm talking about is how. Even if we talk only about men who exclusively like women—like many crossdressers I know—it says nothing about *how* they are heterosexual, which is why labels need to be acknowledged for exactly what they don't tell you.

When I first asked crossdressing men what turned them on, several said things such as "Being the woman sexually." I've talked to women about sex, too, and "being the woman sexually" means almost nothing to them. It just brings up the question of which woman they want to feel like: There's a big difference between June Cleaver and Annie Sprinkle,[13] but they're both women. Of course, I knew what these men meant; they meant they wanted to be the one who was seduced. Some had fantasies of being the one who said no; others just wanted to experience someone else's desire for them in a subjective way—they wanted to feel it without having to return it as directly. As much as I chide crossdressers for such oversimplification, I can't blame them for the way they express their desires. Not only are women supposed to be "the woman in bed," but they're supposed to enjoy that role—getting the attention, accepting desire, being judged on how sexy they are. Plenty of women do enjoy that role, but many women don't. Perfectly regular heterosexual women are not always comfortable feeling desired—maybe it's a personality thing, or an issue with body image, or self-esteem, or maybe they just don't like to feel that it's their body and beauty that makes them attractive to their partner. Some women do feel cheap if a man wants her only for her hair, or breasts, or hips, or even for the whole physical package.

It also seems common knowledge these days that women "prefer" cuddling to sex. Perhaps they prefer cuddling to bad sex. When Ann Landers[14] asked women if they preferred sex or cuddling in 1985, she didn't ask how many of the women responding had been raped or molested or harassed or even just pressured into sex, or whether or not their lovers knew where the clitoris is or what to do with it. I might prefer cuddling too if I'd reached the age of thirty-five and never had an orgasm. I might prefer it if the man I was with refused to wear a condom and I was scared of getting pregnant or an STD. Women dislike, or fear, or dread actual intercourse for a lot of different reasons. Even if they still want the intimacy and human contact sex can bring, sometimes the risks are too great or the pleasures too small. Maybe all the cultural guilt about being overweight means some women prefer cuddling over sex because they don't like and can't enjoy their own bodies. Books about sex may mention all of these things, but the idea gets distilled to "women prefer cuddling to sex" and the message women get from that tidy little summation is that if they're "normal," they don't like sex.

The flip side of the same coin is that fantasy of the shy librarian who, once turned on, becomes a veritable tiger in bed. It's the theme of that famous old-school porn film *Behind the Green Door*,[15] but the idea is everywhere. And yet, who exactly is this tiger going to take by the tail? Obviously, if the woman is heterosexual, she's going to need a man who's willing to be "taken." And that's where fantasy tells us the truth about what's really going on between the sheets. Men may desire the tiger, but they may also feel uncomfortable being taken, and women may want to lead, but they're not "supposed" to, and so it often remains a fantasy. When it isn't, though, you have two heterosexual people playing out nontraditional gender roles, and nothing they're doing makes them any less heterosexual. It's more like good sex.

In so many ways, then, we're pretty much mistaken in thinking "heterosexual" communicates anything much about how a person will behave sexually, or how he or she wants to behave. One of the legacies of gays and lesbians becoming more visible is that it gives straight people more opportunity to learn new tricks. Tristan Taormino said in an interview[16] that she thinks sex is getting more queer as a result of more people coming out. In that same interview Dan Savage agreed that straight people are trying a lot more sexual acts that were previously considered "queer sex," but he quite seriously insisted that he makes a point to emphasize that what they're doing is straight, not queer, "so they don't stop doing it." No doubt he gets a little frustrated with how repressed straight people can be, and he wants them to try new things and not avoid certain things because of the taboos or labels they come with. His comment is telling: People don't want to do anything "queer" because they don't want to lose the "straight" label. There is a point of no return, after which even the most dogmatic heterosexual has to realize that perhaps his straight friends are not having the same kind of sex he is. It's one of the reasons we've seen terms such as "heteroflexible," which describes heterosexuals who might be having queer sex but who don't identify it as such.

Because of my willingness to talk about sexuality, Betty and I were invited to attend a sex conference and getaway that we like to call "sex camp,"[17] which is held at a campground. The workshops offered cover a range of topics, from ones that are more "how-to" where people can learn specific skills (like how to incorporate spanking into a sex life, or how to give a sensual massage) to the kinds of workshops I present, about partnering and gender and role playing, and there are still others about body image or how to mix sexuality and spirituality. But there are also spaces for people to meet, have public sex or watch public sex, and there's a dungeon for the BDSM folks where they can tie each other up and engage in various acts of sadism and masochism. The event draws people who wouldn't usually mix: trans and genderqueer people, BDSM scenesters, pagans, sacred spirituality types, and swingers. We had six days of sun and grass and trees and bad food; six days of nudity, sex, workshops, sex, pagan rituals, sex, naked volleyball, swimming, and yes, more sex. I now know every conceivable way a person can be tied to a tree and flogged. A winter version is held in a hotel and is a lot less muddy, too.

But the sense of camaraderie, the comfort with nudity, sex, and kink are inestimable—like nothing I've ever experienced anywhere else. By the end of the conference, you start to wonder why everyone is so uptight about sex. It becomes so easy and so natural to see people walking around naked or being affectionate or sexual in public spaces. The experience made me question why we restrict desire so much, as if in an attempt to pretend that people don't actually have sex. I was reminded that so many people are longing to try something new and adventurous, to role-play, or to be restrained, and I wondered how many men would love to be seduced and taken and topped by their wives. Since Betty and I don't "play" with others, we tend to enjoy the way camp encourages people to make peace with their desires; the conversations had over lunch or in the more talk-oriented workshops can be quite profound, with people telling stories about how they grew up and why they started to explore their sexual selves, but also to talk about difficult topics such as shame or past sexual problems.

One of the workshops I developed for "sex camp" is called "Uneven Libidos,"[18] in which I talk about how Betty's libido is almost nonexistent and mine is through the roof. Oftentimes Betty chimes in when I talk about how we negotiate the difference. At first it seemed to be the blind leading the blind, but I'd already seen more than once the power in just saying, "We are dealing with this; is anyone else?" This quickly leads to group discussions and turns into what's known as peer support in the therapy community. I tend to do a lot of research, gathering my ideas through reading books and talking to experts. My impersonation of Studs Terkel[19] comes next, and I just start asking people questions. It's always entertaining at dinner parties to ask someone, "So have you ever been with someone who had a way higher libido than you?" But I most enjoy asking a couple, "So which one of you likes to have sex more?"

They always know. There's rarely even a question. Sometimes you find a couple who are evenly matched, but more often than not people's reactions are pretty consistent: One of them looks at his or her feet, and the other looks away, up, off to the side. That's my simpatico—the one looking around, a little guilty, secretly proud of his or her Super Libido. The person looking at her shoes is the one who can't keep up, who feels besieged by demands, who doesn't get what the big deal is about sex, or why the urgency, and doesn't understand the need to try new and exotic things: some of the above, all of the above, most of the above.

That doesn't mean those with lesser libidos are bad lovers, by any means. They might be fantastic, consistent, lovely partners in bed. They may seem so at peace with their need for sex that they come off as having mastered the whole thing. With one simple statement of "I don't get what the big deal is," they leave their partners, who are quietly proud of being both adventurous and willing and able, suddenly feeling like a petulant child for saying, "But I want more, and different, and better, and . . . " and having no reasons that make any sense to a rational person *why* they want those things. "Because it's fun" falls a little flat when your partner is coming off as mature and above *that sort of thing*. Betty always made me feel that I was slightly less evolved than she was because of this animal desire of mine. She, in turn, worried about losing me because we weren't having enough sex, or enough kinds of sex, and started to feel that the pressure was going to make her head explode. As a result, we were both pretty miserable. I felt rejected and atavistic; she felt cold and scared.

Compounding our problem was that just about every book and article I found when I was looking for advice was based on the premise that it's the man who wants more sex. At the time, I just chalked it up to us being us, with our established gender weirdness skewing things as usual. But the advice often wasn't very useful, because it would suggest things such as the less libidinous partner should be willing to have a quickie. But a quickie with a man who isn't turned on is more like three hours of mutual torture. You get the Viagra, the Cialis, the horny goat weed, and the Yohimbe,[20] and you still wind up nowhere. If someone isn't into it, he just isn't.

Every time we watched *Everybody Loves Raymond*, we saw more of the same: Deborah didn't want sex and Ray did. It had to be us: We were gender demented. We couldn't even have gender-normative sex problems like everyone else. But then I started noticing articles about men's low libidos cropping up here and again, plus a crop of articles about how many marriages become sexless after time. I put two and two together: The "miracle cure" of Viagra and Cialis wasn't curing everything. Guys who had physical issues with getting and maintaining an erection could get hard again, but no pill was going to cure an initial lack of desire. Here's the thing: (1) You have to want to take the pill for it to work; (2) fantastic, robust capillaries have nothing to do with the heart and head of the person with the penis; and (3) when someone doesn't want to, he doesn't want to, and no drug on earth will change that.

Whenever I stood in front of a room to lead the Uneven Libidos workshop, more men talked about being the ones with the low libidos than the other way around. These weren't groups of trans people: They were swingers, and polyamorists, and people into BDSM; they were pagans and sexual free spirits. Online I found even more couples who admitted that it was often the guy who had the low libido, and many men, once they admitted that, also confessed to not liking blow jobs (shocker!), or getting more pleasure from pleasuring a woman than in having an orgasm themselves. Men have told me they'd stopped liking the whole business— that performance anxiety or an unreliable penis or demanding partners had ruined their taste for sex, and even for women, or relationships.

I'm not surprised at the humiliation women express because they feel like nags when asking for sex, because not only are we not supposed to like it more than guys, we're not supposed to like it much at all. The guys are often surprised when they realize they're not the only ones in the room who don't want sex more than their girlfriends and wives. In one workshop, an older man raised his hand near the end and said, "I never knew, all these years. I never knew. Thank you," with tears in his eyes. He made me want to go out and smack down every stereotype, every sex book, every everything that always repeats the old saw that men always want a lot of sex. I wanted to go out and hush anyone who repeated that stupid adage about how men give love to get sex. It made me want to give the guy a hug. He was in his fifties at least, and he'd waited all those years for someone to tell him that he was perfectly normal for not living up to a stupid stereotype. That's exactly why this kind of gendered bullshit bothers me so much—because people suffer under these expectations needlessly.

In our relationship, I'd blamed Betty's transness for her lower libido for years. It made sense to me that someone who wasn't quite right with her gender might not be quite right with her body or sexuality; after all, sex is about self and body as much as it is about desire. I had wondered if I shouldn't encourage Betty to transition in order that she might discover a sexuality she was comfortable with and enjoy even if I weren't a part of it.[21] I love sex, and the idea of anyone feeling ho-hum about it was sad to me—sad like a world without chocolate or dancing or birthday presents. It is a simple, beautiful perk of being human and having a body.

One night during an argument about sex, I accused Betty of thinking of me just as a friend who would teach her how to be female and shop with her for clothes. It was the kind of completely illogical thing you say during an argument. If I'd been levelheaded at the time, I would have realized Betty would have chosen a much more feminine woman for her girl training and would have chosen—duh!—a woman who actually liked shopping to shop with her. While I was catching my breath after expressing this sentiment, she said quietly, "But I love making love with you." I stood there like a fool, instantly crying while the rage was still in my lungs. I had been more willing to believe that her less-than-virile libido was caused by her transness and her desire to have a female body than I was willing to believe the small simple truth that she just had a low libido.

A few other partners of post-op trans women confided in me that they'd expected an increase in their partner's libido after surgery, but that things hadn't improved. Rather, some of them reported that the trans person enjoyed sex more than previously, but often the people with low libidos still had low libidos after they developed breasts and had surgery. They were happy in their new bodies, happy to be living in the world as women, but things hadn't improved sexually from the partner's perspective. Some of the trans women had even lower libidos as a result of hormone changes and most functioned differently and experienced orgasms in ways that they hadn't before. If Betty weren't going to love sex just because she'd gotten a vagina, and my passion were to dampen because of that same vagina, then we'd be in real trouble. We'd have no sex life whatsoever. I'd assumed, quite mistakenly, that her dislike of her body caused her lack of desire, but I've never been particularly thrilled with my body, for various reasons, and I love sex. A workshop about body image at the same conference reminded me that a lot of us are willing to forgo body self-acceptance in the context of an orgasm, but that doesn't mean we feel okay naked in front of other people.

It was as if the simple idea that men don't always have high libidos were heresy. Since then I've also talked to more men who have higher libidos than the women they're with, and I've come to the conclusion that people with high libidos just can't comprehend people with low ones. Some women like sex more than other women and don't understand why, and sometimes gay men who like sex a lot are confounded by lovers who don't like it quite as much. Talk about living on different planets. The divide isn't between male and female, it's between libidinous and not-so-libidinous. That is, having a low libido isn't a problem; it's a difference in libidos that is a problem, and then it's not one person's problem or the other's; it's a shared problem.

But guys who have low libidos don't necessarily have low libidos because they're traumatized, or trans, or body dysphoric. It's not always because they were abused or preferred masturbation or are secretly homosexual. Granted, those questions need to be asked; physical problems should also be ruled out by a visit to a doctor, and if there are psychological factors that make people feel bad about themselves, therapy might be useful.

A big change in libido is a red flag in terms of mental or physical health (just like big changes in sleep patterns or appetite are), but if the guy has always had a low libido it's probably just because, like women, men have a range of libidos. Some of them like sex all the time, anytime, with anyone. Others require special circumstances. Others want to feel deeply in love with and connected to their partners before they can have sex. And others just don't like to do it that often, just because they don't, the same way that some people like Mexican food and some people don't. There doesn't have to be a reason. It just is the way it is. Betty has a low libido the same way that I have a high one, and the same way she's got brown hair: Because she does. It could even be genetic, but that's kind of a moot point since I can't go back into her mother's womb to rewire things, can I?

Blaming Betty's low libido on her transness was too simple a solution to a very complex state of affairs. A low libido is most likely the result of a couple of factors, none of which might have anything to do with being unhealthy or deficient. Sexuality is like that box of cords people have stored in a garage or basement because they never want to throw one out, in case they need it "later." Cords from computers you threw out five or ten years ago are in there with numerous phone cords, power cords, adapters, extension cords. After a while you couldn't free one from the mess if you tried. Desire is like that. In Betty's case, maybe the first element was a low testosterone level in the womb, which contributed to her being trans and to having a low testosterone level in general. Added to that was a feeling of being less than virile in high school. A few awkward sexual situations with girls added a few more knots. Hearing guys boast about sexual exploits with women and being offended by the way they talked about women might have been another. Shame about crossdressing or having trans feelings was a great big one. And on and on it might go, and for every man or woman out there with a low libido there are different factors that might contribute. Not all of them have anything to do with being "wrong" or "weird" or "bad." Some of them might be biological and some might be cultural. But for guys, the one huge pressure of being expected to have a high libido knots all the cords that are already in there.

All of this made me think about why it was so hard for me to believe that a man could have a low libido in the first place. Who taught me that? My first boyfriend, who liked sex less than I did? My third boyfriend, who did manage to keep up but who still called me a nymphomaniac? The second, who I assumed had a lower libido than I did because he was more than a decade older? Was it Raymond Romano and all the comics before him who made the same joke about how they're always trying to get laid and their wives are always saying no? Was it the warnings I got when I was young to be wary of perverts in bathrooms? Or the warnings to girls not to wear patent leather shoes so boys can't look up their skirts?

It's yet another case in which gender stereotyping goes unnoticed. When things work out in keeping with those stereotypes, no one notices them. But when problems arise that are not "normally gendered," it's as if we can't see the problems for what they are because we can't even see the gender stereotypes we're carrying around with us. For Betty and me, the gender stereotypes that were keeping us from finding solutions to our problematic sex life centered on the issue of our mismatched libidos. For another couple the minefield of gender might dictate who is "allowed" to like oral sex and who's "supposed" to do it anyway. What roles or acts are considered "appropriate" for men and women might manifest in which positions any given couple thinks are "okay" and which are dirty or taboo.

Or our narrow sense of gender roles might mean that one person in the relationship doesn't have the first idea about how to be the seducer, even if she wants to. There are about a million ways in which expectations around who does what to whom might get in the way of people having great sex. The thing is, you can't start to resolve a problem such as performance anxiety if the guy who has it actually just has a low libido but can't say that out loud for fear of feeling like a sissy. A woman is not going to be able to help her lover bring her to orgasm if she thinks it's wrong or unladylike for her to say, "Touch me there more" very directly. If Ann Landers and Raymond are telling us that it's the guys who want the sex and the girls who say no, then we're never going to know how many of us are lying just to fit in with how we're "supposed" to be. We're not going to get what we want sexually, and neither are our partners, which is a lose-lose situation.

When my friend Vanessa met Betty for the first time, Betty was presenting androgynously, not on purpose but because he'd changed his physical appearance in order to pass as female more easily: tweezed eyebrows, lasered facial hair, and long hair cut into a more feminine style. Vanessa didn't know exactly how to interact, but she connected with Betty as a person, not with his gender. Others, of course, resent not having those kinds of social cues and get confused and angry, especially if their confusion is conflated with desire.

Not long after that meeting, Betty was walking around our living room on a hot Brooklyn night in a green batik sundress of mine. A little while later, she gave up on the sundress and was walking around naked. At home, I often flirt with her girl self—whether she's presenting as female or not. While she stood in the doorway talking to me, I experienced a split second of desire for my male husband. I pretended I didn't, and said something about how hairless she was instead, but he'd seen it.

"When you look at me like that, doll," she said, "I know what you see."

What I see is my beautiful husband. He has all the masculine and feminine beauty the Greeks were after. Betty is naturally hairless, naturally svelte, and has a full head of hair that goes wavy in humid weather. He's a less-muscular David by Michelangelo, with longer legs. His looks both defy gender and confirm it; his beauty is not the type of masculinity we admire now in modern 21st-century America, but it is a classic type of beauty, a little more the aesthetic beauty that men who love men have had a history of portraying. His hairlessness and thinness often make him seem ten years younger than he is, effeminate in a way that a young boy who hasn't fully masculinized can be.

Others who meet him in male mode often remark to me privately that they'd have a difficult time letting go of a man who is so good-looking. That does make it harder. I still go weak in the knees when I see my husband walking around naked, but I still go weak in the knees when he's wearing something silky and leaning over our vanity to apply makeup, too. But in either case, I am responding to his physical beauty, the kind that inspires poetry and love songs. Yet at the same time, people see how beautiful she is and suggest that her looks probably make it a little easier for me to explore any bisexuality I might have, and that is most definitely true as well. So many of us would love to be attractive in only one gender, and Betty is attractive in both.

A magazine with Johnny Depp on the cover a few years back taught me about transness when I wasn't expecting it. As I looked at the photo and considered how Betty had often been compared to him, I wondered why on earth Betty wouldn't want to look like that when just about everyone else I knew—male and female—would give a left leg to look like Mr. Depp. Looking at that handsome man on the cover of a magazine taught me that my husband was trans; he would never feel quite comfortable being a good-looking man. I wasn't sure if he would ever be comfortable as a good-looking woman, either. But he was, at least, more comfortable being desired when he was she.

When I wonder how such a beautiful man ended up with not much of a libido, or how such a beautifully masculine man doesn't feel male, I think someone has played a terrifically bad joke on her. But despite all that, she still wants to be my husband, and we're both the butt of that bad joke. I wish I could bring Betty any kind of comfort or solace in *his* beautiful self. I wish I could help him feel more at home in a male body. I wish I thought I was a sufficient door prize for not transitioning. I also wish I didn't have this feeling that I'm torturing the person I love most in the world. But other times I lay all that aside because it does me a world of good just to say: I married the most beautiful man *ever,* and he loves me.

I'm not supposed to admire or appreciate or desire his him-ness—not according to the rules of the trans community, anyway. But I can't help it. I met him as a man, I first made love to him before I knew about any of this, and I can't change my desire. I will flirt with his femme self; I can compliment how beautiful, how sexy, how pretty she is. I feel impressive when she's on my arm, and content when he holds my hand. When I talk to others like me, people who find a trans person desirable and attractive and a good companion and lover, I hear the same things over and over again.

So many of us love the transness; it's being with someone who expresses both genders that's sexy. A lesbian might appreciate the female body of her boi but love his cocky sweetness; a bisexual wife of one MTF we know loves romancing both the man and the woman she's married to, and she gets off in different ways to the different energies her partner can radiate. But often, trans people don't want that. They want admiration only for their target gender, the person they become through skill or hormones or surgery. I am lucky in that respect: Betty respects that she won me in part because she was a good-looking guy, and that I wanted to have sex with her for the same reason. She doesn't give me a hard time about my desire, but instead she sighs, and flirts, and smiles, but of course I notice how much she beams when I tell her she looks pretty instead. But he will walk around naked or half-naked, as if giving me more permission to desire how I would. There has to be a special alignment of the stars for that to happen, though, or it has to get brutally hot in Brooklyn, so as much as I dislike the heat, I look forward to summer. Even if I am attracted to her male body, and she knows it, I still often let her play a more submissive role anyway, so the issue of whether or not I'm having sex with a man, the way most people might mean they're having sex with a man, is entirely different in our world.

I expect people in the trans community to judge me for not honoring her woman-ness; I fear they'll judge her for not standing up for herself. I expect my fellow feminists will think I've made far too many concessions for the sake of a man, and that some gay men will think I'm fooling myself. Some lesbians might, too.

What I've decided is that I don't care what anyone thinks about my desire or her identity or our relationship. If Betty and I ever did split up,

I have no idea who I would date. I couldn't take "regular" guys anymore, because of the male privilege, and having to fit myself into the "girlfriend" box again, or just because I can't imagine being with someone who identifies with only one gender. But if I wouldn't date guys, I don't know who I would date. It's at times like this when it'd be useful to be bisexual. I wouldn't have the first clue how to date women raised female. I couldn't ever date another crossdresser, either, because with my luck, he'd want to transition too. Trans men, and bois, and others on the FTM end of the spectrum pique my sensual curiosity. But ultimately it's a damn good thing there is no breakup on our horizon because I've been ruined for dating. I used to joke about being *Betty-sexual,* but apparently that was one truth initially said in jest. It's a relief to know that Betty probably couldn't ever date a woman who didn't look good in trousers, either.

I do like men, and I desire them; I enjoy having sex with them, too. I am hardly an archetypal female, especially from the vantage point of most heterosexual man. I don't wear heels. I do expect to lead at least some of the time. I'm not very good at being submissive, or coy, and I am not the type to assuage a man's ego and tell him I came when I didn't. At the very same time, I would love for Betty to keep looking more like Johnny Depp than not, but asking her to be as masculine as that would be kind of hypocritical if I'm not also willing to look like Kate Winslet all the time. But for us, gender is a tricky thing when it comes to desire; it feels unfair to be attracted to a type when you refuse to be one.

A recent Campari commercial[22] reflected my sexuality in a way I could actually relate to. It starts with a smooth-faced, good-looking male-presenting person with dark hair, in a suit, scoping a room. A tall figure in a slinky, backless gown ascends a staircase. The pursuer pursues, through hallways and balconies, past swimming pools and bars, and comes upon the object of desire a little too quickly—spilling a glass of Campari onto the beauty's dress. The beauty undoes the halter top and lets the front fall to reveal a male chest—hairless and svelte, with perfect nipples. The seducer looks surprised and then also reaches back to release long, silky black hair from where it was tucked up near the suit's collar. With another hand, the seducer pulls away a dress shirt to reveal bound breasts.

And they stand looking at each other; the looks on their faces reveal a kind of Rorschach test for the viewer. Some people see them as mutually baffled, or even disappointed. But I saw me and Betty, and a kind of desire that doesn't have a name. I want porn like that. I want to know other couples like that. I don't want people to come to the immediate conclusion that two people who are gender variant could not desire each other, nor do I want anyone to think they're doomed because they couldn't possibly desire each other.

They can.

Some people may never know what it's like to be "the man" sexually if they're female, or "the woman" if they're male, which is a shame. It can be so liberating, or at the very least, educational. In an interesting essay[23] about the existence of female transvestites, Raven Kaldera interviewed Shannon, who explained, "I couldn't find my boy side until I unbrainwashed myself. . . . I had to get past all those things that I'd been told I ought to want, and then I could do what I really wanted. That took until I was twenty-five." If there are still heterosexual women who haven't had an orgasm by the age of thirty-five, and heterosexual men who completely flip out the first time they lose an erection or come too soon, some of us are going to be a lot older than Shannon's twenty-five before we figure out where our other gender is sexually, what it feels like to be in it, and what it wants exactly. That "unbrainwashing" Shannon refers to could take a very long time, depending on how you were brought up and how many of those voices you bring with you to the bedroom. Women don't have to be trans, or even gender variant, to explore kinds of male sexual energy. At the start of a workshop about strap-on sex, the incomparable Nina Hartley[24]—who is very feminine, very sexy, and even petite—joked that the first time she strapped it on she understood instantly why men always want to stick it into things. Any insight into "how the other half lives" could be useful for a couple. Likewise if a man is willing to be "pegged"[25] by his girlfriend. Being receptive might teach him a lot about that kind of sensual pleasure (and will simultaneously teach him how intensely pleasurable prostate stimulation is). Every woman should put on a strap-on once in her life, even if she doesn't get to stick it in anywhere; she should try it on just to feel what it's like, just to explore a different kind of sexual power that she might otherwise not give herself permission to feel. (Women should shave their heads at least once, for similar reasons.) Interestingly, the reports I've gotten from women are that they don't feel more masculine as a result of strapping it on, just more powerful—which is a very heady and sexy feeling, indeed. Guys who are willing do not have to be queer or gay or submissive or trans to enjoy giving it up to a female partner, either—just a little adventurous.

I wonder what I would do about sex if Betty did get "the surgery." Having nearly had sex with women in my past, I always had a visceral dread of having to make a vagina other than mine happy.

Mine I know, but women's orgasms strike me as so complicated and as unsatisfying for the satisfier. I'm clearly and painfully heterosexual in that sense, because getting another woman to orgasm would be a chore, not a pleasure. The other side of my brain says I might actually enjoy it, because I do like strapping it on, and I might enjoy being able to please Betty that way. We have talked about my having sex with a woman before Betty transitioned to see if I could enjoy sex with someone with a vagina, but she wouldn't be Betty, and after so many years of intimacy with her, sex with another woman wouldn't give me any clue as to whether I would or wouldn't like having sex with Betty if she had a vagina. Sex has become entirely different to me in the years we've been together, complicated and deep, more about trust than pleasure. There's also that little hurdle of our monogamy, too, which kind of prevents us from ever acting on a theoretical idea like that.

I can't turn myself into a lesbian just because it would be useful to my relationship if Betty transitions. I can't become asexual, either, like so many other trans couples seem to do. There is a third option for partners of people who transition: staying with a partner by taking outside lovers—either one or both of them—or becoming polyamorous[26] in some way. If that works for a couple, and it's how they can stay together when that's what they want, that's fantastic. I can't do it. My natural bent is monogamous—not because that's what you're "supposed to do," but because I'm naturally shy about my body and don't trust others very easily, and I've become much less casual about sex since I've been with Betty. Betty is similar about her own sexuality, so for us monogamy has been a careful choice: It allows us a deep trust and commitment, which then enables us to experiment with each other, to have an erotic life that we can explore together. The truth of it is that despite our uneven libidos, and despite our gender weirdness, our whole relationship—the sexual one included—has very much been about compromise. We've learned to trust each other in very deep ways about very difficult, intimate things. But it's been a choice that both of us made freely, that we talk about a lot, that we've weighed the pros and cons of. I would love it if taking another (male) lover would allow me to tell Betty to go ahead and transition, but it's not that easy. I would love it if my enjoying sex with a woman raised female were any kind of bellwether for whether I'd enjoy sex with Betty if she developed a female body, but it wouldn't. We both believe that we wouldn't be us if we weren't monogamous, and as much as our friends at sex camp are often bewildered by our choice, we can say that at least in one way, we are deeply conservative. When I'm in a room full of kinky people and self-declared perverts of various stripes, I always joke that I have accidentally stepped into the only situation where monogamy is possible for someone with a high libido: I have a husband and a girlfriend on the side, but they both happen to be the same person. Except that's not a joke, not really. I feel like the cat who ate the canary, because Betty truly is the hottest thing ever to me, in either mode. Honestly, there are times when it's almost reassuring that in one instance, we're kind of old-fashioned and square: When most people think of you as "out there" or radical or freaky or queer, it's nice to have that one thing in your pocket that will *really* surprise them.

love is a many-gendered thing.

It's rare now when Betty and I actually look like a heterosexual couple, or at least when we actually pass as one. Most of the time, I'm not sure what we look like to other people, because often Betty decides to look like my husband for the day and dresses like a guy, only for us to be called "ladies" when we're out having lunch. We might run into someone we know on the street afterward, and it might be a fellow actor friend of his, and suddenly he's male again, and we're straight again, at least in the eyes of the person we're talking to, even while at the very same moment people are passing by who are reading us both as women. I occasionally have moments when I wonder to myself why I make such a big deal of her transitioning when it's as if she already has, sans the name change and gender marker on her driver's license.

The moments I have as "his wife" are fleeting while we're in New York, since more and more people know us as a trans + female couple. It was only when we went to Betty's family reunion in Colorado that we were reminded of what it was like to pass as a heterosexual couple again, and it was downright weird.

Betty decided to go as her guy self mostly because we didn't want to do Trans 101 with every aunt, cousin, and grandparent. We are fully aware of how much attention could be drawn away from the event if Betty were to show up as her female self—enough so that no one would really enjoy the stories and would seem kind of relieved when we left. Since this trip was to be the first time Betty had seen her extended family in more than a decade, we wanted the trip to be about catching up and meeting new in-laws and the next generation.

Most people who express their trans selves as fully as Betty couldn't have pulled it off; most wouldn't want to or wouldn't on principle, although I do know one trans woman who went to a family wedding as her former male self to walk her daughter down the aisle because her daughter wanted "him" to. Betty is, however, a very talented actor and pulled it off. We were more put off by her looking and acting like a guy than anyone else was. No one else seemed to notice, because most of the people we were with didn't know anything about her trans stuff; they hadn't seen him since he was twelve. We discussed telling certain family members during quiet moments because we really liked a lot of people and thought the younger generations especially would "get it," or at least not get hung up on it, and we wanted to tell them because we felt like phonies otherwise. One of his nieces, despite having been told nothing about her "Aunt Betty," kept pointing out that her friendly, fun uncle "seems more like a girl." Betty thought it was his long hair that tipped her off, but she could just tell, the way kids can. Kids are not only generally more accepting than adults, but they're also famous for "clocking" crossdressers and bluntly asking, "Are you a girl or a boy?" and other indelicate questions. When Betty was asked that once by a friend's child, she answered, "What do you think I am?" and he stopped for a minute, thought about it, and said, "I think you're a girl who's a boy." And that was that.

The whole experience was surreal—like going back in time to when we were first together and meeting each other's families. People kept introducing me as his wife, not as her partner or spouse. We had left those gender-neutral terms back in New York; we were back in the land where men were men, and women were women, and only they shall marry each other. We were in Colorado.

Betty likes to joke about what a New Yorker I am because

once I leave "the city" (by which I always mean New York City), I walk around like an anthropologist marveling at the way people live. In a small city outside of Denver, a hip little coffee shop/bookstore we visited had no gay and lesbian section at all, and no women's studies or gender studies books, either. A slew of those *How to Get That Numbnut to Make a Second Date*[1] titles were stocked in the self-help section. We sat and talked with the clerk about the new Neil Gaiman novel that was due out, drank chai tea, and went mostly unnoticed. Later the same day, when Betty dropped me off for a massage appointment, the masseuse asked where I was visiting from and if "that guy" was my brother. It took me a minute to realize she was asking about Betty, who was standing outside bored like a regular boyfriend, leaning against our borrowed car, looking all sorts of studly in jeans and sunglasses. I laughed when I realized whom she was referring to, but I passed off my delayed response as having been confusion about the brother reference. When I say, "No, he's my husband," people tend to get a little embarrassed, but we've gotten used to joking about marriage between siblings as "that sort of thing not being legal around here," and they relax again. When women ask me about Betty they're often trying to find out if he's single, which always makes me think, *Sure, you like him now, but if you saw what he looked like most of the time* . . .

One of my close friends asked me early on how I felt about dating such a handsome man, if I wouldn't feel a lot of pressure because other women would hit on him all the time. One of my gay friends told me to stay in shape and not be jealous and be cool and independent to keep such a catch. But that was long, long before any of them knew he was trans, after which people tended to be not so impressed with my mate-catching skills. "Oh" is often all they said after it all came out. The women who used to have crushes on him treat him now, by his own description, more as a person to be pitied than someone to steal away from his wife. Other than that week in Colorado, the only times I see my husband as he once was, as he was when we met, are when Betty performs as a guy onstage. If he is playing a male role he becomes more "male ascendant" in our personal life, and I find myself walking with a lighter step, dreaming consciously and unconsciously of him during those times.

The rare family reunion and the occasional play that inspires him to take a male role onstage may be what's getting me through. I feel like a romantic camel, storing up those hearts-and-flowers feelings to get me through the long dry desert of endless days of femininity. I can catch a glimpse of him getting dressed when he thinks I'm sleeping, or admire his male self quietly without his noticing, or remember scenes he's done onstage as Algernon or Bluntschli or Melchior in an old Tom Stoppard play[2] to connect with the guy I'm in love with. When I watched him perform this past year bare-chested in Glyn Maxwell's *Wolfpit*, I could glimpse him from my seat in the theater: my once-confident, nearly cocky husband, rising star.

I used to fit into a world of wives who know their brilliant husband's secret selves: the girlfriend who sees her award-winning screenwriting beau biting his nails till they bleed; the spouse of a world-class scientist who loses his wallet, his glasses, and a briefcase in the span of a week; the partner of an inspiring lawyer who sees him shaking with nerves before a court battle. The world may see brilliance, even genius; the wife sees a man who can't remember his mother's birthday.

Everyone has an underbelly.

The transness used to feel more like an underbelly, an eccentricity, a quirk. He was well liked, so people found it odd, but interesting, and certainly not weird enough or crazy enough to like him any less. What it did for some people is explain how exactly he'd ended up with a wife who looked like me instead of a beauty of an actress or a model or whatever exactly is the crème de la crème of women these days. Gay men were often impressively funny about how astonishing it was that he liked women at all, but if he must, surely he could have come up with a little more of a trophy than I am. I don't even remember to reapply my lipstick, after all.

But now that's all turned around. Now people tell me I'm doing him a favor, that I'm kind and courageous and all those other things that I'm not. I am a romantic, as is he, which is really all that's ever explained why the two of us are for each other and have been since we met. But that my partner in life slid in status is not debatable: It's a fact. The room afforded a good-looking, charismatic young man is legion: He'd leave work at five and arrive closer to ten o'clock than to nine and no one would say a word. But once Betty was out of the bottle, and he started looking more like her, people found fault with character flaws that had been there the whole while. I did it myself first—saw myself do it and watched as others followed suit. He started to be excluded from conversations he used to lead; he was talked past and stonily excluded, especially when straight men were involved. I found people looking to me for conversation instead. I was only ever the straight man to Betty's showman, and I couldn't offer them what he had given them: the chance to stand, just a little, in the spotlight that seemed to follow him around. They were orphaned fans of a light that had dimmed.

The irony perhaps is that she is as much of a star as he had ever been. She's charming and well-read and tech savvy and funny. She flirts shamelessly, almost to the point where people want to follow her around. People like Betty an awful lot; lesbians she worked with had crushes on her. But anyone who had known the pull of his charm isn't as impressed with the new, improved, genderqueered individual with the unusual voice, not even the ones who counted bravery and honesty in his favor. The charisma and social points he had stored up lasted only so long: Memories fade, and people adjust to the new you and forget the old one.

Seeing him onstage now is like having a dream about my grandmother who died more than a decade ago. I've woken from a dream of her, feeling happy and loved, as if the wrongs in the world have been righted, my life made whole. Then comes that moment when I realize it had been a dream, that I can't see her or help her find her glasses and never will. I'm not filled with despair but more a sense of longing, the colors of my world a little more flat than they had been just moments earlier. The part of me made from my grandmother's rib says there's no use living in a fantasy world, no use dreaming of shining palaces while cat hair and dust clump under the couch. What is, is. There's no use in feeling sorry for yourself, wondering what could have been.

I still do, though.

We came home one night after a dinner with friends and a long cab ride to discover that Betty had lost his forty-gig iPod. It was a bonus he'd earned at work, and its loss seems oddly symbolic to me now, as it was only after he lost it that his coworker started complaining about his coming in a little too late and leaving a little too early, that my sister and her husband told us they were worried for us, for our future: We had no children, we had no savings, we had no house. I wanted to say: *We had even less a year ago; why are you noticing only now?* But I knew the reason. It had become obvious to others that Betty had changed: Her appearance demasculinized, she didn't command the same kind of respect he had. My husband had gone from having luck on his side to hoping he might be lucky enough to be one of those fools or drunks, thankful to be watched over. He'd fallen from grace, and that shiny future everyone had imagined had turned to rust, overnight, all because of gender.

Some days my husband's being a woman just doesn't seem possible.

Some days I don't want to see her transsexualism still.

But it's as if every day brings a new way for me to see the woman I am married to, that forces me to see her, no matter how much I'd rather see him. I can stick my head in the sand only so far. But Betty hasn't made the decision to transition. She tells me all the time she doesn't have the necessary blinders, by which she means that she knows transitioning will create more problems than it will solve. It may solve a vital one, but she's not convinced it will fix her gender dilemma; she will not forget she is trans whether she lives in a male or female body, and it's the transness, right now, that's the hardest aspect of this. What she'd like to be is not trans, and that's not possible. She can't go forward with transition just hoping that I'll hang around and that people will accept her as a woman or that she'll accept herself as a woman. She is, fortunately or unfortunately, with me, and I won't let her delude herself into thinking that living as a woman is going to be easy for someone who grew up with the perks of male privilege, especially since hers was embellished by her own charm and looks. She is almost too aware of what transition might bring to forge ahead.

The dilemma is that too much of her may have to be left behind if she decides to live as female full-time.

At a recent party we went to, Betty decided to experiment by retaining more of his "male" personality even while presenting as female. The party was thrown by a couple we know, and because the husband is also transgendered, most of their friends have already heard a good deal of Trans 101. Betty was unlikely to pass as female, but she presented as female and before long she was in the heart of a group on the outdoor patio, telling stories and jokes and sharing random bits of interesting things she'd read on blogs. When politics came up she found herself doing a Lewis Black[3] impersonation and reverting to a voice more like his than hers.

When we got back home, we talked about how she felt about being more "him" while presenting as female. She was happy to have tried it and felt that perhaps there was a chance she would be able to bring all of herself forward into femaledom. She had noticed that things had grown a little awkward toward the end of the party, and I had too. There are times when people seem bothered, as if they can't cope; they'll be laughing along with a story she's telling and you can almost see the thought bubble that expresses their confusion appear above their heads. Both men and women seem disturbed by his looking like a woman because they don't know how they're supposed to like the person they're talking to. They can't categorize her quickly as "okay to be attracted to" or "not okay to be attracted to." They run into the same kind of discomfort I run into when I find myself drawn to something masculine about her or vice versa. It seems to upset people that she has the audacity to be both.

We thought of a woman friend of ours who is a female drag queen and a punk rock free spirit. We both love her for her larger-than-life personality: She could be a character on *Absolutely Fabulous*.[4] Women who have those kinds of large personalities have adapted to having them by signaling that they are outside of "regular woman" in one way or another. Betty's transness would make standing out like that problematic because her transness already does that. We both realized, sadly, that a woman who is an aggressive enough conversationalist to pull off doing a Lewis Black impersonation successfully is never quite going to feel like "one of the girls," because she isn't. Betty knows her opinionated, hard-headed wife is also soft-spoken and sees how uncanny it is that I am two seemingly diametric things at once. But she also knows that one of the reasons I get away with being as opinionated and hard-headed as I am is exactly because I'm soft-spoken; the most trenchant attitude can be made more palatable with the right tone of voice. My barely audible voice is an accidental apology for being the type of woman who has the nerve to argue with men about politics or music, one I never meant to proffer but that developed unconsciously. I've described how slow and almost undetectable female socialization is, a kind of slow wearing down, or wearing out, of whatever parts of your personality don't meet with social approval. She knew what I was talking about because she's seen me not argue with groups of guys about music when they're shouting past me at each other, as if I'm not there at all, and she knows I used to make a point of arguing anyway but grew tired of having to put so much energy into just being included.[5] Instead I mumble things to her about the utter crap they're talking, and she's come to see how many social calluses I've had to develop just as a result of knowing something about music. The thought that becoming female would mean her opinions about music wouldn't be respected anymore either is a bitter pill to swallow.

It's been a steep learning curve for her to see how sexist people can be. One of the reasons it kills me to see Betty leaning toward transition is the same reason it kills me that I have ten nieces: The world has changed some, but not enough, for women.[6] There is no doubt in my mind that Betty would not be able to be a woman in the same way that he is a man; she would lose the vibrant, outgoing personality he expresses as a guy. Even now the world doesn't prefer women who break certain rules of femininity by being too aggressive or too much the center of a conversation. Transition might mean she would have to give up big parts of who he is now in order to "pass" as female. What would happen to the Lewis Black impression? What about his longshoreman's language? His acting would have to go because his experience is in playing male leads, and he has no life experience to invest in a female character. His ability to use his resonant voice to get someone's attention from a block away would be no longer. Even the women I know who burp in public giggle or boast about it afterward; they can't just burp.

Perhaps some personality differences between men and women are innate, but perhaps not. Betty and his sister are like siblings written by Brontë or Alcott: Betty is the eldest son, the black sheep, the ne'er-do-well. His sister stayed home, and by her own admission compensated by being as good as her brother had been bad. She is active in their parents' church and has given her parents four grandchildren. But she also quit pursuing a career as a concert pianist in order to be a wife and mother, despite being as talented a musician as her brother is an actor. She's Judith Shakespeare to his William,[7] and the thought is especially sobering because once you've had William's life you could never adapt to Judith's: It would be too much to give up. But since trans women do profess a desire to be "one of the girls," they have to chip away at parts of themselves that women aren't allowed to have.

Seeing trans women learn decades of female socialization as adults is almost as painful as watching their genital surgery, except that the socialization can "invert" a lot more of them than a flap of skin.[8] When transitioning doesn't invert people's personalities, it can actually seem anomalous and awkward, as when, at a trans conference, one trans woman stood up, cleared her throat, and then proceeded to interrupt the keynote speaker with a point of disagreement. That's just not the kind of thing I'd ever expect in a lecture hall full of women, and I go back and forth between thinking that's a good thing and finding it terribly,

terribly unfair that they should be able to be women without having to be hemmed in by all the rules of being a woman. (On the other hand, female socialization seems to do great things for FTMs; so many I've met have both a masculine earnestness and the kind of sensitivity that comes from years of living as female.)

Being a woman, for me, is a remarkable thing. I look at the lives of Flannery O'Connor, Ursula LeGuin, Simone de Beauvoir, Katherine Mansfield, Edna St. Vincent Millay, Margaret Atwood, Kathy Acker, Susan Sontag, Wendy Wasserstein[9] (yes, all writers), and I know what it is to be a woman. But I wouldn't wish female socialization on my worst enemy, not even for the way rebelling against that socialization "builds character." It doesn't build character; it wears you down. The socialization girls get is to be obliging, indirect, and insecure. I'm a feminist for a reason, after all, and the main one is to show girls that how they're "supposed" to be is a plan to rob them of everything they can be. People raised to be direct, secure, and not obliging are going to have a hard time fitting themselves into that much smaller frame.

That's not to say I haven't met both women raised female and trans women who've just said, "Fuck it" to the whole thing, and who took as their archetypes Amazons or Roller Derby queens. They are occasionally apologetic about asserting their aggressive tendencies because, as I've found personally, it takes years, and a good excuse, to stop apologizing for it, and you don't quite shake the feeling that you're still "wrong." Trans people feel wrong for such a long time in their lives that their chances at throwing off those voices are less likely; they often have a greater need to feel right, to be gendered correctly, at long last.

I once told a crossdresser who was having a hard time meeting a feminine ideal that maybe, if he really wanted to pass, he should try to be a different kind of woman—a woman who drives a city bus, or who works in vice, or as an EMT. He was a little insulted by my suggestion, but I asked him if women who work in tougher jobs aren't also women. He agreed that of course they were women, but they weren't what he wanted to be, which was feminine. If women can be women without being feminine—that is, if femininity isn't actually connected to woman-ness—then why shouldn't men be feminine if they want? That left him in a pickle. Similar lines of questioning have driven Betty to distraction on occasion, so much so that after a workshop where a crossdresser asked if there were any more like me at home, Betty responded, "Be careful what you ask for." Like a lot of feminists, I'm generally suspicious of what people mean when they say they have a "woman's brain," or "feel like a woman," but transsexual people are content after they transition, feel they've fixed something, and while I'll never understand it, I've met too many people now who have given up too much to transition to doubt that what is going on is legitimate.

Unfortunately, not all feminists know as many trans women (and men) as I do, and they come to largely negative conclusions based on theory, gynecentric ideas of woman-ness, and poor research. The sins of some feminists are often held against any feminists who come in contact with the trans community, because a few feminists have said or written really nasty things.[10] They see the sexualized aspects of MTF lives and decide it's all about sex. Others see, the same way I did, the uberfemme presentation, the seeming obsession with nails and hair and makeup (what I call NTHH, for "nails, tits, hair, and heels") and dismiss it all as masquerade or dress-up, especially if that dress-up seems to be covering up otherwise masculine features and appearance. Or they see masculine behaviors or attitudes in trans women and call them "men in dresses," or worse. As a feminist, I find these attitudes a little embarrassing, since I grew up being told by feminists that *biology is not destiny.* I don't remember a caveat about that slogan not "counting" if the woman happens to be masculine.

But I can also see what these feminists are seeing. What is "the sincerest form of flattery" does look like an insult sometimes, and it offends me, too. That's one of the reasons I keep talking to MTFs about the way they present as female, because I don't appreciate—as any feminist doesn't—having it assumed that "becoming a woman" is about the trappings of it. After you've gotten to know a lot of MTFs, it's easier to understand that they are trying to learn how to look like women, and they see—just as all of us do—the commercial and fashion and media images of women, most of which are limiting and plenty of which are sexist. Most trans women I've known eventually figure it out and drop the dragon-lady nails and start wearing heels only when they need to, like the rest of us. But in the beginning stages of transition, or out crossdressing, it's as if the pendulum has to swing fully the other way from years of manly overcompensation. Dangerous jobs and driving fast or drinking a lot are the ways many MTFs try to prove to themselves and the world that they were men. Once they realize what's going on, the pendulum swings the other way. Eventually it will come to a rest, though sometimes it takes years. People who feel such intense confusion about their gender are desperately trying to find ways they can feel normal. While I understand what feminists "see" in terms of the way trans women and MTF crossdressers mock women with their own presentations of us, it's an underinformed opinion.

I've come to the conclusion that transsexualism is not going anywhere, and as long as people raised male will continue to transition later in life, the least I can do is present an image of woman-ness that isn't about the trappings. I can ask them to read feminist books. I'd rather be in the trenches helping new women become women I can like instead of standing at an arm's distance full of criticism and mockery.

They can't go back and grow up women and get the female socialization that has such a significant impact on the lives of women raised female, but the parallels trans women experience are intensely reflective of the struggles women raised female face. Growing up trans has to suck. As much as female socialization is my personal bugaboo, I still wouldn't trade growing up socialized female for growing up trans, not for a second. Trans people express such deep levels of shame and repression and outright unhappiness. My version of feminism has always been about recognizing oppression caused by gender—not just the oppression of women by men, or by patriarchy, but also the oppression of men by unfair standards of masculinity. I have always been a feminist because I believe boys do, and should, cry. I agree with the smart blogger who wrote, "Feminism has never been at its best or strongest when saying 'keep out' to oppressed minorities."[11] When it comes to transness, feminism is hitting a very low mark, indeed.

If I didn't think my husband would actually become a woman, I wouldn't be having half as hard a time with this. Then again, I don't think I'd be asking him to be very careful about deciding to transition if I believed he were a woman already. For a gender feminist such as myself, whether or not someone is a woman on the chromosomal level is hardly important, because living in the world as a woman is the defining characteristic of woman-ness. Living as a woman may be what "makes" you a woman. Maybe all the trans women who feminists such as Germaine Greer and Janice Raymond have met are more recently transitioned; maybe the ones who don't pass as well are the ones who would seek out that kind of validation. Trans women need a while to experience sexism and patriarchy firsthand, and like women raised female, often experience something that triggers their need to get a feminist education. Others are more like feminine gay men who grow up relating more to women. One trans woman told me that her mother, at the end of her rope, had told her father that she was leaving. Her father, pulling aside his young son and explaining the finer points of male privilege, reassured the boy, saying, "Don't worry, she'll be back because she has no place to go." That child got a first-row seat into patriarchy, and "he" became a feminist long before she transitioned.

Transitioning brings up more questions than it answers. When transsexual women express the need or desire to transition, many of them are not aware that they're going to have to figure out what kind of woman they are. They are sure they are not men, don't feel comfortable as men, don't fit in as men, but their desire to be women can eclipse the many ways to be a woman, and very few of them have anything to do with how women look. But they do want to fit in. "Fitting in" as a woman, and being considered "one of the girls," is variable and iffy even for women born female. Butch women get chased out of bathrooms when people think they're men.[12] I've certainly been in situations where I feel as if I don't belong and where I'm not accepted, and I used to get funny looks in bathrooms, too. I've been made to feel as if I didn't count unless I was a certain kind of woman, which left me to go find other spaces where I did count and where I did fit in. Just think about the way Anne Coulter gets accused of supposedly having been a man by the people who hate her and her aggressive politics.[13]

What I ask Betty regularly is whether she wants to be "one of the girls" shopping for shoes, or "one of the girls" at a feminist rally, or "one of the girls" buying graphic novels in a sci-fi shop. We went to see the first screenings of all three Lord of the Rings movies, for instance, where the crowd was predominantly male and the women all seemed a lot like me—certainly a lot more like me than a group of women whom I might have found at a screening of *The Sisterhood of the Traveling Pants*.[14] Granted, categories overlap. Some women in one group will fit just as easily into another: I might run into the women I saw at the *Lord of the Rings* screening at a rally, or in the medieval section of the Met, or buying clothes in the downtown boutiques of the East Village. Different groups of women have different standards for membership, and even different beauty standards. What I need Betty to be is the kind of woman I would go with to see the first screening of *Lord of the Rings*, the kind of woman who recommends novels such as *Neuromancer*, who loves The Smiths and yes, who does Lewis Black impersonations at parties. If she can keep all of that, I might be able to buy that "being the same person inside" line. And she has to figure out how to look like the person who likes that stuff, too. When she tells me that I'm the girl she always wanted to meet, I ask her to try to be more like the kind of girl that the girl she always wanted to meet wants to meet. She needs to figure out how to be the kind of girl she might have been, not the girl she wanted to be. That girl is way too gendered for me, and I suspect the girl she might have been won't be.

My friend Peter once told me a story about a friend of his who insisted on playing with female cats more gently than he did with male cats, and we had a good laugh over that because anyone who has ever known a female cat knows they are no less ferocious than the males. We extend our own sense of gender roles even to animals and objects, where it's often obviously inaccurate, but that's how pervasive the need is. Female lions do all the hunting and killing for the pride, as do a lot of other female animals, yet this guy, raised in the human world, had to be gentle with an animal whose playtime is all practice for killing. I'm going to hope that he'd realize the error of his ways if he were around one of the big female cats. I'm just glad I'm not that guy's girlfriend or his boss.

Some people really do give everything in their world a gender, including living things and inanimate objects. Nouns are gendered, after all, in most Romance languages.[15] One transsexual woman told me she assigns everything a gender, even numbers and the letters of the alphabet and lampposts and mailboxes. That completely baffled me, the same way it baffled me that my grandmother always used to refer to all cats as she and all dogs as he. She knew that was an illogical thing to do, but she insisted. But it still bothers me that once we gender a thing (or a person), we have all these rules about how that thing is supposed to behave as a result. A chair may be female in French, but that doesn't imply that all chairs should be pretty or soft. In grammar, it's really just a way of dividing up nouns, and it otherwise doesn't mean anything about the nature of the thing being named. But when we divide human beings by gender, it comes with all these expectations that seem about as silly as expecting all chairs to be pretty and soft, or saying a chair that isn't pretty and soft isn't a chair.

This world of seeing everything as male or female is new to me. When I was a tomboy I wasn't doing "boyish" things; I was doing what I liked to do, what made me feel good. It never occurred to me to think of carrying my wallet in my back pocket as a masculine thing to do; I just didn't like purses and tended to lose bags, so I bought small wallets—in men's departments and in women's. I knew that other women in my life carried purses, but I didn't think I was masculine for not carrying one. The first time I felt awkward about not carrying a purse was in a Baby Gap, buying a present for friends. I was standing in line in tandem with a woman at another register; when she pulled out her purse, I reached for my back pocket and experienced a sudden pang of wrongness. No doubt my experience was exacerbated by its being a Baby Gap store, since I don't want children, either, which is another reminder that how I am is gendered even if I've never seen it that way.

I miss living in a gender-free or gender-neutral world, which is what mine was before I met Betty. The problem is that it's difficult to talk about gender without going on assumptions, and no matter how much it chafes me to call any physical or aggressive play on the part of a girl "boyish," other people will see it that way. To me, physical and aggressive play is neither boyish nor girlish—it's what kids do because they're growing and they have landfills of energy. I've seen girls steal bases and knock over goalies and dislocate their shoulders climbing monkey bars. I've seen them play with Barbies and nurse dolls back to health, too. We don't see boys choose dolls[16] over baseball because there is absolutely no positive reinforcement if they do, and even if they do get it from their liberal parents, it's not going to be consistent from everyone else in the world. We simply haven't removed enough obstacles to see how people might naturally express their gender.

Having only two boxes in which to place the numerous traits and habits and sensibilities and types of bodies restricts who we allow ourselves to be. I'd prefer more genders, or at the very least something less like a wall and more like a membrane between the categories. I suspect that the way so-called "innate" traits seem to cleave to gender may turn out to be more a funhouse mirror's reflection of the biology than an accurate reflection, because it's apparent throughout history that our biases are very firmly entrenched. We've always thought we were being objective about gender, and we've always been wrong. I don't see any evidence that we've managed it this time around, either. As a culture, we pretend that sexism is no longer an issue and that social inequities based on gender are in our past, and as a result some people defend the current system—one that is far from free of discrimination. As a feminist I'm suspicious of research that posits innate differences because sexist apologists would prefer it that way; after all, if we found that sex differences are innate we could feel relieved of the pressure of making sure women have equal representation and opportunity. As long as there are inequities in the way men and women are treated, I fear, one will always be considered better than the other, and the chasm between Mars and Venus will persist.

While it would be lovely to have three or eight or four hundred genders, the man on the street will tell you there are only two. I'd love it if we lived in a world where people who don't fit into "man" and "woman" very tidily weren't considered weird, scary, and duplicitous. But we don't live in that world, and glossing over the ways gender plays out on the ground prevents people from acknowledging how hard it is to live in the world as gender variant. It belittles the struggles trans people and tomboys and sissies go through. Right now it's as if everyone were expected to use one hand or the other but not both. We should at least have the freedom to pick which hand if we're forced to use only one, or at least be allowed to switch off occasionally, and some of us are going to continue using both hands, no matter how much we're told it's unseemly to do so or how much it makes us suspect.

The feeling that I am supportive of Betty's transness only

for the sake of the man I met creeps up on me now and again. Betty worries that out of love for him I "put up" with her. If she gets to the point where she has no male left for me to connect to, there is a chance I will wake up one day and realize I am not in love with and feel no loyalty toward her. This is why when a trans person uses that "but I'm the same person" argument, I want to say, "Well, I sure as hell hope not," because we had better not be dealing with all this crap without its effecting any real change. That's the point, that the trans person's change will be enough to make living in the world easier and more comfortable for him, whether that's done through crossdressing or transition.

Betty knows, at the very least, that transitioning will not necessarily help her feel more normal, that she will not be able to believe she is no longer trans afterward. Living with someone who looks as if she's transitioning and seems to want to transition but isn't transitioning is a little like living with post-traumatic stress disorder, feeling as if every bit of you is hair-triggered, waiting for the announcement, waiting for the crisis. Walking around like an adrenalized superpower is not what human beings were meant to do, and being in a marriage that poses that "fight or flight" question every day is not conducive to long-term happiness. It's not even conducive to a more Buddhist "in the present moment" kind of happiness. It is nothing: a void, waiting to be filled.

You can't build a future on a void, and you can't tell someone you love her when you wonder if you'll still be able to in the next year or ten.

There's a Rufus Wainwright song called "Low Grade Happiness"[17] in which he prays, in the song, for the ability to stay in love. It's reassuring to know that my question is more a broad-reaching, romantic concern—that it's not just mine. I wonder if others know why they're waiting to find out. I know. It seems as if my husband is willing himself to become a woman, that he'd like to be able to live as one, that he'd like to make physical changes that would enable him to be accepted as one socially. Others maybe worry for completely different reasons, if they worry that their passion will dry up, that their taste will change. I don't worry about that. I worry about my tastes not changing, or not changing fast enough, if my husband becomes a woman. I worry about not feeling desire for breasts that might appear or feeling disgust at seeing those straight boyish hips become rounded with fat. I worry that his ass, which I find the most perfect ass ever, will someday be unrecognizable to me.

Maybe for other people, time will do that to a body they love. Betty jokes about her transition's going at "glacier speed" and wonders whether she can transition so slowly that her transformation will seem as if only time is turning her into a woman, and not sheer will or actual hormones. Tiny, incremental change seems so much less drastic, so much more organic, and for me, so much easier to roll with. There is nothing selfish about wanting to be whole. There is nothing wrong, either, with self-expression. The problem with living with transsexualism is that the trans person so often hopes and more rarely expects the rest of the people in his or her life to be okay with it, to accept the new self as having been the only self all along. But partners, friends, and family really liked the old "self." We fell in love with the old self. We made a commitment to the old self. We don't like being told that there's a (wo)man behind the curtain, because we feel foolish, tricked, and stupid for having believed the lie or for not having seen before what we know now.

The only way I can live with Betty's not transitioning for my sake is to realize that it is, ultimately, her decision. She could gamble and lose. She could gamble and win. But it's her decision. Mine is to stay, or to go, to be generous or vindictive. But I can't change what I've been handed. Neither can she. Most days, that's what helps us: knowing that neither of us wanted this, that both of us would rather have it otherwise, and that all we can do, at the end of the day, is try to find our love in the shared difficulty of knowing we have to deal with this. But we have our bad days, too.

The most fundamental problem for partners who didn't know about their spouses' gender issues or desire to transition before marriage is that there is no one to blame. Most partners will, rightly or wrongly, blame their trans spouse, because the whole idea of "I knew but I didn't really know" just doesn't make any goddamned sense to anyone who hasn't been inside the brain of someone who has lived it.

The sense of betrayal is huge but not even half so huge as the sense that the trans person knew something, anything, the whisper of a hint of an idea, that there might have been a problem all along, but went ahead and fell in love and got married before resolving it. No way can anyone apologize for completely disrupting and in some cases ruining someone else's life; there is no way to make up for it, to fix it, to take back the love and optimism that have been crushed. I'm not surprised that some women go ballistic, or that others are out for revenge, because there is that very real sense that partners have that "you knew this was a possibility and yet you went ahead with our relationship *anyway?*" And that's exactly what it feels like, because there is no way to comprehend what "I knew but I didn't really know" means. None. It means nothing, ultimately, to anyone but the trans person.

But even if it were comprehensible, when you're standing there with your life shattered because of what your partner didn't know, chose not to know, did not have the courage to deal with before meeting you, the only person who looks responsible is the one who's trans. As the partner you resent him for not saying up front, "After we're married for x years, and we've merged our lives in inseparable ways, after you've hitched your wagon to my star, I will become a woman, and there's not a goddamn thing you or I or anyone else will be able to do about it, and I won't have any money after transition to even pay you for your heartbreak, and not only that, but I'll resent you for not loving the person I've known myself to be all the while even though I will not resemble, in any way, shape, or form, the person you married anymore at all." There is almost no way for the partner not to feel used, above and beyond everything else she feels. In my cynical moments, I've thought that the trans person ought to have something on hand to offer as a consolation prize. All too often, instead, I've heard the trans person rage about the wife's anger or have difficulty understanding why she went ballistic or why she couldn't or wouldn't try to love a woman. They object that they've "always been the same person" inside and mention the "in sickness and in health" clause of most marriage vows.

The real kicker is when they ask why a change of gender should be such a big deal to anyone, even though they're turning their entire lives upside down and emptying their 401k for that same change of gender that shouldn't be a big deal to a wife. One friend explained that of course her gender was important to her, but she still couldn't imagine why it would be important to anyone else. Then she asserted she'd be a-okay with it if her female partner became male. In her case, it's probably true, but I thought I would have been a-okay with Betty's transitioning too.

It's not just the overall change that makes women angry. It's not just that transition uses up the family resources, and it's not just the confusion and fear wrought by the issues of identity and sexuality. It's having your former husband tell you she can't put up bookshelves because she might break a nail while the unspoken assumption is that it's okay for the woman raised female to put them up. The trans person absconds from the roles they've both been playing without acknowledging that the rules have changed. Wives implode because their partners express such a sheer lack of comprehension that a change of gender should upset someone so much. In a nutshell, it's the tragically funny way that male privilege (or what a friend of mine calls "male autism") intersects with notions of woman-ness that makes wives hell-bent on revenge. I'm lucky because Betty's gender issues upset her so much that she doesn't have a hard time appreciating why they might upset me, too. But neither of us has a hard time understanding the desire for revenge, either. I'm not a vengeful person, but in this case I wholly understand wanting that pound of flesh, and in the case of some wives, even being willing to take it. I wish I didn't. I wish I could say I find that desire totally incomprehensible. But unfortunately I understand it perfectly well and have gone through my mind, many times, for something, anything, that Betty could do that would make me feel compensated for the sheer, unrivaled disappointment I feel some days.

Nothing, nothing at all, could ever make up for the feeling that the friendship and love I believed in—that we both put all our effort into building, that brought me solace in a world that is too frequently remorseless—was a sham, a kind of way station or second womb that Betty hid in while delaying the inevitable. It feels as if she built a fort while I built a home.

When the wife stops screaming and crying, when she realizes the pointlessness of getting the pound of flesh, she realizes that she is alone, her life in tatters, and that she and she alone will be able to sew it back together. As C. S. Lewis wisely wrote in *The Silver Chair,* "Crying is all right in its way while it lasts. But you have to stop sooner or later and then you still have to decide what to do."[18]

What is there to do? She can choose to see that the connection between her and her partner gave him the courage to face one hell of an evil dragon, and that that in itself is inestimable and invaluable. She can realize that there is a tenacity in her that is strong in ways she's never given herself credit for, strong with hundreds of years of sheer, bone-splitting endurance. She can do for herself what she did for her spouse and re-create her own life in ways that would make her happier. She can give birth to herself fully grown, to a self that she never gave a chance because she didn't think she had it in her. She can recognize that she is ultimately a more powerful person than she ever knew, and that she can use that power badly or well. She can realize that she may as well take the companionship her partner has offered, even if it has taken a new form, just for the sake of the help and the humor and the conversation and the shared grief that only they can understand.

A wife can just leave, too. Sometimes it's the best thing for her to do. Partners who separate from transitioning husbands can have a life afterward; Katie, who in Chapter 5 of *My Husband Betty* tells the story of how her crossdressing husband started taking steps toward becoming a woman, which ultimately led to the end of their marriage, has since gotten remarried and is very, very happy. But no matter what path a wife chooses, the desire for revenge, or justice, will ultimately only destroy her, and one way or another, she has to find a way not to give in to it.

My personal goal is to be able to look at our wedding photos after Betty transitions and still be able to say, "That was the beginning of the rest of my life." When I get to the point where I would marry Betty if I met her tomorrow, and marry her with the same surety with which I married her male self five years ago, I will be ready for her to transition. I probably won't ever know that, but I also don't know whether I would make it through transition with her. That's all a matter of considering a kind of risk that neither of us is willing to take right now.

Too often, I've tried to predict the future. I've tried to understand "transsexualism" as if it were a monolithic thing, but it's very subjective, and it's described in very different ways by good writers who happen to be transsexual. Jenny Boylan calls it "a knife wound"; Dallas Denny describes it as a pebble in her shoe.[19] Another friend once remarked glibly that for her it was just like wearing the wrong shoes, so she got new ones. So which is it? I can't figure out how all of these can be true, or which is most accurate in describing Betty's feelings about her own transness. Clearly, different people experience transness differently, and the same person may experience it in different ways at different times in his or her life. The standard notion of a "man trapped in a woman's body/woman trapped in a man's body" strikes me as the most simplistic explanation ever. That shorthand might be useful for people who need to know only a little, just in case their good manners fail them and they decide to treat a trans person they work with like a nonentity. People who don't have a personal relationship with someone trans don't need to know much more than "you knew her as Laura, and now you can call him Larry" and move on. But people have all sorts of moral indignations and crazy beliefs that what they think about something gives them the right to treat other people like crap. But in a world where it seems better to self-righteous types to let foster children go homeless than to let gay people give them loving homes, I really shouldn't be that surprised.

Still, people do think they need to know what causes transsexualism—what it is, whether there's a genetic determination or a hormonal one, whether trans people are just messed up. I've always been partial to Dr. Harry Benjamin's[20] take on it; he didn't know the cause, but he figured out that the brain and the body didn't always match, even if he didn't know why. Looking a little into the way trans people had already been treated by previous psychiatrists, he realized that the only way to ease their suffering was to change their bodies, since decades of trying to change their brains hadn't worked. That was all. There is something practical-minded and humanitarian in his thinking that people could learn a lot from, and not just medical professionals who deal with trans people.

What we do know is that there are people who detransition[21] after realizing for whatever reason that their sense of being "trapped in the wrong body" wasn't totally accurate after all. I want to know how those people experienced their transness, if they were guilty of simply being too repressed as men and thought the only door out of that was marked WOMAN. I don't know what they do after they realize they weren't good at being men but can't live as women. Some of them retransition later. But my guess these days is that many people who identify as trans are in that middle group. They are the ones who aren't really aren't male *or* female, or they are fully male *and* female. Kate Bornstein had to transition to figure that out, and she now sees the way trans people identify as MTF or FTM (that is, as still defining themselves as gendered according to M and F) as a failure of imagination.[22] Some trans people identify as neither/nor, and others live dually gendered lives. The rough part is that there's not much room in the world for those who would live in the middle, whether they're there because that's what feels right or because they're trying to honor the commitments they made before the gender issues made themselves known.

It's not as if I don't have enough to think about if Betty doesn't transition; there's a lot more to consider if she continues to live with a male self and a female self, or as a neither/nor self. There will always be days she comes home exhausted from having heard the string of "ma'am . . . uh . . . sir" all day from deli clerks and baristas. She's not sure if she should be in the men's or women's section of our favorite spa, and we're not sure we should ask, either, for fear she'll be put in the men's section on a day when she just doesn't pass for a man. We will always have to let people know that when she has breasts she should be referred to as Betty and that she is a "her" and not a "him." We will continue to wonder if there is a gender-neutral name she might use that would suit all of her, or whether a gender-neutral name might cause more problems than it solves. We wonder if we will ever feel that we can "settle down" the way people do when they have children and move to the suburbs. And though we're sure we want neither suburbs nor children, we would like that sense of taking your shoes off at the end of a day that we imagine the folks who have those things feel. We will have to figure out if we'll ever feel wholly at home again in places outside of close family and friends or queer spaces; we'll have to figure out how to deal with being who we are in "regular" bars, whether we'll want to be visible as a lesbian couple or whether we'll pass as friends in public spaces and then deal with guys hitting on one or the other or both of us all night.

We took a cab home not long ago with a friend of ours who is queer, and we happened to get a famous cabbie who runs a matchmaking service out of his cab. He told us uncommon love stories about people he had introduced to each other; in one case, an Irishman had told the cabbie he missed home and wanted a girlfriend. A week later, an Irishwoman from the same part of the country as the guy was in his cab; he gave the woman the man's number, and several months later they called him to tell him they were getting married. I wanted so much to share our fantastic love story, but I sat there mum until he eventually asked, "Do you all have boyfriends? Husbands?" and I stammered. Our friend piped up, "Some of us have girlfriends!" quite happily, and with pride, and I was still at a complete loss for words. Betty was sitting next to me, and of course I could have said I had a husband (without pointing out that he was the woman sitting in the cab next to me), but I also wanted to put my arm around Betty and just say, "Yes, her." Or "Yes, him." Or . . . and that was the problem. I don't know how to answer simple questions anymore. Betty said, "I'm happily married, too," but of course that implied she was married to a man, which left me with fewer possibilities. I wanted to add that she was happily married to me, but I didn't because I started worrying about whether saying that might out her and whether he'd assume we'd gotten married in Massachusetts, and then I started getting angry that people are so upset by the idea of same-sex marriage and how idiotic it is that I've had to spend time educating people in the trans community that the legalization of same-sex marriage will benefit not just gays and lesbians, but trans people too. I didn't answer because I didn't have an answer that wasn't a dissertation.

I miss knowing answers to simple questions about my life and my identity. I miss having people assume there's nothing interesting about our sex life. I miss the days when people didn't ask about what genitals my partner had. I miss not worrying that I'm going to do, say, or actually be something inappropriate. I miss not making people uncomfortable when I kiss the person I love. I miss being able to say, "This is my husband," and having people be impressed. It always seemed such a victory to me, on behalf of tomboys everywhere, that a not-skinny, too-smart-for-her-own-good, aggro punk rocker of a girl married a talented, handsome, charming man.

But of course I didn't, not really. That was all just an illusion.

Many years ago a gay friend of mine and I were talking about where we might live if not in New York City. New Yorkers are like that; even those who have grown up elsewhere, sometimes especially those who have grown up elsewhere, can't fathom living anywhere else. But he mentioned how, as a gay man who wanted to date openly, he would be comfortable only in maybe six other places: Austin, San Francisco, Chicago, Atlanta, D.C., plus a handful of small university towns scattered across the country. Now, when I plan for Betty's and my future together,

I remember the places my friend listed, the unflinching quality in his voice when he said he could live only in *maybe* six other places, and I remind myself that I have to think like that now, too. The more queer we look, the fewer places we can live. We are thankful for New York every day, that there is at least somewhere we can be who we are, where people know that everyone's a little different. We are thankful that bookstores have gay and lesbian sections that aren't always hidden in the back, and that you do see people reading Judith Butler[23] books on the F train. I am personally thankful that when I ask a clerk at a lingerie store if the shop serves trans folk, and she answers simply, "We'd love to but we only have dressing rooms for women," that there is a way to help the store become trans friendly, so the next time someone calls she will say yes instead.

I would be more thankful if people didn't think our marriage shouldn't be legal if Betty transitions. I'd be a lot happier if same sex-marriages were legal so I wouldn't have to worry about it. I'd be a lot happier if there were no gender markers on driver's licenses and other ID cards,[24] and I'd be happy if charisma and confidence didn't seem a requirement for getting by in the world as trans. Even shyness can be a downfall; Betty often has no problem using her male ID at airports because while the guard is looking at it, she chimes in, "I've changed a lot since this picture was taken." I would be very pleased if Betty didn't feel so at odds with the world when she gets called "ma'am" (when he thinks he's presenting as male), or when she gets called "sir" (when she thinks she's passing as female).

I'd also be happier if more people knew about transness, because so many trans people are living visible lives. I could worry less if some heterosexual men didn't think that beating up effeminate men was acceptable, and if men who respond to finding out a woman they are attracted to has a penis didn't think it was okay to hurt her. I'd be relieved if the guys who've committed atrocious violence against trans people spent the rest of their lives in jail. I'd be relieved if all the difficulties trans people face weren't exacerbated by class and race, and I'd be thrilled if journalists could get pronouns right and not insist on mentioning what gender the murder victim "really" was.[25]

Our response to Betty's transness has been to make lemons from lemonade. Our activism has actually been what therapists might call a "positive coping strategy," the same way art can be. When people have asked us why on earth we put ourselves out there the way we do, our answer has always been, "Because we can and others can't." We became Helen and Betty because we were being blackmailed a long time ago, an experience that planted a seed in us to never allow anyone to hurt us in that way again. Initially, we started using these names to avoid that person. We never imagined that names forged as a result of secrecy, the closet, and blackmail would become the names that would carry us into the light, into activism and education, names that would carry us into whole new selves. They say that when a door closes, somewhere a window opens. Apparently, they're right.

betty's afterword.

"So . . . yeah. That's all true."
—Eddie Izzard

I'm tempted to say that it isn't really me Helen describes in this book. But she mentioned the Britney Spears phase, and if she's going to tell you about that, well then, all bets are off: She's going to tell you everything.

For the record, it's all true.

I do, however, have an opportunity to tell you a few things. So, here goes:

I'm trans. Not a transsexual or a transvestite, a crossdresser, genderqueer, drag queen, whatever. Just trans. Although I am reflected in any number of those monikers, I don't want to be known as any of them. Trans will do, thank you.

I don't like the labels. They imply hierarchies and theories and formulations and lions and tigers and bears, oh my! I'm not saying they aren't necessary; I'm just saying I don't like them, and if I have to live in a world that considers labels important, then I want to be "trans." It'd be even better if people thought of me as a person and we could go from there.

However, I look more and more like someone who could be female and that mucks up the whole "person" thing. Because I'm not a woman (I don't have enough hubris to claim that) and people don't like blurriness and I am nothing if not blurry these days. I still have moments when I look in the mirror and think, *Wow. You really don't look like you used to.*

I walked into a meeting with Helen recently and someone we both know said, "Betty, I didn't recognize you. I thought you were a woman," when she first saw me. She was looking for "Betty," and all she saw was "some woman" with Helen, instead. She meant I didn't look trans, and that made what I see in the mirror more real. It was a backhanded compliment, of course, but the nut of it really struck me. More and more, I really do look like a woman.

Jeebus, does Helen know this?

Yes, she does.

It's odd, this life of ours, and I'm terribly aware of my culpability in said oddness. It is our life, though, and there is no one on the face of this earth that I'd rather be with than Helen. She really is the girl I always wanted to meet. And wouldn't you know it? I met her . . . and she liked me back. And we got married. And I feel like a lottery winner. I'm amazed that she feels even remotely the same about me—the guy who looks like a woman a lot these days. But she does.

I'd rather remain blurry if blurry means walking along the beach with her rather than being some woman sitting in the sand, alone. I wish I could guarantee that I won't, someday, tell her that I have to live my life fully and 100 percent as a woman. But I can't: Such is being trans. But I'm hoping for the beach, with Helen, regardless. If that sounds starry-eyed and impractical, I don't care. That's how I feel.

It makes Helen uncomfortable when I say such things. She's afraid she'll come across as some kind of gatekeeper, or that she's "holding me back." Bullshit. I'm a grownup, and I make my own choices. I'm not going to knowingly jeopardize the single best thing to ever happen to me.

Don't get me wrong. I don't have my head in the sand around my trans stuff. I can't. It won't let me. The dysphoria is real. I feel more comfortable in this world being thought of as female, and I've felt this way since I can remember, but I refuse to be a slave to something I didn't ask for. I'll deal with it the best I can and get on with my day.

I wish that I had something more pithy or profound to say, something that might be a balm to some hurting soul, because I've met so many hurting souls. I don't have a balm, or a secret, or a magic wand. But here at the end, I can say that while love won't "cure" me, it gives me a reason to wake up each day. That I can kiss Helen before leaving for work and know that I'm coming home to kiss her yet again is the coolest thing I've ever known. And I won't willingly or knowingly throw that away.

So, yeah. That's true too.

notes.

one

boy meets girl.

1. Eowyn is the name of the human heroine in *The Lord of the Rings;* Arwen and Galadriel are both Elven women.

2. The original quote is actually by St. Cyril of Jerusalem, who said: "The dragon sits by the side of the road, watching those who pass. Beware lest he devour you. We go to the Father of Souls, but it is necessary to pass by the dragon." What Flannery O'Connor said was her own take on that dragon: "No matter what form the dragon may take, it is of this mysterious passage past him, or into his jaws, that stories of any depth will always be concerned to tell, and this being the case, it requires considerable courage at any time, in any country, not to turn away from the storyteller."

3. Some of our story is told in *My Husband Betty,* such as why I named her Betty in the first place.

4. I will refer to my husband as both she and he, to him or to her. The pronouns only

begin to demonstrate the confusion that living with someone trans might bring, but eventually you get used to it. Please read the author's note: on language, & pronouns, & taxonomy (page 17) for more language/terminology issues.

5. Dagny Taggart is the steel-nerved heroine of Ayn Rand's ode to capitalism, *Atlas Shrugged*. She is a railroad baron, the owner of the fictional Taggart Transcontinental, a captain of industry. She is a very powerful woman, who appreciates only other powerful people and especially very powerful men.

6. "Pants" is actually a term invented by the fashion industry to sell women on wearing them. They called women's trousers "pants" to demasculinize them, and it worked. That said, when I talk about wearing pants, I'm just using common American parlance, because in fact I often wear (men's) trousers— usually vintage.

7. Gregory Hemingway, the author Ernest Hemingway's son, used the names Gloria or Vanessa when he presented as female. He had one breast implanted and also underwent SRS (sex reassignment surgery, or genital surgery), even though he still appeared in public as male. Most trans people would assume he was trans and either had intense body dysphoria (i.e., the need to change his physical body from male to female) or couldn't transition socially for personal reasons. As the unconfirmed story of Larry (occasionally Laurenca, or Lara) Wachowski, of *Matrix* fame, points out, being both trans and famous can be very, very complicated. Betty happens to think Michael Jackson is trans, too, but couldn't ever give up being "Michael Jackson" and so is stuck between genders. Transness and fame don't seem to be very good bedfellows, and the tabloids don't present these issues sympathetically at all, instead harping on the "freakiness" or "perversion" of the people involved.

8. There are no good statistics on nearly anything trans, much less how often trans couples stay together. But from where I'm sitting, it doesn't look good. It's gotten so common for couples we meet to break up when transition happens that I've come to feel gun-shy about befriending female partners of trans people, as after the breakup they tend to be the ones who leave the trans community, and thus, our lives.

9. For trans people, family law issues such as divorce and child custody are a minefield. Richard Juang of National Center for Transgender Equality (NCTE) states: "Transgender people have been particularly hard-hit in cases concerning marriage and family law. Going to the courts is risky in marriage and family law cases, even if a person believes that he or she has a strong case. Trans people have lost cases because of the continuing presence of strong biases or irrational and incorrect beliefs against trans people that have been eroded in other areas of law" (from private correspondence). For more information, check Taylor Flynn's essay in the book *Transgender Rights,* plus the websites of organizations such as NCTE, www.nctequality. org; SRLP (the Sylvia Rivera Law Project), www.srlp.org; The Transgender Law Center, www.transgenderlawcenter.org; Gay and Lesbian Advocates and Defenders, www.glad.org; Lambda Legal, www.lambdalegal.org; National Center for Lesbian Rights, www.nclrights.org; and the Transgender Law and Policy Institute, www.transgenderlaw.org.

10. Many men see feminism as having improved women's lives but not having changed men's much at all; where women gained freedom and status, men often saw gender fluidity as a loss of manhood and privilege. Culturally that indicates our bias against femininity; for a woman to gain masculinity is empowering, but for a man to gain femininity is almost always seen as a loss. But of course in either case there are restrictions and exceptions.

11. Harvard president Larry Summers stated publicly that the probable reason for the lack of women in science is an innate lack in women, not institutionalized discrimination and sexism. Ben Barres, a scientist and FTM trans person, rebuts Summers's thesis in an article he wrote for the journal *Nature* (Vol. 442, No. 7099, 133–136) and submits a few ideas for encouraging diversity in science.

12. PCOS is also known as Stein-Leventhal syndrome. It's an endocrine disorder that affects 5–10 percent of women and occurs among all races and nationalities. It is a leading cause of infertility. The symptoms and severity of the syndrome vary greatly among women, with symptoms such as:

- irregular or absent periods,
- infertility,
- elevated blood androgens (testosterone and others),
- obesity,
- acne,
- male pattern balding,
- patches of skin discoloration/darkening,
- sleep apnea,
- prolonged or extreme symptoms of PMS (bloating, etc.),
- insulin resistance.

Yes, it's a real blast. More important, many women who have it don't know they have it or go untreated until and unless they are trying to get pregnant and can't. For more information and resources, check www.pcosupport.org and www.soulcysters.com.

13. Neil Gaiman's The Sandman is a collection of comics (ahem, graphic novels), ten in all, about a fictional set of siblings called The Endless. The books are probably best known in the trans universe for an empathetic portrayal of an MTF in *Book 5: A Game of You*.

14. The Borg is a race of cyborgs in the *Star Trek* fictional universe. Being "assimiliated by the Borg" means losing all individual thought and identity; they are a hive mind, or a collective, or the ultimate in communism— depending on how you interpret the idea.

15. Betty preferred the term "transvestite" to "crossdresser," though she's really never preferred to identify as anything in particular, being naturally not a "joiner" and despising labels. Still, there are specific reasons she preferred transvestite to crossdresser, all of which are in the glossary of *My Husband Betty*.

16. Cher was born Cherilyn Sarkisian, Sting as Gordon Sumner, Jon Stewart as Jon Leibowitz, and Mark Twain was christened Samuel Clemens.

17. She is not typical of trans people in this respect; most have a pronoun of

preference, and Betty in her heart of hearts prefers "she." She's just the type who'd rather earn it than insist, and she understands that those who have known her as male her whole life tend to continue to see her male self, no matter how pretty she gets.

two
confessions of a grown-up tomboy.

1. More on what parts are required to be sexed as female in Chapter 4.

2. In Kate Bornstein's *My Gender Workbook: How to Become a Real Man, a Real Woman, the Real You, or Something Else Entirely.*

3. Although it horrifies me somewhat that people may not know anymore who Adam Ant is, in the eighties he was a pop star who had a hit with "Goody Two Shoes" and who was the lead of his band Adam and the Ants before that, which was a huge hit in most of the world and an underground one in the United States. He often showed up in those "best-looking" lists back then, and he wore pounds of makeup but also leather trousers and in that sense was a descendent of a long line of musicians who played with gender. His last hit was with "Wonderful," released in 1995. *Stand & Deliver: The Autobiography* was published in 2006, and details both his fame and his lifelong struggle with manic depression.

4. In a film called *Girl Wrestler* (directed by Diane Zander), which aired on PBS, the girl wrestler in question explains that boys would often quit wrestling altogether after she beat them. She gave up wrestling because at high school age she was prohibited from wrestling with boys by the state of Texas, and there were no other girls to wrestle with. For more, www.pbs.org/independentlens /girlwrestler/film.html.

5. I was the youngest of six, and none of my siblings had shown a calling to the priesthood, and anyone with a Catholic mom knows nearly all Catholic moms want a child who is a priest. I was an excellent Sunday school student and thought I'd be a shoo-in. Not very surprisingly, my good relationship with the church came to a pretty abrupt halt after I learned the church's sexist policies. While I know my mother would have still loved a nun in the family, I wasn't

really hip to being "second class," though I have found that nuns, when they are radical and kind, are often more radical and more kind than most people. For the record, our current pope—whom I prefer to call Pope Maledict—is not doing women any favors. His antiwoman policies are turning off even committed Catholic women. His stances on homosexuality, birth control, and AIDS are equally deplorable.

6. That Annie Lennox wasn't a lesbian was important only in the sense that a lot of women who wear suits are, and trying to find a reflection of a heterosexual woman who was masculine was nearly impossible—actually, it still is. I wanted a role model who was "like me" and probably also to quell my own confusion about my sexual orientation. That is, I used her as a kind of diagnostic tool; she was "proof" that not only lesbians could be masculine women. Adam Ant and Nick Rhodes are both hetero, too. More on the intersections of gender variance and sexual orientation in Chapter 4.

7. The national average is 1 in 8; for FTMs it's 1 in 4. See A. H. Balen et al. (1993). "Polycystic Ovaries Are a Common Finding in Untreated Female-to-Male Transsexuals." *Clinical Endocrinology* 38 (3), 325–329. Thanks to gender.org for the information: www.gender.org/resources/dge/gea02005.pdf.

8. I'm also halfway convinced that because they don't grow up perceived as women, they don't know what being uberfeminine can mean in terms of the way people treat you. More than one crossdresser and trans woman has had her eyes opened by the first time she experienced sexual harassment or condescension; also, because they're not socialized female and don't first experience harassment or the objectification of their bodies at young, impressionable ages, they have better life skills to deal with those occurrences when they do happen. Many also may understand intellectually what harassment or sexism is like, but experiencing it emotionally can be a whole different story.

9. Margaret Atwood's novel *Cat's Eye* is about the cruelty of girls directed at other girls, and her novel *The Robber Bride* is about the cruelty of adult women directed at other adult women. Tina Fey, queen of geek chic, wrote the movie *Mean Girls*.

10. Everyone except for John Irving, who portrays a couple in *A Prayer for Owen Meany* who are married, heterosexual, but who seem to have reversed gender roles (and, if I remember correctly, are always going on about it). His latest novel, *Until I Find You*, involves crossdressing.

11. The assumption in much research about tomboys is that the most likely scenario is that they either grow up to be lesbians, or, if they're heterosexual, tomboyism was only a "phase" in which they learned more about who they were and what they liked but eventually gave up. None of the research seems to credit heterosexual tomboys with having to give up being visibly tomboy because they otherwise won't or can't date. As Judith Halberstam says in her book *Female Masculinity:* "I have no doubt that heterosexual female masculinity menaces gender conformity in its own way, but all too often it represents an acceptable degree of female masculinity as compared to the excessive masculinity of the dyke." While what she's saying is true in the larger (cultural) context, dyke female masculinity is in some ways more acceptable within lesbian culture than heterosexual female masculinity is in the het world. The grass is always greener, I suppose. Life is not easy for a masculine lesbian, by any stretch, but I'm a little tired of having my own struggles fitting in as a masculine woman dismissed because I'm het.

12. "Genderqueer" is a term used by people who are intentionally subverting the binary, who choose not to use "he" or "she" or use one when their appearance is to the contrary, and so on. "Trannyfag" is a term used by some FTMs who identify as gay men posttransition.

13. Transsexual genital surgery was largely developed as a result of experimental reparative surgery on soldiers with war wounds, which is one of the reasons it's so funny that we met over *The Sun Also Rises.*

14. As much as I wanted Sadie Hawkins to be a kick-ass woman who didn't wait to be asked on dates, which she was in her way, she was really a misogynist joke from a comic strip (Andy Capp's *L'il Abner*, 1937). At the ripe old age of thirty-five, "ugly" Sadie was becoming a "spinster" and her father called all the eligible bachelors to his farm and announced it "Sadie Hawkins Day." He

declared that when he shot his rifle, whichever man ran slow enough for his daughter to catch would have to marry her. Despite its origins, Sadie Hawkins Day is still recognized in American culture as the one day it's "acceptable" for girls to ask boys out. Sadie Hawkins dances seem to have died out, mostly after the day itself was moved to February 29. (Apparently once a year was just too much for women to be so forward, so now it's once every four years. I think it's a conspiracy.)

15. Jamison Green is one of the most out FTMs imaginable and has been running groups, speaking on trans issues, and influencing trans-related law and policy for nearly twenty years—and that on top of two decades of queer activism. His book *Becoming a Visible Man* is an invaluable resource about the experience of FTMs.

16. Dr. Richard Docter, who has been studying transgender identities for well over twenty-five years now, said in an interview: "My guess is that a lot of transgender expressions will turn out to be built on brain-based propensities." For now, it remains a guess, as no proof has yet been found. ("Five Questions with . . . Richard Docter," an interview from my blog: www.myhusbandbetty.com).

17. In Virginia Erhardt's new book, *Head over Heels: Wives Who Stay with Transsexuals and Crossdressers* (Haworth, 2007), she mentions that while transitioning women do start to notice men sexually, they often return to having a primary sexual attraction to women. Erhardt's observation rings true with my experience; many trans women (who were hetero males before transition) I've known seemed antsy to have sex with men close to transition but found female partners eventually, instead. I'm pretty convinced at this point that it's the liberation of letting themselves be themselves that allows them to acknowledge an attraction to men even if they don't feel compelled to act on it. The removal of the homosexuality taboo has to help, too. Many would probably love to avoid being lesbian posttransition, especially because so many have that urge to be "normal" for once and for all, and also because it can be easier to feel validated by men's sexual energy and attentions. I'm pretty sure the change in orientation is not caused by the hormones. Doctors used

to treat effeminate homosexuals with testosterone, on the assumption that they were lacking, and instead of making them more manly it only resulted in their wanting to have more sex with men—because it increased their libidos. That said, more than one trans woman seems to have pointed out that it was stubble that first got their attention, and I wonder if the skin-sensitizing effects of estrogen contribute to their suddenly noticing men sexually—that it's not a change in orientation, but a change in sensuality.

three
the opposite of 49.

1. One of the problems is that people are oversimplifying a very complicated process. Changing a male body to a female one is more complicated than just having "the surgery," for starters. What people are talking about when they refer to "the surgery" is what's referred to in the trans community as SRS (sex reassignment surgery) or GRS (genital reconstruction surgery, or gender reassignment surgery). Acquiring a vagina is not all it takes to pass as or be accepted as a woman: Imagine any guy you know going in for a six-hour surgery and coming out with a vagina—he wouldn't be a woman if he hadn't done anything else, would he? MTFs who are transitioning usually also take hormones, which changes secondary sex characteristics such as fat distribution and the quality of body/facial hair. They may also (or instead, or in any combination) have facial feminization surgery (FFS), hair implants, tracheal shaves, permanent body and facial hair removal via electrolysis or laser. An orchiectomy is the surgical removal of the testicles, which some trans women opt for in order to stop taking testosterone blockers or while saving up money for SRS. And that's only the physical side of transition, and only for the MTF side of things. Socialization, gait, manners, voice, demeanor, conversational style: All of these are things transitioning people examine, and may or may not alter in their attempts to change sex. Personally, I find it insulting that people think that getting a vagina is what makes a transsexual person "become" a woman, as I don't really like to think of my whole experience of being a woman

as summarized by what I've got between my legs. Further: You can't really talk about "the surgery" at all when you're talking about people who transition from female to male, because there are a variety of surgeries FTMs could have: chest surgery, complete hysterectomy, and then whatever kind of genital surgery they choose, if they choose any. For FTMs, too, testosterone proves more powerful for them than estrogen for MTFs, resulting in increased body hair, muscle mass, a deepening of the voice, and depending on the age of the FTM, even male pattern balding. The term "sex change" is out.

2. Because it's impossible to portray all the varieties of partners, from sexual orientations to attitudes about gender, I generally "default" to talking about the heterosexual female partners of MTFs, though of course there are bisexual and lesbian partners of MTFs, too. For a small sampling of the experiences of wives who stay with MTF transsexuals and crossdressers, Virginia Erhardt's *Head over Heels* is a good anthology. The women's stories are told in their own words, with some commentary from Dr. Erhardt. There are also female partners of FTMs, hetero and lesbian and bisexual; and there are male partners of all sexual orientations who are with MTFs and FTMs, though finding male partners online and in "support group culture" is much rarer. Plus, there are partners of trans people who are trans themselves, in trans-trans relationships.

3. In a qualitative survey I did of partners to give myself a better sense of who we are, I found it nearly impossible to summarize anything, except this: If the partner was with the trans person pretransition, the state of the trans person's genitals figured significantly as to whether or not the couple made it through transition with a sex life intact. Ironically, although genital surgery for FTMs is inferior to genital surgery for MTF, the less radical change in genital configuration and the decision not to undergo bottom surgery at all might be one of the factors that enables lesbian-identified partners to stay with their formerly female partners even after they become male. I was very, very surprised by that information, to be honest, because I'd like to think genitals are not so important—and for social passing, or outward gender, they aren't—but for sexual intimacy, they seem to matter a lot.

4. Although some transsexual women are aware of their need to transition for much longer than that, once they begin the process it's usually only a few years between living as a man and living as a woman. Most transitioning transsexuals try to take a very short time to transition physically, so as to not disrupt their jobs too much. Looking like a transsexual person or being out as one can still come with significant job discrimination, so most people try to transition and return to work as their new gender. Sometimes couples make decisions together to stall the transition until children are grown, or until the trans woman is approaching retirement, or for the partner to finish a degree, and so on. It may also be years between when some trans people realize their transness and tell their partners or decide to do anything about it. Sometimes other life changes—death of a parent, something such as 9/11, a cancer scare—motivate the realization and subsequent decision to transition.

5. For most people, living a dually gendered life requires living in the closet—as many crossdressers do. Betty and I are lucky in that she can be out and visible as trans without too much hassle; her workplace is highly tolerant, and so is New York City. That doesn't make it easy—just possible. Betty is also lucky to be able to pass as female without hormones or other significant body modifications, which is not true of many MTFs. In other words, Betty started much further along the feminine spectrum than other MTFs do, at least physically, which meant that I needed to confront the issue of permanent body modification only after she'd been out passing as a woman for some time. Other wives have to be okay with the body modifications long before their partners are out in the world as women. Many MTFs never crossdress at all until after transition, or just before. Neither situation is easy, but I often thought that Betty's not needing to do any body modification would mean she wouldn't want to. Ah, delusions.

6. The irony of my wishing this way is that there are plenty of fantasy stories for crossdressers that feature "magical" transformations such as this, in which the person "must" live as a woman because of a (usually contrived) plot device, such as being cursed. See www.fictionmania.com for a treasure trove of those kinds of stories.

7. Legal issues surrounding transition, genital surgery, and bathroom usage vary from state to state, city to city, county to county, and of course, from country to country.

8. Betty does occasionally act, but playing male roles has gotten more difficult, and she doesn't pursue acting anymore as a career as she once did. We used to joke early in our relationship that we'd be a "power couple" like Tim Robbins and Susan Sarandon, but we didn't know who would be whom. Now, as that famous Smiths song puts it, "that joke isn't funny anymore."

9. Described in Jennifer Finney Boylan's *She's Not There*. Many transsexuals and crossdressers admit to hoping the same thing. Because there does often seem to be a cessation in the transgender feelings due to the euphoria of falling in love, or the busy-ness of having a new family, setting up house, and so on, the trans person can often feel as if the transness has gone away. One of the reasons Boylan's narrative is particularly interesting is how functional "he" was for many years as a writer and teacher and husband and father, until that day the transness insisted on being heard.

10. Nancy Friday, who has been writing and talking about women's sexuality for a couple of decades now, wrote about how she learned to appreciate women's bodies and find them sexy, but that her appreciation for women doesn't have the same primitive charge for her as seeing a man's body. A crossdresser named Marlena explained it thusly: "I've learned to appreciate a nice set of pecs, but they don't have the straight-to-the-groin zing that seeing the wiggle of a woman's ass can." It's that zing I want to keep in my life, and I'm not sure at what point it might go away if Betty altered her body with hormones or surgery, that is, at what point I wouldn't be viscerally responding to a male body even while seducing someone feminine.

11. I applaud anyone who can make this work in any way they can. When I was looking around for ways to do this, however, I was repeatedly told about relationships in which the couple weren't having sex and were living "like sisters." It got my back up after a while. In a lot of cases, some of these relationships were between people who were much older than us, and sex had already petered out, and both

had accepted their relationship as platonic long before transition. That said, it's not necessarily the age of the couple or the partner that determines whether or not that's an acceptable outcome: Older women can be just as concerned about wanting an ongoing sex life with a partner as younger women. Some women recognize an innate bisexuality and encourage it in themselves. Some couples try being poly (which can work, but it doesn't seem to if the couple started out as monogamous). One couple I met would occasionally find a guy to have sex with together (as the trans woman had discovered an erotic attraction to men). It's very highly variable and based on the couple's own needs, desires, sexual relationship, and emotional commitment. I have often felt very drowned out by the "like sisters" set and often find in support groups that women who are very concerned about having a satisfying sex life are often pooh-poohed as if they're being shallow, or they are indirectly told that if they *really* loved their partners, they could give up sex. It's one thing, in my opinion, to give up sex with a man and another thing to give up sex altogether. For couples who are monogamous, this issue can become the deal-breaker. If the partner isn't willing to be sexual with her new female partner, still wants a sex life, and is monogamous, there's really just no good solution.

12. There's also a history of transphobia within the gay and lesbian community, unfortunately.

13. I know some people hate the term "faghag" or are offended by it, but I'm using it in the casual, lighthearted way my generation of gay men and their straight female friends use it—just as a way of expressing the unique and interesting and compassionate friendship that can exist between them. I've used "fruit fly"—which is a little too cute—and I like SWISH (Straight Women in Support of Homosexuals) but neither of them are used in wide circulation. Thus, faghag. The original use of the term—for older women who preyed on gay men and vice versa—has gone out of general use, as far as I can tell, but I know there are both older women and gay men who resent the term, which was about as derogatory as "queer" when it was used as an insult. My apologies to them.

14. The LGBT Community Center provides meeting spaces, support services, therapy, and a panoply of resources to LGBT people, and it specifically has a Gender Identity Project that focuses on trans and gender issues: www .gaycenter.org for more information.

15. Ray Carranente, Rosalyne Blumenstein, Carrie Davis, Katie Douglas, Rita Hernandez, the late Arlene Hoffman, and Barbara Warren were the movers and shakers who got the T added to the GLBT Center in the West Village. Rosalyne Blumenstein helped found the Gender Identity Project (GIP) at the center, and she is a heterosexual woman of transsexual experience. There is often still some confusion—not from the folks who work there but sometimes from volunteers—about why there are heterosexuals coming to the center at all and to the GIP in particular, even though one of its originators is straight and trans (private correspondence with Rosalyne Blumenstein). There are also heterosexual male partners of pretransition FTMs and heterosexual female partners of posttransition FTMs.

16. As it turns out, he managed not to crossdress for a couple of years but has started again. (They always do. That said, it's not the worst thing in the world for the couple to be able to take a huge break from CDing, either, especially because it can come to dominate a relationship rather easily.)

17. The whole scandal about gay priests existing completely baffles me, as I was raised in a parish where everyone knew that some priests were gay—at least anyone paying attention did. It was at one time the "proper" thing for a Catholic family to do with one's gay son, as priesthood meant celibacy, and celibate homosexuality was, in the opinion of many Catholics, about as close as a homosexual could get to a sin-free life. It makes perfect sense if you believe that anyone can be celibate. But I have to add that the whole conflation of gay man/pedophile really pissed me off, and so did the anti-Catholic taint a lot of those reports carried. Vern Bullough's article, "Homosexuality and Catholic Priests," in *Free Inquiry* (Vol. 22, No. 3), elaborates on distinctions between being homophilic and homosexual, among other things.

18. Lesbian partners of FTMs ask a lot of the same questions of themselves in

reverse, as in: Does having an FTM partner now make me straight? Am I allowed to think of my boyfriend's clitoris as a clitoris, or do I have to think of it as a penis? Am I still queer? How can I take part in the lesbian community when no one who sees me with my partner thinks I'm a lesbian? They also contend with FTMs who are actively distancing themselves from woman-ness, and who (sometimes, and only some of them) act out in sexist ways.

19. *The Aggressives*, 2005, directed by Daniel Peddle.

20. Aaron Devor differentiates between (1) fantasies (stuff you enjoying thinking about but don't want to actually do), (2) desire (stuff you'd like to do regardless of whether you've done it), and (3) actual behavior. See Aaron H. Devor. (1993). "Toward a Taxonomy of Gendered Sexuality." *Journal of Psychology and Human Sexuality* 6 (1), 23–55.

21. *Winterset* is a play by Maxwell Anderson, and Sacco and Vanzetti were two Italian anarchists who were convicted and sentenced to death in Boston in 1927. Their case was a cause célèbre throughout the world, usually vis-à-vis the death penalty in America, or in the treatment of "foreign radicals," and is sometimes revisited on the anniversary of their executions.

22. A "beard" is slang for a disguise; I had a gay friend whose family didn't know he was gay, so whenever they would come to New York for a visit, I would be his "beard" by pretending to be his girlfriend for the night.

23. Tristan Taormino is a writer, sex educator, and equal-opportunity pansexual. The review in question was one of her columns for *The Village Voice*, "Husband Betty."

24. Deborah Feinbloom. *Transvestites and Transsexuals.* New York: Dell, 1977.

25. Frank Lewins. (2002). "Explaining Stable Partnerships among FTMs and MTFs: A Significant Difference?" *Journal of Sociology* 38 (1), 76–88.

26. Grayson Perry is a sculptor who won the coveted Booker Prize for his pottery a few years ago, and who is also a crossdresser who received his award in a little girl's frock he'd had made for the occasion.

27. From Chaucer's *The Canterbury Tales*, "The Wife of Bath's Tale," from the J. U. Nicholson translation, New York: Covici-Friede, 1934, 338–39.

28. The capitalization of D/s is meant to describe the relationship—Dominant capitalized, submissive lowercase. Minna was the wife of a crossdresser who came to understand her husband's need to crossdress through their D/s relationship. Her notes on the way D/s intersects with crossdressing and ways to play out those dynamics are in *My Husband Betty*. I miss her very much; Minna was diagnosed with breast cancer and fought all the way, but she didn't beat it in the end.

29. Caroline Dryden's book *Being Married, Doing Gender* details the way gender plays out vis-à-vis feminism in a couple's life, decisions, and especially housework and child rearing.

30. Michael Kimmel's *Manhood in America* talks about how this was a common problem during the Great Depression in families in which the husband was out of work for a long time. He cites a quote from one wife who said something along the lines of, "I still love him, but I don't *respect* him."

31. In a publication called "Having a Daughter with a Disability: Is It Different for Girls?," by the National Information Center for Children and Youth with Disabilities (NICHCY), the authors write: "How do stereotypes of male and female behavior and potential affect children with disabilities? To begin with, many adults feel that children with disabilities need more help. Boys with disabilities can often escape the disability stereotype of helplessness or dependence by aspiring to such traditional male characteristics as competence, autonomy, and work. Girls with disabilities, however, confront two stereotypes—the 'passive, dependent' female and the 'helpless and dependent' person with a disability. As a result, they often get a double dose of assistance that can lead to a kind of a dependence called learned helplessness (Lang, 1982)." 31. Merle Froschl, Ellen Rubin, and Barbara Sprung, et al. (1990). *NICHCY News Digest* 14. Retrieved July 30, 2006, from www.kidsource.com/NICHCY/girl_disability1.html.

four
snips & snails & sugar & spice.

1. The reverse is not true. Women raised female generally do not like to be asked if they are the trans person. I've been asked it myself, usually by a trans person, who says something along the lines of, "Are you a real girl?" And while I can often think of a few annoying ways to answer that question, along the lines of "I'm older than eighteen," or "What do you mean by 'real'?," I usually just nod so the person will move along. It's often been asked of me when someone wants to know what I'm doing in a trans space, whether I'm supposed to be there, and what my right to be there is.

2. Trans men generally have an easier time passing than trans women, because 1) short men are far less noticeable than tall women, and 2) testosterone is a really remarkable hormone, causing the voice to drop, weight to shift to the face and midsection, hair to grow (on the face and body), and baldness to happen (depending on the age of the man in question).

3. Likewise, "passing" as one gender and being "discovered" to be another, or being discovered to have the genitals of another, can often be life-threatening. Stories such as Brandon Teena's and Gwen Araujo's—both young adults who were passing as their target gender and killed when young men discovered their genitals didn't match their gender—happen far more often than they should, and the trans person is often painted as intentionally deceptive. (Gwen Araujo's story was just made into a movie called *A Girl Like Me* by Lifetime television, and Brandon Teena's story is told in the film *Boys Don't Cry*.) Yet trans people who live their whole lives working hard at being the gender that matches their genitals, but who come to be so miserable they come out when older, are also often accused of deceiving people. When people are damned if they do or damned if they don't, that's a pretty clear case, in my opinion, that the deck is stacked against them.

4. For an interesting examination and rebuttal of that kind of conclusive, gendered research, try *Same Difference: How Gender Myths Are Hurting Our Relationships, Our Children, and Our Jobs* by Rosalind Barnett and Caryl

she's not the man i married

Rivers. A good example from the book breaks down Deborah Tannen's sweeping generalizations about gender and communication by pointing out other studies that controlled for a power differential and found that power influenced who interrupted whom far more than gender (pp. 103–106).

5. It was commonly understood that women were less intelligent than men because female skulls are generally smaller than male skulls (because female bodies are generally smaller than male ones). That seems a rational conclusion and doesn't seem biased, but it took only a few small-skulled male Nobel Prize winners for it to be debunked.

6. "No matter where they stand on the question of biology versus culture, social scientists agree that the sexes are much more alike than they are different, and that variations within each sex are far greater than variations between the sexes." L. Shapiro, "Guns and Dolls," *Newsweek*, May 28, 1990, 56–65.

7. *Suits Me: The Double Life of Billy Tipton*, by Diane W. Middlebrook (Houghton Mifflin, 1998). Some female-bodied people who have passed as male are considered women, albeit "passing women" by the lesbian community, or they are seen as male, and trans, by some trans people. I'm not sure it's acceptable to make a decision about people's identity if they didn't say anything about it themselves, and I am also hesitant about giving people an identity that wasn't around when they were. If I took myself as a historical subject, say, I could easily call my teenage identity genderqueer, but that word wasn't in common parlance then, and/or I certainly didn't know it. It would diminish the sense of isolation I felt to call me that in retrospect, and that skews my sense of my identity at that time, and would even more so if the word gains in popularity in the next ten years. Identity is the most important to the person who lived it, or claimed it. Other kinds of identity-making bother me too, as when Virginia Woolf or Edna St. Vincent Millay are declared lesbian, when the evidence is that they were bisexual. Of course, as Patrick Califia points out, "The most common response to the accusation of fomenting bisexual invisibility or biphobia among gay social-science researchers is to claim that any heterosexual behavior on the part of

our long-ago heroes and heroines was made necessary by life in a repressive heterosexual society." He makes a good argument. From *Sex Changes: Transgender Politics,* Chapter 4: *The Berdache Wars and "Passing Women" Follies: Transphobia in Gay Academia.*

8. In the case of Jacobellis v. Ohio, 378 U.S. 184, 197 (1964), Justice Potter Stewart tried to explain "hard-core pornography," or what is obscene, by saying in his concurring opinion, "I shall not today attempt further to define the kinds of material I understand to be embraced . . . [b]ut I know it when I see it."

9. John Money. *Gay, Straight, and In-Between,* Oxford, Oxford University Press, 1988, 28–29, *id.* at 28–31. While many of Money's theories have been dismissed (see John Colapinto's book about David Reimer, *As Nature Made Him,* for more about why), these eight characteristics used to sex a child if there is a question of indeterminate sex have not.

10. Anne Fausto-Sterling's book *Sexing the Body* is a remarkable exposition of how sex became binary. Alice Domurat Dreger's *Hermaphrodites and the Medical Invention of Sex* makes a nice companion to it, explaining how the study of hermaphrodites—people who are now referred to as intersexed—cemented the idea of the sex binary.

11. A treasure trail is the line of hair that goes from navel to pubis.

12. This late development of our genitals apparently creates "androgynies" that some cultures are uncomfortable with, resulting in circumcision—both female and male. A recent apologist for these operations, Robert Daniels, explained it thusly: "The cutting in each case removes our inherent androgynies, taking away the most feminine aspects of boys' genitalia and the most masculine aspects of girls' genitalia, so that we are truly made men and women." I really can't begin to comprehend or explain how anyone can see labia as masculine, or a foreskin as feminine, but what's interesting to me is that androgyny is considered a sufficient reason to "correct" these genitals. See Marissa Heyl, "It's About Tradition," *Patchwork* (Summer 1.2), 2005. See http://patch.unc.edu/tradition.htm.

13. My suspicion is that "gender" is becoming used more often in lieu of "sex"

because of good old-fashioned American prudery. It doesn't matter that "sex" in this instance means more like "sexual function" and has little to do with sex as in "sexual intercourse"—we still prefer leaving sex out of it.

14. According to the U.S. Census Bureau, in 2004 there were 10 million single mothers living in the United States with children under eighteen years old. Other facts: 5.6 million are stay-at-home moms, 55 percent of mothers in the workforce have infants, 80 percent of mothers who had a child twelve or more years ago (at the ages of fifteen–forty-four) are working, 51 percent of women went back to work within four months of giving birth, and 9 million women reported making an average weekly childcare payment of $92. See www.census.gov/Press-Release/www/releases/archives/facts_for_features_special_editions/006560.html.

15. In Norah Vincent's *Self-Made Man,* she passes as "Ned" Vincent—who she admits is not perceived as being of the same class as the men she befriends in a bowling alley. She draws a lot of conclusions about how men are friends with each other—and how they aren't friends with women—from that experience. My experience growing up working-class is that it was often more important for someone to be working-class for there to be a kind of trust that might lead to friendship. Gender and race often seem less important; the friendships among union members, for instance, are a good example of the way class can trump race and gender.

16. Specifically in "A Black Feminist's Search for Sisterhood," in *Invisibility Blues.*

17. Granted, as Western culture engulfs the globe, Western standards of beauty are invading other cultures. Bollywood actresses, for instance, who in my opinion are often outstandingly beautiful women, are more frequently getting surgery to get rid of their epicanthic fold if they have one.

18. Interestingly, feminists and health experts (and even some commercial enterprises, such as Dove) are now starting to get out the message that girls should not overexercise and should certainly not become anorexic, and they are pushing "love the body you're in" messages instead. Black feminists are concerned that once again, African American teenagers will be done a

disservice as they're often more prone to obesity and diabetes and shouldn't be getting the same "accept yourself as you are" messages for the sake of their health. It's a good example of how anything written about "women" or "girls" is not universally applicable.

19. From a January 1916 article in *The Atlantic* called "Further Notes on the Intelligence of Woman": "I think she will succeed, for I doubt whether any mental power is inherent in sex. There are differences of degree, differences of quality; but I suspect that they are mainly due to sexual heredity, to environment, to suggestion, and that indeed if I may trench upon biology, human creatures are never entirely male or entirely female; *there are no men, there are no women, but only sexual majorities*" (italics mine). See www .theatlantic.com. Turn-of-the-20th-century sexologists, including people such as Magnus Hirschfeld and Havelock Ellis, believed that if you were to exclude anyone from the categories of "man" or "woman" based on gender variance, there wouldn't be anyone in those categories at all. Hirschfeld specifically had a system based on Primary, Secondary, Tertiary, and Fourth-Order Features. His orders still apply, but we call them different things. His Primary order included things such as "oviduct or spermatic duct" and is what we'd call sex; his Secondary Order mentioned things such as hair distribution and is what we still call secondary sex characteristics, but his Tertiary included things we'd call sexual orientation and gender presentation, while the Fourth Order describes things we'd now call gender, gender roles, or gender identity. Still in all, his "man" and "woman" needed to have sixteen variables all line up on one side or the other for anyone to be considered 100 percent, which is akin to my feeling that most people, depending on context, culture, or the viewer, could have their gender called into question. In some ways he was trying to make the point that while gender variance is often viewed as being determined by sexual orientation or genitals, it could as easily be determined by the size of a larynx, which then raises the question as to who wouldn't be gender variant, depending on which variables are used to determine sex and gender variance.

20. Intersex activists object to being "made to fit" since that often requires surgery at birth, to which an intersexed child cannot give consent. See www.isna.org for more information.

21. Matthew Rottnek, ed. *Sissies and Tomboys: Gender Nonconformity and Homosexual Childhood.* New York: New York University Press, 1999.

22. "T-girl" is another type of MTF and seems to be used mostly to describe the more party-oriented types.

23. Once, in India, I had an American woman express surprise at how "out" homosexuals were in India, and I asked her where all these out homosexuals were. She immediately pointed to a couple of young men who were walking down the street with their arms around each other's shoulders. She would not and could not believe me when I told her they were straight, that physical affection between men was far more commonplace in India than it is in America, but that what she was seeing certainly didn't signal that the guys were gay or that India was entirely accepting of homosexuality. Since there are prohibitions against homosexuality in India, it's very unlikely these men were gay, but I suppose she didn't know that homosexuality is still illegal in a lot of countries.

24. The way femmes are appreciated or not within lesbian culture is explored in Joan Nestle's *The Persistent Desire: A Femme-Butch Reader,* but loosely, it was because they could pass as straight, because they were seen as normatively gendered, or their feminine expression was interpreted as their being co-opted by heterosexual beauty standards.

25. The article is called "Gay Shame Is a Drag," written by Q. Allen Brocka in the *Advocate* (Issue 965): www.advocate.com.

26. The way I see it, some trans people and gay people and lesbians are gender variant, but there are also gender-variant people who are not gay, lesbian, or trans. Myself, for instance.

27. J. Michael Bailey's recent study on bisexuality basically stated that there is no such thing as bisexuality. This guy is obsessed with telling people that he knows them better than they know themselves. A queer woman I know said

she's often told by lesbians, "But you're mostly gay," as if that somehow makes her own sense of herself—which includes enjoying sex with men—somehow less important than their sense of her sexuality. Interestingly, I find that people who are trying not to honor the gender binary now often identify as queer, and who perhaps, a decade or so ago, would have identified as bisexual *and* queer, where queer is something more like a political affiliation as well as a sexual orientation.

five
wearing the pants.

1. *Rubyfruit Jungle* is a coming-of-age novel about a young lesbian by author Rita Mae Brown.

2. *The Sims* is a computer game that simulates people's lives. Not only can women do the seducing, but female Sims can seduce other female Sims, have same-sex relationships, and have civil unions with their same-sex partners.

3. *Thelma & Louise* is a movie about a frustrated housewife, Thelma, and her waitress friend, Louise, who go on a "girls' night out" that turns into a road trip and crime spree. The road trip starts because they need to run from the law—after Louise kills a man who rapes Thelma. So many women loved it, and I thought, *Wow, rebellious women die at the end, how—overdone.* There's a whole tradition of women's breaking social conventions and dying (by suicide or otherwise) by the end. The most frequently cited example is Kate Chopin's *The Awakening.*

4. "talking about the iSsues that no onE's eXpressing," by Heather Franek in *Anything That Moves* (Issue 17).

5. *puta*—Spanish for slut.

6. Many of the (masculine) women Aaron Devor interviewed for his book *Gender Blenders* also came from families where men were highly valued.

7. *Self-Made Man,* by Norah Vincent, describes Vincent's experiment in passing and living as a man.

8. Actually men *are* given permission to express some emotions—such as

anger or competitiveness, among others. These are emotions that women are culturally trained to be the least comfortable with. But "difference feminists" framed this argument, and they paint women as benevolent, nurturing earth mothers. Granted, they started doing so precisely because so many "womanly traits" (such as gentleness) were considered so negative. As a result, "male emotions" such as anger and competitiveness don't "count," and thus the mythos that men don't express emotions. Or as Ben Barres recently pointed out in an interview in *The New York Times,* "It is just patently absurd to say women are more emotional than men. Men commit twenty-five times the murders; it's shocking what the numbers are. And if anyone ever sees a woman with road rage, they should write it up and send it to a medical journal." See www.nytimes.com.

9. *Talk to Her,* a film by Pedro Almodóvar, the famed Spanish director. Many of his movies play on binaries (masochist/sadist, male/female) with his particular sense of humor and commentary. *Talk to Her* is, in my opinion, one of his best films to date. He also portrays MTFs with great empathy.

10. It's important to point out that I am not saying I *am* the butch to her femme, but that I'm *playing* butch to her femme. It's an important distinction. To me, being a butch (and a femme) is a lesbian identity, and one I don't want to claim—out of respect for the butches of the world. I use "playing butch" the same way I've used "playing the male role" to indicate a temporary way of role-playing gender, not as an identity. For a good modern book on what being butch is about, try S. Bear Bergman's *Butch Is a Noun.*

11. A "trouser role" was the term used when women played the parts of boys in opera and theater. Loosely speaking, Mary Martin's playing Peter Pan is an example, though of course Peter's costume required only tights, not trousers.

12. *The Rules* is the only actual book, and its subtitle, "Time-Tested Secrets for Capturing the Heart of Mr. Right" pretty much sums up the contents. The others are titles I made up, though with the way things are going, they might exist by the time this book does.

13. In the fake textbook entry, "How to Be a Good Wife," one of my favorite tips

goes like so: "Prepare yourself. Take fifteen minutes to rest so that you'll be refreshed when he arrives. Touch up your makeup, put a ribbon in your hair and be fresh-looking. He has just been with a lot of work-weary people. Be a little gay and a little more interesting. His boring day may need a lift." See www.snopes.com/language/document/goodwife.htm.

14. My favorite historical example of the way women can enforce masculine codes comes out of World War I, when a sizable population of English men had taken a pacifist stance. Women were known to go around giving out white feathers, which symbolized cowardice, thereby shaming the men for not being manly and enlisting like "real men" did.

15. *The Persistent Desire: A Femme-Butch Reader*, edited by Joan Nestle, is an anthology by butches and femmes about their relationships and social scenes in the recent past.

16. In a recent *San Francisco Chronicle* article, Steve Winn writes: "Maybe one of the 'problems' boys and young men face today is the gradual disappearance of the monolithic male role model that used to loom over the culture like those mighty, jaw-jutting stone figures on Easter Island. They are, increasingly, confronted by more textured, provisional, authentically flawed images." See www.sfgate.com. The "monolithic role model" and tight restrictions on "how to be a man" have always been a more accurate articulation of what I'd consider a "crisis of masculinity," but recently there's been a rash of articles about how most people in college are women and everyone getting an advanced degree is a woman, and so on, when in fact, women are barely reaching majorities: At Harvard, 55 percent of women graduated with honors this spring and it just admitted 52 percent women to the freshman class, and somehow this means boys suddenly need special classes—especially boys who are being raised to even try to get into Harvard. Doubtful. In a recent *NYT* article on this so-called gender divide, you'll find this sentence: "'Over all, the differences between blacks and whites, rich and poor, dwarf the differences between men and women within any particular group,' says Jacqueline King, a researcher for the American Council on Education's

Center for Policy Analysis and the author of the forthcoming report." Race and class trump gender—*go figure.*

17. In a recent ESPN article, Bill Simmons talks about the recent increase of men—and even manly athletes!—crying openly. While he doesn't encourage it per se, he doesn't discourage it, either. See http://proxy.espn.go.com.

18. "The Yellow Wallpaper," by Charlotte Perkins Gilman, is a story that illustrates the sad lives of women forced to sit and look pretty in sitting rooms. By the end, the protagonist goes mad out of boredom. It reflects actual advice Gilman was given by a doctor she saw to relieve her postnatal depression, who said: "Live as domestic a life as possible" and "Never touch a pen, brush, or pencil as long as you live." The story was published in 1892. See www.kirjasto.sci .fi/gilman.htm. "Mother's Little Helper" is a song by the Rolling Stones about how Valium helped so many 1960s housewives get through their day:

Mother needs something today to calm her down
And though she's not really ill
There's a little yellow pill
She goes running for the shelter of a mother's little helper
And it helps her on her way, gets her through her busy day

The song ends with "mom" dying of an overdose.

19. Mark Mothersbaugh was lead of the eighties geek band Devo; Prince still performs in heavy makeup and three-inch heels; Henry Rollins, former frontman for the band Black Flag, is heavily tattooed and has a neck as thick as his head. Tina Fey is the ruling queen of "geek chic," Ellen DeGeneres is often given as an example of a "Chapstick" lesbian (meaning gender neutral), and Julia Roberts is both glamorous and goofy.

20. *The Twilight Zone,* a sci-fi TV show that premiered in 1959 and ran through 1964, and which was narrated and originated by Rod Serling, represented a kind of dystopian sci-fi that resembled and commented on the heavily conformist 1950s. The sci-fi of that time is something like a bellwether for the

rebellions that would take place later in the 1960s (during which, of course, men grew their hair long and women started being more open about having casual sex).

21. In fact, there's a long tradition of considering left-handed people strange, wrong, or weird. Some of it, in Western culture, comes from an unfortunate etymology: Left in Latin is "sinister," the root of which is "sinus," or pocket. The pockets in togas were on the left side.

22. The Japanese think of blood types the way Americans think about horoscopes. See www.bellaonline.com/articles/art22988.asp.

23. *House,* a TV show about a misogynist, grumpy, rude doctor, is one of my favorites, but unless I was dying of something no one else could diagnose, I don't think I'd want to see him.

24. A mash note is an old-fashioned term for a love letter.

25. There is no female form of avuncular, which is a shame considering I'm an aunt to thirteen nieces and nephews. It'd be mighty useful.

26. G. Alexander, "Sex Differences in Response to Children's Toys in Nonhuman Primates *(Cercopithecus aethiops sabaeus),*" *Evolution and Human Behavior* 23 (6), 2002, 467–479. A wonderful explanation of why this research doesn't hold water, unlike the cooking pots, can be found at the Blogspot blog *Mixing Memory:* http://mixingmemory.blogspot.com/2006/04/monkeys-playing-with-boys-and-girls.html.

27. Researcher J. Michael Bailey often comes to conclusions that seem to be biased to his own beliefs. In this case, "(Promiscuous gay men) . . . are doing what most heterosexual men would do if they could." Later, "But women do not, in general, benefit at all from having more than one sex partner." (*The Man Who Would Be Queen*, pp. 87 and following.) He determines what might be a "benefit" by evolutionary needs—*not* exactly what most women are thinking about when they're trying to figure out who they're going to have sex with. I'm not the only one who thinks Bailey's research is flawed and his conclusions biased: For more information about Bailey, Wikipedia has a nice summation: http://en.wikipedia.org/wiki/J._Michael_Bailey.

28. Who is viewed as a "problem solver" in terms of gender role is an issue that draws on other aspects of culture. It's possible to see much older traditions within our current ones, sometimes within family structures. In a Catholic family, for instance, especially Catholics from Ireland and other Catholic countries that were matriarchal before the church showed up, but where Mary is still central to the faith, it can seem obvious that the women are more the "stop complaining, make a decision" types. Similarly, in African American culture, because of the racism implicit in our criminal justice system, you often find women are the source of decision-making in families. I often think that one of the big divides between the way we view gender roles and gender in general is whether or not we are matriarchy's descendents or not. Matriarchy was alive and well in my family structure, as my grandmother was the only surviving grandparent by the time I was born. Interestingly, the folks I knew at City College who came from extended families, or who grew up with grandparents living in their home, understood my grief over my grandmother's death in a way my wealthier friends did not, which leads me to wonder if the person who produces the wealth eventually supplants the more family-centric matriarchal role as "head of household" as the family moves up the economic ladder.

29. *Sex and the City* is the show about single women who live in Manhattan. I don't know anyone like any of them.

30. George Saunders, "My Amendment," *The New Yorker*, March 8, 2004. See www.newyorker.com/shouts/content/?040308sh_shouts.

31. Janet Reno (former U.S. attorney general) and Margaret Thatcher (former U.K. prime minister) are both older, heavyset women who are often mocked for their masculinity (whether in terms of their personality or appearance) but who are definitely not trying to occupy a gender-neutral space. Marlene Dietrich, on the other hand, was famously bisexual and always traveled with several of her own suits. Her masculinity was sensual, sexual, and decadent, and it wasn't just whom she played in the movies. David Bowie's androgynous glam in the 1970s continues to inspire fashion, including this year's Gaultier line, which features skirts for men.

32. Trans-amorous is a word coined to describe people who find trans people sexually attractive. (It's a sexual orientation in its own right, in my opinion.) Woman-raised-female is one way I have of distinguishing a woman who was assigned female at birth, as I was, from transsexual women. Non-op means no surgery. Noho means no hormones. Not-currently-socially-transitioning clarifies that some trans people do live full-time in their target gender without hormones and surgery, which is referred to as a social transition (as opposed to a medical transition).

33. When I've told media people that Betty is transgender, they often come back with, "So he's had the surgery?" and I always have to say, "That's transsexuals. Transsexuals have the surgery. People who identify as transgender might or might not have surgery, and Betty is one of the 'might nots.'" I often want to add, "What kind of genitals does *your* partner have, and why on earth do you think it's acceptable to ask me that?" (But she also started using trans because she got tired of people wanting her on their "team" in the ongoing border wars and infighting of the trans community.)

34. Alfred Kinsey, namesake of the Kinsey Institute, was a sex researcher whose *Sexual Behavior of the Human Male* (1948) and *Sexual Behavior of the Human Female* (1953) contributed significantly to the gay rights movement and toward the sexual liberation of the 1960s.

six
genitals are the least of it.

1. Havelock Ellis's *Studies in the Psychology of Sex* and Richard von Krafft-Ebing's *Psychopathia Sexualis* were the ones I read in the public library, along with others whose titles/authors I can't remember.

2. Case 34: "A man had an inamorata who would allow him to blacken her hands with coal or soot. She then had to sit before a mirror in such a way that he could see her hands in it. While conversing with her, which was often for a long time, he looked constantly at her mirrored hands, and finally, after a time, he would take his leave, fully satisfied." What I am amazed by is how clearly this description

had remained in my memory. I hadn't read the actual entry since I was a teenager, twenty years ago. It appears in a section about the defilement of women. Richard von Krafft-Ebing. *Psychopathia Sexualis: The Case Histories*, p. 45.

3. Neal Stephenson, *Cryptonomicon*. New York: Avon Books, 2002, pp. 447–448.

4. Castration anxiety, the incest taboo, anal retentiveness, oral fixations, repression: These are some of the ideas that "explain" why people are sexual in the way they are. Some of them make sense with some sexual practices and not others.

5. Although Hirschfeld never mentioned in his own papers that he crossdressed, Christopher Isherwood did say he saw Hirschfeld crossdressed. Charlotte Wolff, his biographer *(Magnus Hirschfeld: A Portrait of a Pioneer in Sexology)* mentions that Hirschfeld did enjoy the company of crossdressers, but so have more-current researchers such as Dr. Richard Docter and the late Vern Bullough, and they are not crossdressers. Many assumed that because Hirschfeld wrote about transvestites he was one, as he also wrote about homosexuality and certainly was homosexual (Vern Bullough, from private correspondence).

6. Lee's Mardi Gras Boutique was a drag/crossdressing emporium on West Fourteenth Street in Manhattan and was owned and operated by Lee Brewster. You could enter the third-floor store only by buzzing the downstairs doorbell and having someone buzz you in, which protected the privacy of the clients (many of whom were closeted). Brewster also pushed for the legalization of public crossdressing. He died in 2000, and shortly thereafter Lee's Mardi Gras shut its doors. His obituary appeared in *The New York Times,* and you can read excerpts from it at the International Foundation for Gender Education's (IFGE) website: www.ifge.org/news/2000/may/ntc00may15.htm.

7. Sometimes it's a box, sometimes a bag, sometimes a whole storage trailer, but almost every CD I've ever met has a compact stash of women's clothes and shoes and breast forms that they keep tucked away somewhere. Because of the shame and embarrassment of being a CD, sometimes these items have been taken from mothers, sisters, girlfriends, or female friends. The discovery of a crossdresser's kit ends up outing plenty of crossdressers to

their wives, who often think (at first, incorrectly) that their husbands have another woman on the side. Some are more horrified when they realize the truth, others relieved.

8. Dan Savage, sex advice columnist who writes the column "Savage Love" for *The Stranger*, which appears in other weeklies. Tristan Taormino, sex educator and columnist, writes "Pucker Up" for the *Village Voice*.

9. Cherríe Moraga, in *The Persistent Desire*, p. 245.

10. In the first season of *The Sopranos*, Episode 9, titled "Boca," Junior's girlfriend, Roberta, lets it slip that Junior likes to go down. The gossip gets around until Tony is needling Junior about it, and Junior breaks up with Roberta because of it. *Boca* is Italian for "mouth," of course.

11. The new "Man Law" Miller Lite commercials are actually an attempt to make up for the commercial featuring women in bikinis wrestling in wet cement. I can't really figure out why the company seems to think the "Man Laws" are less offensive, though the guys around the table in the commercial do argue that smashing a beer can on one's forehead isn't cool anymore. Score one for civilization.

12. Kevin Aviance, a self-confessed freak and downtown diva, was gay-bashed just as Pride Month 2006 was starting in New York. Gang members were arrested, but Aviance was admitted to the hospital for a few weeks and had to have his jaw wired for nearly a month. Clarence Patton of the NYC Gay and Lesbian Anti-Violence Project (www.avp.org) also pointed out that gay-bashings often increase in the months leading up to Pride Month. Interestingly, many who report being gay-bashed also mention that they "looked gay" at the time, which is another way of saying they looked gender variant. Aviance, it should be noted, was six feet two inches and very well built, not someone who would physically radiate "easy target," and his publicist was very clear about his having been dressed in "boy clothes" at the time of the attack.

13. June Cleaver was of course a fictional woman, but a symbol of prim 1950s womanhood. Annie Sprinkle, on the other hand, is a former porn star, sex

advocate, and pro-sex feminist who gives workshops for women on how to female ejaculate, among other things.

14. Ann Landers conducted the survey in 1985 and got ninety thousand responses; 72 percent of respondents said they preferred cuddling over "the act." Obviously "the act" means intercourse, and anyone who's had good sex knows it requires a lot more than just intercourse, which may in itself explain why these readers preferred cuddling. But calling sex "the act" connotes a certain prudishness around sex in the first place.

15. *Behind the Green Door* is a 1970s artsy porn film, in which Marilyn Chambers (who was otherwise the Ivory Snow model) is kidnapped and made to perform sex acts at an underground club with the result that she is ultimately liberated by doing so.

16. The interview with Dan Savage and Tristan Taormino was in the *Metro Times,* www.metrotimes.com.

17. The name of the event is Dark Odyssey: www.darkodyssey.com.

18. I don't just talk about the difference couples can experience in frequency, but in different sexual styles, locations, where on their priority list they put sex, and even what they think it does for them (i.e., some people prefer sex only when they're already relaxed, and others use it *to* relax). Since the frequency issue is the most gendered of these differences, I'm focusing on that, but I wanted to acknowledge there are many other ways to have uneven libidos. For that matter, people mean different things when referring to a libido: Some are talking more about function (i.e., if they respond physically to sexual stimulation), or desire, horniness, or even just how much they think about sex.

19. Studs Terkel, famous journalist and radio show host of Chicago, whose books feature people's answers to the questions he asks, but very rarely his questions. They're usually thematic, covering topics such as race *(Race),* the Great Depression *(Hard Times),* or working *(Working).*

20. Viagra and Cialis are medical solutions for men with erection problems.

Viagra, it's now been discovered, makes some men blind, which would be funny considering the old masturbation myth, but it isn't at all. Horny goat weed and Yohimbe fall more into the "aphrodisiac" category.

21. I had in fact hoped that Betty's comfort with a change in gender, or gender role, might "free up" her sexuality in *My Husband Betty*, specifically on p. 161. I've come to change my thinking about that, mostly because that theory situates a trans person's low libido solely in body dysphoria and rules out many other factors that could be contributing. It also precludes the idea that a low libido is completely functional, because if two people in a relationship have a low libido there is no problem; it's only when people with mismatched libidos are together that there is. When I stopped trying to "fix" Betty's "problem" and stopped thinking of it as a problem altogether, we made a hell of a lot more progress toward a good sex life.

22. Campari Group, "The Secret," directed by Tarsem Singh. See www.campari .com/pdf/Issue16-P24-25_The_Secret.pdf.

23. Raven Kaldera's essay, "When Sex Is a Drag—Part III: Uncharted Territory: FTVs (Or Girls Who Get Off on Being Guys)" can be found on his website, www.cauldronfarm.com. Raven Kaldera's book *Hermaphrodeities: The Transgender Spirituality Workbook* discusses the place of trans and intersex people in spiritual traditions.

24. Nina Hartley is a porn star, sex educator, knockout, and feminist. Not necessarily in that order.

25. "Pegged" is the term used to describe when a woman straps it on and bends her boyfriend over to penetrate him anally. The video *Bend Over Boyfriend* has instructions.

26. Polyamory is a practice of having more than one sex partner, or romantic partner, or both, at a time. Different people who are poly practice it in different ways—some with a primary relationship of two or three people, others with multiple equal partners, and so on.

seven
love is a many-gendered thing.

1. Another fake title. But the Neil Gaiman novel that was about to come out was his *Anansi Boys*, which like my nom de plume, is a play on the slang term "nancy boy."

2. Algernon is the "Oscar Wilde" part in *The Importance of Being Earnest;* Bluntschli is the male lead in Shaw's *Arms and the Man,* and Melchior is a minor but funny character in an old Stoppard play called *On the Razzle.* Betty played them all. For the first five years we were together, Betty worked at a repertory theater company, which meant she was onstage eleven months out of the year and was in at least five plays in that time. Now she does a play or a reading every once in a while, not even once a year, so my chances to see "my guy" onstage are quite rare indeed.

3. Lewis Black is an angry, smart comedian who's known for an aggressive style and the way his own anger makes him spit his lines out. He's best known for his spots on *The Daily Show.*

4. *Absolutely Fabulous* is a British TV show about two dissolute women who work in the world of fashion. Just about every character on the show is over the top.

5. The way certain guys talk to women about music has frustrated me my whole life. If I do express an opinion—say that I prefer the drummer Rat Scabies from The Damned over Neil Peart of Rush—often a guy will throw off this attitude that I'm so dumb I'm practically unteachable, and not only is it useless to try but it's useless for him to even get me to understand exactly how wrong I am. I find this doubly irritating (and amusing, depending on my mood) when I know the guy in question hasn't even heard a song by the Damned but won't admit it. But if Betty chimes in and says Rat Scabies is a pretty great drummer, they all stop and listen and ask what he thinks is the best of his work. She doesn't even have to be in guy mode for them to listen; they just have to know there's a guy under there somewhere. My vagina apparently affects even my hearing. Some guys tend to get kind of gear-headed about music and quantify things they like about musicians, literally, even how many notes a guitarist can

play per minute. Other guys who aren't hung up on the "swinging dick" factor of rock music are much better at treating me as a fellow musichead.

6. Frankly, sometimes I think we're going backward as far as women are concerned, what with Maureen Dowd's reporting (in *Are Men Necessary?: When Sexes Collide*, P. G. Putnam, 2005) on women's devaluing their own worth by referring to their salaries as "girl money," and in a recent *Rolling Stone* article by Janet Reitman ("Sex and Scandal at Duke," June 1, 2006. See www .rollingstone.com/news/story/10464110/sex_scandal_at_duke), young Duke women's admitting that their mothers didn't raise them to pander to men the way they do.

7. As in the sisters Charlotte "Jane Eyre" Brontë and Emily "Wuthering Heights" Brontë, and Louisa May Alcott, who wrote *Little Women*. "Judith Shakespeare" is a fictional character Virginia Woolf made up for her essay "A Room of One's Own" to illustrate what might have happened to a gifted female writer who had lived at the time Shakespeare was writing his world-making plays and poems.

8. Genital surgery isn't "cutting a dick off" as people popularly refer to it—the penis is actually sliced longways and inverted back into the body cavity.

9. Flannery O'Connor, probably the finest short story stylist of the 20th century (in my opinion); Ursula LeGuin, crossover science fiction writer and humanist; Simone de Beauvoir, French feminist and novelist; Katherine Mansfield, mother of modernism; Edna St. Vincent Millay, the 20th century's most popular poet, who supported her whole family on the earnings of her poetry books; Margaret Atwood, dystopian novelist; Kathy Acker, experimental novelist; Susan Sontag, cultural theorist and author; Wendy Wasserstein, playwright. All worth looking into, if you haven't read them.

10. Janice Raymond is the mother of all antitrans feminists, having written the book *Transsexual Empire* in 1979; Norah Vincent called murdered FTM Brandon Teena "she" and "her" throughout her *Village Voice* articles (1994) but expressed empathy for trans people during interviews for her book tour of *Self-Made Man;* Germaine Greer castigated MTFs in a chapter called "Pantomime Dames" in her book *The Whole Woman* (1999), and Sheila Jeffreys's chapter "Transfemininity,"

in her *Beauty and Misogyny* (2005), makes a tidy argument about the way MTF femininity is actually a form of masochism. I was left with a feeling that her argument was just a little *too* tidy, and that she didn't know any of the women she calls "he," either. I do. People suppose that not personalizing things makes them more objective, but I find it makes them less likely to be challenged by their prejudices. Once you connect with someone as a human being, it's much harder to vilify the person. The undercurrent of condescension aimed at Peggy Rudd (the first woman to write publicly about her experiences as the wife of a crossdresser) bothered me even more, since Rudd and I are in the same boat.

11. Barry Deutsch, one of the contributors to *alas, a blog,* at: www.amptoons.com /blog/archives/2006/04/27/on-transgender-transsexuals-and-entrenching-the-binary-gender-system.

12. An essay by Amy Groshek called "Me in the Bathroom" appeared in *The Anchorage Press* and tells the story of a woman, not trans identified, dealing with bathrooms and other places where gender becomes a point of contention: www.anchoragepress.com.

13. I'm really tired of the fact that liberal/lefty bloggers seem to come up with only one way to insult Ann Coulter—and that's by implying she's transsexual. It aggravates me not just because it's ignorant and mean-spirited name-calling, but because it's lame and sinks to her level. Not only that, but there are so many cool trans women that it's insulting to them to be grouped with Coulter. And while she is masculine in some ways, it's about time people grew up and stopped trying to discredit a woman because she is confrontational and aggressive about getting her point across. Who and how she is has nothing to do with her masculinity, but more to do with her being heartless and opportunistic, and neither of those traits is exclusive to men or women.

14. Plenty of women are into fantasy novels, and specifically the Lord of the Rings trilogy, but they are far outnumbered by male fans. *The Sisterhood of the Traveling Pants* was originally a YA (Young Adult) novel about four girls who share a pair of "magic jeans," which make them look sexy and long-legged, and which was turned into a movie.

15. Ships are referred to as "she" even in genderless English because our words come from languages in which nouns were either masculine or feminine (but sometimes neuter). I don't know why ships are considered female, whether it has anything to do with the sea or the moon and its tides, or even the metaphors of lonely sailors, but some things that don't have a sex still have a kind of cultural, symbolic gender that may or may not have anything to do with their grammatical gender.

16. A recent study showed that playing with dolls improved Alzheimer's patients' ability to communicate. The gendered ramifications of that might put Deborah Tannen out of a job.

17. Rufus Wainwright, musician. This song is not yet on a CD—it's one I've seen him perform live.

18. C. S. Lewis, *The Silver Chair*, New York: Collier Books, 1970, p. 15.

19. Jennifer Finney Boylan is the author of *She's Not There*, and Dallas Denny's pebble metaphor is from the essay she wrote that appears in the anthology *Crossing Sexual Boundaries: Transgender Journeys, Uncharted Paths*, edited by Ari Kane and Vern Bullough (Prometheus Books, 2006).

20. Harry Benjamin, after whom the "Standards of Care" are named, was the primary doctor and champion of transsexual treatment. His 1966 book *The Transsexual Phenomenon* lays out distinctions between types of transsexuals, treatment options, and overall does so with an empathetic but medical tone. The "Standards of Care," often referred to as HBIGDA (because they were created by the Harry Benjamin International Gender Dysphoria Association), are the protocols determining treatment of transsexualism—requirements such as therapy and cross-living before surgery, and so on. Their usefulness is hotly debated.

21. To detransition is when transsexuals or those who are cross-living as their target gender return to living in the gender they were declared at birth. People detransition because they may find it difficult to get jobs, or because of social ostracism, not passing in their target gender, family responsibilities, and so on.

22. Kate Bornstein, in *Hello, Cruel World: 101 Alternatives to Suicide for Teens, Freaks, and Other Outlaws* (Seven Stories, 2006).

23. Judith Butler's *Gender Trouble* is a groundbreaking work on gender, specifically on the notion of performativity.

24. Quite to my surprise, I found out not too long ago that race used to be on ID cards such as driver's licenses, too. Working to get race removed from ID cards was also once thought of as futile because it was seen as such an important way to identify someone. *Ahem.*

25. Amnesty International's report on the treatment of LGBT Americans by police is a very disturbing indictment that if you are poor, a person of color, and LGBT, your chances of being treated well by a police officer are very, very slim: http://web.amnesty.org/library/Index. Too frequently when a trans person is murdered—which is a little too often, if you look at the statistics on www.rememberingourdead.org—the news reports often make the murder victim out to be a freak. They use the wrong pronouns, they imply that the trans person intentionally deceived someone, and they often sensationalize the transness itself. The supplement to the National Lesbian and Gay Journalists' Association says quite clearly: "When writing about a transgender person, use the name and personal pronouns that are consistent with the way the individual lives publicly." The NLGJA's stylebook is here: www.nlgja.org/resources/NLGJA_Stylebook.pdf and the supplement is here: ww.nlgja.org/resources/stylebook_english.html.

bibliography.

Nonfiction

Angier, Natalie. *Woman: An Intimate Geography.* New York: Anchor Books, 2000.

Anzaldua, Gloria, and Cherrie Moraga, eds. *This Bridge Called My Back: Writings by Radical Women of Color.* New York: Kitchen Table, Women of Color Press, 1983.

Bailey, J. Michael. *The Man Who Would Be Queen: The Science of Gender-Bending and Transsexualism.* Washington, DC: Joseph Henry Press, 2003.

Barnett, Rosalind, and Caryl Rivers. *Same Difference: How Gender Myths Are Hurting Our Relationships, Our Children, and Our Jobs.* New York: Basic Books, 2004.

Bergman, S. Bear. *Butch Is a Noun.* San Francisco: Suspect Thoughts Press, 2006.

Bornstein, Kate. *Gender Outlaw.* New York: Vintage Books, 1994.

Bornstein, Kate. *Hello, Cruel World: 101 Alternatives to Suicide for Teens, Freaks, and Other Outlaws.* New York: Seven Stories, 2006.

Bornstein, Kate. *My Gender Workbook: How to Become a Real Man, a Real Woman, the Real You, or Something Else Entirely.* New York: Routledge, 1998.

Boylan, Jenny. *She's Not There: A Life in Two Genders.* New York: Broadway Books, 2003.

Bullough, Bonnie, Vern Bullough, and James Elias. *Gender Blending.* Amherst, NY: Prometheus Books, 1997.

Bullough, Vern, and Ari Kane. *Crossing Sexual Boundaries: Transgender Journey, Uncharted Paths.* Amherst, NY: Prometheus Books, 2006.

Butler, Judith. *Gender Trouble: Feminism and the Subversion of Identity.* New York: Routledge, 1999.

Califia, Patrick. *Sex Changes: Transgender Politics.* San Francisco: Cleis Press, 2003.

Colapinto, John. *As Nature Made Him: The Boy Who Was Raised as a Girl.* New York: Harper Perennial, 2001.

Corber, Robert J., and Stephen Valocchi. *Queer Studies: An Interdisciplinary Reader.* Malden, MA: Blackwell, 2003.

Currah, Paisley, Richard M. Juang, and Shannon Minter. *Transgender Rights.* Minneapolis: University of Minnesota Press, 2006.

David, Deborah S., and Robert Brannon. *The Forty-Nine Percent Majority: The Male Sex Role.* Reading, MA: Addison-Wesley, 1976.

Devor, Aaron. *Gender Blenders.* Bloomington: Indiana University Press, 1989.

Dreger, Alice Domurat. *Hermaphrodites and the Medical Invention of Sex.* Cambridge, MA: Harvard University Press, 1998.

Dryden, Caroline. *Being Married, Doing Gender: A Critical Analysis of Gender Relationships in Marriage.* London: Routledge, 1999.

Ekins, Richard, and Dave King. *Blending Genders: Social Aspects of Cross-Dressing and Sex-Changing.* New York: Routledge, 1996.

Eller, Cynthia. *Am I a Woman?: A Skeptic's Guide to Gender.* Boston: Beacon Press, 2003.

Ellis, Havelock. *Studies in the Psychology of Sex: Sexual Inversion.* Honolulu: University Press of the Pacific, 2001.

Erhardt, Virginia. *Head over Heels: Wives Who Stay with Transsexuals and Crossdressers.* Binghamton, NY: Haworth Press, 2007.

Faludi, Susan. *Backlash.* New York: Crown, 1991.

Fausto-Sterling, Anne. *Sexing the Body: Gender Politics and the Construction of Sexuality.* New York: Basic Books, 2000.

Feinbloom, Deborah Heller. *Transvestites and Transsexuals: Mixed Views.* New York: Delta Books, 1976.

Green, Jamison. *Becoming a Visible Man.* Nashville: Vanderbilt University Press, 2004.

Halberstam, Judith. *Female Masculinity.* Durham: Duke University Press, 1998.

Heilbrun, Carolyn. *Toward a Recognition of Androgyny.* New York: Harper Colophon Books, 1973.

Hirschfeld, Magnus. *Sexual Anomalies.* New York: Emerson Books, 1948.

Katz, Jonathan Ned. *The Invention of Heterosexuality.* New York: Plume Books, 1995.

Kimmel, Michael. *Manhood in America: A Cultural History.* New York: Free Press, 1997.

Krafft-Ebing, Richard von. *Psychopathia Sexualis: The Case Histories.* London: Velvet, 1996.

Lady Chablis. *Hiding My Candy: The Autobiography of the Grand Empress of Savannah.* New York: Pocket Books, 1996.

Lev, Arlene Istar. *Transgender Emergence: Therapeutic Guidelines for Working with Gender-Variant People and Their Families.* Amherst, MA: Haworth, 2004.

Middlebrook, Diane W. *Suits Me: The Double Life of Billy Tipton.* New York: Houghton Mifflin, 1998.

Nestle, Joan. *The Persistent Desire: A Femme-Butch Reader.* New York: Alyson, 1992.

Pollack, William. *Real Boys: Rescuing Our Sons from the Myths of Boyhood.* New York: Henry Holt, 1998.

Rottnek, Matthew, ed. *Sissies and Tomboys: Gender Nonconformity and Homosexual Childhood.* New York: New York University Press, 1999.

Roughgarden, Joan. *Evolution's Rainbow: Diversity, Gender, and Sexuality in Nature and People.* Berkeley: University of California Press, 2004.

Thurer, Shari L. *The End of Gender: A Psychological Autopsy.* New York: Routledge, 2005.

Vincent, Norah. *Self-Made Man*. New York: Viking Books, 2006.

Wallace, Michele. *Invisibility Blues: From Pop to Theory*. New York: Verso Books, 1990.

Woolf, Virginia. *A Room of One's Own*. New York: Harcourt, Brace, Jovanovich, 1929.

Fiction

Atwood, Margaret. *Cat's Eye*. New York: Anchor Books, 1998.

Atwood, Margaret. *The Robber Bride*. New York: Anchor Books, 1993.

Brown, Rita Mae. *Rubyfruit Jungle*. New York: Bantam Books, 1983.

Chopin, Kate. *The Awakening*. New York: Avon Books, 1982.

Feinberg, Leslie. *Drag King Dreams*. New York: Carroll and Graf, 2006.

Feinberg, Leslie. *Stone Butch Blues*. New York: Alyson Books, 2004.

Gaiman, Neil. *The Sandman: A Game of You*. New York: DC Comics, 1992.

Gilman, Charlotte Perkins. *The Yellow Wallpaper and Other Writings*. New York: Doubleday, 1989.

Hall, Radclyffe. *The Well of Loneliness*. New York: Anchor Books, 1990.

Hemingway, Ernest. *The Sun Also Rises*. New York: Scribner Books, 1996.

Irving, John. *A Prayer for Owen Meany*. New York: Ballantine Books, 1991.

Irving, John. *Until I Find You*. New York: Random House, 2005.

McCullers, Carson. *The Member of the Wedding*. New York: Bantam Books, 1981.

acknowledgments.

First, to all the good folks at Seal Press: Brooke especially.

Thanks to my agent, Nancy Ellis, and her assistant, Maureen.

Thanks to my unofficial research assistants, Emilia Lombardi & Marlena
Dahlstrom & Donna Levinsohn, & to Angus (Andrea) Grieve-Smith
for linguistics help.

To the people who gave me comments and questions and feedback when
they read drafts of chapters: Megan & Marlena & Johanna.

& Of course to those who did the same with the whole of the book, too:
Donna Levinsohn & Betty & Doug McKeown.

Thanks to Deborah for helping to heal my various ailments.

To my friends and family for their insights and patience: Guy, Jule, Lara,
my sister Kath and her husband, Ian, the Phoenix Theatre cadre,
and Ernesto.

Also thanks to NYC & all of the people in our queer community here who have welcomed us, challenged us, & flirted with us. A special thanks to Tristan & Colten, for being them.

Thank you to the trans activists, educators, and artists who have been willing to answer questions or talk shop.

& To anyone anywhere who is helping to create safe spaces for trans people and/or for their partners, children, and families, especially the folks who moderate the various online support groups and wade through a daily deluge of enthusiasm and sadness to help others.

Much thanks to the always challenging people who post on the mHB community forums for giving me somewhere to bounce ideas around, & to the members of the various partners' support groups I met online and in person who shared their stories with me, & to the people who've sent me their stories through the years, & to Caroline and Caprice, who help me run the online support groups I started with nary a hitch.

Of course this book could not and would not have been written but for the okay from my beautiful wife, Betty, who allows me to tell our stories so that they might help others, & whose love knows no bounds, & who is loved at least as much as that, if not more.

© Ashley Thayer

about the author.

Helen Boyd is the author of *My Husband Betty,* which was a finalist for a Lambda Literary Award. Her blog *(en)gender* is a journal of gender and trans issues that is widely read within the gender community. She lives with her partner, Betty, in Brooklyn, New York. She can be found online at www.myhusbandbetty.com.

Selected Titles from Seal Press

For more than thirty years, Seal Press has published groundbreaking books. By women. For women. Visit our website at www.sealpress.com.

The Testosterone Files: My Hormonal and Social Transformation from Female to Male by Max Wolf Valerio. $15.95, 1-58005-173-1. A gripping transsexual memoir that focuses on testosterone's role in the author's emotional, perceptual, and physical transformation.

Nobody Passes: Rejecting the Rules of Gender and Conformity by Mattilda a.k.a. Matt Bernstein Sycamore. $15.95, 1-58005-184-7. A timely and thought-provoking collection of essays that confronts and challenges the notion of belonging by examining the perilous intersections of identity, categorization, and community.

Incognito Street: How Travel Made Me a Writer by Barbara Sjoholm. $15.95, 1-58005-172-3. From the founder of Seal Press comes this eloquent coming-of-age travel narrative about her beginnings as a writer.

Intimate Politics: How I Grew Up Red, Fought for Free Speech, and Became a Feminist Rebel by Bettina F. Aptheker. $16.95, 1-58005-160-X. A courageous and uncompromising account of one woman's personal and political transformation, and a fascinating portrayal of a key chapter in our nation's history.

One of the Guys: Women as Aggressors and Torturers edited by Tara McKelvey, foreword by Barbara Ehrenreich, afterword by Cynthia Enloe. $15.95, 1-58005-196-0. In this bold anthology, McKelvey and her contributors tackle complex issues of women and their involvement in torture and the abuse of power.

Indecent: How I Make It and Fake It as a Girl for Hire by Sarah Katherine Lewis. $14.95, 1-58005-169-3. An insider reveals the gritty reality behind the alluring facade of the sex industry.

CPSIA information can be obtained
at www.ICGtesting.com
Printed in the USA
LVOW11s2102011216
515300LV00003B/14/P

9 781580 051934